MORE IN SORROW

Wolcott Gibbs

MORE IN SORROW

HENRY HOLT AND COMPANY : NEW YORK

Copyright © 1958 by Wolcott Gibbs

Copyright, © 1938, 1939, 1940, 1941, 1948, 1949, 1954, 1956, 1957, 1958, by Wolcott Gibbs.

Except for "The Country of the Blind" and "Robert Benchley: In Memoriam," all the material in this book originally appeared in *The New Yorker*.

"Robert Benchley: In Memoriam" originally appeared in *The New York Times*.

"The Country of the Blind" originally appeared in *The Saturday Review*.

The following stories are reprinted by permission of Dodd, Mead & Company from *Bed Of Neuroses* by Wolcott Gibbs. Copyright, © 1929, 1932, 1933, 1936, 1937 by Wolcott Gibbs: "Feud," "The Factory and the Attic," "Glorious Calvin," "Outwitting the Lightning," "Ring Out, Wild Bells," "Time . . . Fortune . . . Life . . . Luce," "Death in the Rumble Seat," and "Topless in Ilium."

The following stories are reprinted by permission of Random House from *Season In The Sun & Other Pleasures* by Wolcott Gibbs. Copyright, © 1937, 1938, 1939, 1940, 1941, 1942, 1943, 1944, 1945, 1946 by Wolcott Gibbs: "Shad Ampersand," "The Education of Henry Apley," "Eva's Deathbed Revisited," "Shakespeare, Here's Your Hat," "Song at Twilight," "Crusoe's Footprint," "The Courtship of Milton Barker," "The Personality Kid," "Adultery Makes Dull Bedfellows," "The Mantle of Comstock," "The Secret Life of Myself," "The Country of the Blind," "O.K., Zanuck, Take it Away," "The Big Boffola," and "Battle's Distant Sound."

FIRST EDITION

83109-0118
Printed in the United States of America

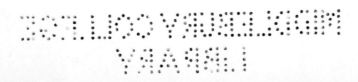

TO WILLIAM D. BIRMINGHAM

Foreword

About a quarter of the material in this book appeared in a collection of mine published in 1937; another quarter turned up in a second collection ten years later; and the remainder has never been assembled between covers, other than those of *The New Yorker* magazine, up to now. It is hard to say what conclusions can be drawn from these facts. It occurs to me that writers don't change much from the time they are thirty or thereabouts until they are laid away—permanently, I trust. As they grow older, they are apt to perform at somewhat greater length, age being garrulous, and their prose is perhaps a little more ornate, conceivably because they have so much time for the superfluous decoration on their hands; but the essence remains the same. An author is either competent or horrible in the beginning, and he stays that way to the end of his days, unless certain pressures force him into other and shadier occupations, like alcoholism or television.

I can see now that this has little bearing on this book. Well, what *is* there to be said about it? For one thing, I guess, I'd like to point out that several articles in it were written at least twenty years ago so that the subjects are left more or less in midstream. I think here specifically of a short biography of Henry Robinson Luce, founder of *Time* and kindred enterprises, which takes rather abrupt leave of him at the time he was just starting a magazine called *Life*. It seemed to me at first that Mr. Luce's career ought to be

brought up to date, but my second, and final, decision was
that this would be superfluous, not because of the extra effort involved, a matter naturally of small concern to me, but
because whatever changes have taken place in him have had
to do with increasing celebrity and scope rather than any
fundamental shifting of personality. It is obvious that Mr.
Luce occupies a more obtrusive position in the nation than
he did in 1935, but I see no reason to suppose that he is
a different man. There are several other cases where history
has altered circumstances, but none, I think, where it has
rearranged my opinions. The articles in this book therefore
are printed just as they were in the first place. Among other
things, this makes for brevity, a quality high on any list of
literary virtues.

The only other thing I wish to say about this collection is
that, as far as I know, it contains no references to juvenile
delinquency, the atomic bomb, supersonic flight, Miss Mari-
lyn Monroe, or any of the other phenomena peculiar to our
times. This may easily lead a good many readers to suppose
that I died several years ago, probably in the explosion of
the first electric icebox, but the truth is that these subjects
are just a little beyond my range. I am content to leave them
all, including Miss Monroe, to the science-fiction writers.

Unlike most authors, I am a victim of almost totally defective recall, so that the autobiographical notes that customarily accompany such essays as this will be uninforma-
tive, to put it mildly. I do remember that we were an
unusually peripatetic family, and that I spent considerable
segments of my childhood in the states of New York, Vermont, Maine, Pennsylvania, Maryland, Wisconsin, New Jersey, Connecticut, Rhode Island, and Massachusetts, not necessarily in that order. They all looked much alike to me, only
the girls shifting a bit in size and shape from place to place.
The reason for all this gadding about was that my father
was an inventor, always under the impression that the cli-

mate for invention would be a little more favorable in another town. Once, when some particularly preposterous invention made us rich, I had an English governess, who made it practically unthinkable for me to spell words like "honor" without a "u." Then, with the failure of a considerably more rational device, I went to a succession of public schools where I learned a good many things that appeared to surprise my mother, and then, finally, to three or four private ones where it proved substantially impossible to teach me anything whatever. The fault here, I realize in retrospect, was principally my own. As nearly as I can put it, I held strong and wayward opinions on practically every subject in the world, and when I found that they seldom coincided with those forced upon me by my instructors, I simply stopped listening. The years and increasing tolerance have convinced me that a man can simultaneously imagine that a book called *Kim,* by Rudyard Kipling, may be read for pleasure and still be capable of instructing the young in the English language. At the time, however, it struck me that I was holed up in some American version of Dotheboys Hall, and I kept out of everybody's way as much as was feasible.

After the collapse of my education, I was employed, again in no recapturable sequence, as an insurance clerk, an unpaid apprentice in an architect's office, a chauffeur to an 87-year-old actor, a timekeeper, a brakeman, and a newspaper reporter. It was like almost any career you can read, synopsized, on the back jacket of a mystery story, except that at no time, even during the year or so I spent on something called *The East Norwich Enterprise,* did it occur to me that writing might be a rational or profitable occupation. Practically no one, of course, is without some dream of what the future holds for him, however incoherent it may be. As much as anything else, I guess, I would have liked to instruct an endless succession of beautiful young women to play tennis. The only trouble with that was that I didn't really play tennis very well. Magazine writing, I suppose, simply occurred to me as the next easiest way to make a living, and I applied to an obliging relative who happened to have access to an editor for such employment. It was as simple as that.

The time I spent on *The New Yorker* (from 1927 up to now) has been covered by Mr. James Thurber in his book called *The Years with Ross* in a manner that should serve always as a model for such reminiscences. In addition to a phenomenal memory, Mr. Thurber has enormous perseverance in research, a wit and style that have always commanded my stunned admiration, and, I should say, a romantic heart that has enabled him to think of his place of business as the most picturesque establishment in publishing history. This is a touching illusion, and I hesitate to correct it. Instead, I think, we will just pass on to something else. Because of a late-blooming and therefore more than usually passionate energy, I have contributed more words to *The New Yorker* than anybody else in its thirty-odd year span. It is certainly unnecessary to go into the nature of these works, except to say that they included practically everything this side of women's fashions and horse racing, two fields in which my information was generally felt to be inadequate, though not by me. The important, or perhaps the merely numbing, thing is the matter of sheer volume, and here I yield to no man. Year in and year out, regardless of the world's condition or my own, I thumped away, and the drifting pages were gathered up, numbered, and, after some superfluous hocus-pocus known as editing, despatched to the Condé Nast Press in Greenwich, Connecticut, where they were translated to type and eventually distributed to the public as part of a magazine. In my opinion, the selection that follows contains the best of this staggering output, or at any rate the part that pleases me most. I will be grateful, and rather startled, if anyone agrees.

WOLCOTT GIBBS

Contents

PARODIES REGAINED

Time . . . Fortune . . . Life . . . Luce

Sad-eyed in October, 1936, was nimble, middle-sized *Life*-President Clair Maxwell as he told newshawks of the sale of the fifty-three-year-old gagmag to *Time*. For celebrated name alone, price: $85,000.

Said he: "*Life* . . . introduced to the world the drawings . . . of such men as Charles Dana Gibson, the verses of . . . James Whitcomb Riley and Oliver Herford, such writers as John Kendrick Bangs. . . . Beginning next month the magazine *Life* will embark on a new venture entirely unrelated to the old."

How unrelated to the world of the Gibson Girl was this new venture might have been gathered at the time from a prospectus issued by enormous, Apollo-faced C. D. Jackson, of Time, Inc.

"*Life*," wrote he, "will show us the Man-of-the-Week . . . his body clothed and, if possible, nude." It will expose "the loves, scandals, and personal affairs of the plain and fancy citizen . . . and write around them a light, good-tempered 'colyumnist' review of these once-private lives."

29,000 die-hard subscribers to *Life*,* long accustomed to he-she jokes, many ignorant of Duke of Windsor's once-private life (*Time*, July 25, 1936, *et seq.*), will be comforted for the balance of their subscription periods by familiar,

* Peak of *Life* circulation (1921): 250,000.

innocent jocosities of *Judge*. First issue of new publication went out to 250,000 readers, carried advertisements suggesting an annual revenue of $1,500,000, pictured Russian peasants in the nude, the love life of the Black Widow spider, referred inevitably to Mrs. Ernest Simpson. By March, 1937, circulation had touched a million; form and content remained essentially the same.

Behind this latest, most incomprehensible Timenterprise loomed, as usual, ambitious, gimlet-eyed, Baby Tycoon Henry Robinson Luce, co-founder of *Time*, promulgator of *Fortune*, potent in associated radio & cinema ventures.

"HIGH-BUTTONED . . . BRILLIANT"

Headman Luce was born in Tengchowfu, China, on April 3, 1898, the son of Henry Winters & Elizabeth Middleton Luce, Presbyterian missionaries. Very unlike the novels of Pearl Buck were his early days. Under brows too beetling for a baby, young Luce grew up inside the compound, played with his two sisters, lisped first Chinese, dreamed much of the Occident. At 14, weary of poverty, already respecting wealth & power, he sailed alone for England, entered school at St. Albans. Restless again, he came to the United States, enrolled at Hotchkiss, met up & coming young Brooklynite Briton Hadden. Both even then were troubled with an itch to harass the public. Intoned Luce years later: "We reached the conclusion that most people were not well informed & that something should be done. . . ."

First publication to inform fellowman was *Hotchkiss Weekly Record;* next *Yale Daily News,* which they turned into a tabloid; fought to double hours of military training, fought alumni who wished to change tune of Yale song from *Die Wacht am Rhein.* Traditionally unshaven, wearing high-buttoned Brooks jackets, soft white collars, cordovan shoes, no garters, Luce & Hadden were Big Men on a campus then depleted of other, older Big Men by the war. Luce, pale, intense, nervous, was Skull & Bones, Alpha Delta Phi, Phi Beta Kappa, member of the Student Council, editor of the *News;* wrote sad poems, read the *New Republic,* studied political philosophy. As successful, less earnest, more convivial, Hadden collected china dogs, made jokes.* In 1920 the senior class voted Hadden Most Likely to Succeed, Luce Most Brilliant. Most Brilliant he, Luce sloped off to Christ Church, Oxford, there to study European conditions, take field trips into the churning Balkans.

BEST ADVICE . . . DON'T

Twenty months after commencement, in the city room of Paperkiller Frank Munsey's *Baltimore News,* met again Luce, Hadden. Newshawks by day, at night they wrangled over policies of the magazine they had been planning since Hotchkiss. Boasted the final prospectus: "*Time* will be free from cheap sensationalism . . . windy bias."

In May, 1922, began the long struggle to raise money to start *Time.* Skeptical at the outset proved Newton D. Baker, Nicholas Murray Butler, Herbert Bayard Swope, William Lyon Phelps. Pooh-poohed *Review of Reviews* Owner Charles Lanier: "My best advice . . . don't do it." From studious, pint-sized Henry Seidel Canby, later editor of Lamont-backed *Saturday Review of Literature,* came only encouraging voice in this threnody.

Undismayed Luce & Hadden took the first of many

* Once, watching Luce going past, laden with cares & responsibilities, Hadden chuckled, upspoke: "Look out, Harry. You'll drop the college."

offices in an old brownstone house at 9 East 17th Street, furnished it with a filing cabinet, four second-hand desks, a big brass bowl for cigarette stubs, sought backers.*

JPMorganapoleon H. P. Davison, Yale classmate of Luce, Hadden, great & good friend of both, in June contributed $4,000. Next to succumb: Mrs. David S. Ingalls, sister of Classmate William Hale Harkness; amount, $10,000. From Brother Bill, $5,000. Biggest early angel, Mrs William Hale Harkness, mother of Brother Bill & Mrs. Ingalls, invested $20,000. Other original stockholders: Robert A. Chambers, Ward Cheney, F. Trubee Davison, E. Roland

* In return for $50 cash, original investors were given two shares 6% Preferred Stock with a par value of $25, one share Class A Common Stock without par value. 3,440 Preferred, 1,720 Class A Common were so sold.

170 shares of Class A Common, 8,000 shares of Class B Common, also without par value, not entitled to dividends until Preferred Shares had been retired, were issued to Briton Hadden, Henry R. Luce, who gave one-third to associates, divided remainder equally.

In 1925, authorized capital of Time, Inc., was increased to 19,000 shares; of which 8,000 were Preferred, 3,000 Class A; as before, 8,000 Class B.

In June, 1930 (if you are still following this), the Preferred Stock was retired in full & dividends were initiated for both Common Stocks. Corporation at this time had 2,400 shares Class A, 7,900 Class B outstanding.

By the spring of 1931 *Time* had begun to march, shares were nominally quoted at $1,000. Best financial minds advised splitting stock on basis of twenty shares for one. Outstanding after clever maneuver: 206,400 shares Common.

In 1933, outlook still gorgeous, each share of stock was reclassified into 1/10th share of $6.50 Dividend Cumulative Convertible Preferred Stock ($6.50 div. cum. con. pfd. stk.) and one share of New Common Stock. New div. cum. con. pfd. stk. was convertible into a share and a half of New Common Stock, then selling around $40 a share, now quoted at over $200.

Present number of shares outstanding, 238,000; paper value of shares, $47,000,000; conservative estimate of Luce holding, 102,300 shares; paper value, $20,460,000; conservative estimate of Luce income from *Time* stock, $818,400; reported Luce income from other investments, $100,000; reported Luce bagatelle as editor of Time, Inc., $45,000; reported total Lucemolument, $963,400.

Boy!

Harriman, Dwight W. Morrow, Harvey S. Firestone, Jr., Seymour H. Knox, William V. Griffin. By November Luce & Hadden had raised $86,000, decided to go to work on fellowman.

"SNAGGLE-TOOTHED . . . PIG-FACED"

Puny in spite of these preparations, prosy in spite of the contributions of Yale poets Archibald MacLeish & John Farrar, was the first issue of *Time* on March 3, 1923. Magazine went to 9,000 subscribers; readers learned that Uncle Joe Cannon had retired at 86, that there was a famine in Russia, that Thornton Wilder's friend Tunney had defeated Greb.

Yet to suggest itself as a rational method of communication, of infuriating readers into buying the magazine, was strange inverted Timestyle. It was months before Hadden's impish contempt for his readers,* his impatience with the English language, crystallized into gibberish. By the end of the first year, however, Timeditors were calling people able, potent, nimble; "Tycoon," most successful Timepithet, had been coined by Editor Laird Shields Goldsborough; so fascinated Hadden with "beady-eyed" that for months nobody was anything else. Timeworthy were deemed such designations as "Tom-tom" Heflin, "Body-lover" Macfadden.

"Great word! Great word!" would crow Hadden, coming upon "snaggle-toothed," "pig-faced." Appearing already were such maddening coagulations as "cinemaddict," "radiorator." Appearing also were first gratuitous invasions of privacy. Always mentioned as William Randolph Hearst's "great & good friend" was Cinemactress Marion Davies,

---

* Still framed at *Time* is Hadden's scrawled dictum: "Let Subscriber Goodkind mend his ways!"

stressed was the bastardy of Ramsay MacDonald, the "cozy hospitality" of Mae West. Backward ran sentences until reeled the mind.

By March, 1924, the circulation had doubled, has risen since then 40,000 a year, reaches now the gratifying peak of 640,000, is still growing. From four meagre pages in first issue, *Time* advertising has now come to eclipse that in *Satevepost*. Published *Time* in first six months of 1936, 1,590 pages; *Satevepost*, 1,480.

NO SLUGABED, HE . . .

Strongly contrasted from the outset of their venture were Hadden, Luce. Hadden, handsome, black-haired, eccentric, irritated his partner by playing baseball with the office boys, by making jokes, by lack of respect for autocratic business. Conformist Luce disapproved of heavy drinking, played hard, sensible game of tennis, said once: "I have no use for a man who lies in bed after nine o'clock in the morning," walked to work every morning, reproved a writer who asked for a desk for lack of "log-cabin spirit."

In 1925, when *Time* moved its offices to Cleveland, bored, rebellious was Editor Hadden; Luce, busy & social, lunched with local bigwigs, addressed Chamber of Commerce, subscribed to Symphony Orchestra, had neat house in the suburbs. Dismayed was Luce when Hadden met him on return from Europe with premature plans to move the magazine back to New York. In 1929, dying of a streptococcus infection, Hadden still opposed certain details of success-formula of *Fortune*, new, beloved Lucenterprise.

OATS, HOGS, CHEESE . . .

In January, 1930, first issue of *Fortune* was mailed to 30,000 subscribers, cost as now $1 a copy, contained articles on branch banking, hogs, glass-blowing, how to live in Chicago on $25,000 a year. Recent issue went to 130,000 subscribers, contained articles on bacon, tires, the New Deal, weighed as much as a good-sized flounder.*

Although in 1935 *Fortune* made a net profit of $500,000, vaguely dissatisfied was Editor Luce. Anxious to find & express "the technological significance of industry," he has been handicapped by the fact that his writers are often hostile to Big Business, prone to insert sneers, slithering insults. In an article on Bernard Baruch, the banker was described as calling President Hoover "old cheese-face." Protested Tycoon Baruch that he had said no such thing. Shotup of this was that Luce, embarrassed, printed a retraction; now often removes too-vivid phrasing from writers' copy.

¶ Typical perhaps of Luce methods is *Fortune* system of getting material. Writers in first draft put down wild gossip, any figures that occur to them. This is sent to victim, who indignantly corrects the errors, inadvertently supplies facts he might otherwise have withheld.

¶ *March of Time* in approximately its present form was first broadcast on March 6, 1931, paid the Columbia System for privilege, dropped from the air in February, 1932, with Luce attacking radio's "blatant claim to be a medium of education." Said he: "Should *Time* or any other business feel obliged to be the philanthropist of the air; to continue to pay for radio advertising it doesn't want in order to provide radio with something worthwhile?" So popular, so

---

* Two pounds, nine ounces.

valuable to the studio was *March of Time* that it was re-
stored in September of the same year, with Columbia do-
nating its time & facilities. Since then *March of Time* has
been sponsored by Remington-Rand typewriter company,
by Wrigley's gum, by its own cinema *March of Time*, has
made 400 broadcasts.* Apparently reconciled to philan-
thropy is Luce, because time for latest version is being
bought & paid for by his organization.

¶ No active connection now has Luce with the moving-
picture edition of *March of Time*, which was first shown on
February 1, 1935, appears thirteen times a year in over
6,000 theatres, has so far failed to make money, to repay
$900,000 investment. Even less connection has he with
Time's only other unprofitable venture. Fifty-year-old *Architectural Forum*, acquired in 1932, loses still between
$30,000 and $50,000 a year, circulates to 31,000.

¶ *Letters*, five-cent fortnightly collection of *Time's* correspondence with its indefatigable readers, was started in
1931, goes to 30,000, makes a little money.

¶ For a time, Luce was on Board of Directors of Paramount
Pictures. Hoped to learn something of cinema, heard nothing discussed but banking, resigned sadly.

FASCINATING FACTS ... DREAMY
FIGURES ...

Net profits of Time, Inc., for nine years:

1927	3,860
1928	125,787
1929	325,412

* By some devious necromancy, statisticians have calculated that *March of
Time* ranks just behind *Amos & Andy* as most popular of all radio programs; reaches between 8,000,000 and 9,000,000 newshungry addicts.

1930 818,936
1931 847,447
1932 .... 613,727*
1933 1,009,628
1934 1,773,094
1935 .... $2,249,823†

* Hmm.
† Exceeded only by Curtis Publishing Co. (*Satevepost*): $5,329,900;
Crowell Publishing Co. (*Collier's*): $2,399,600.

In 1935 gross revenue of *Time-Fortune* was $8,621,170, of
which the newsmagazine brought in approximately $6,000,-
000. Outside investments netted $562,295. For rent, salaries,
production & distribution, other expenses went $6,594,076.
Other deductions: $41,397. Allowance for federal income
tax: $298,169.

Time's books, according to Chicago Statisticians Gerwig
& Gerwig, show total assets of $6,755,451. Liabilities, $3,-
101,584. These figures, conventionally allowing $1 for name,
prestige of *Time*, come far from reflecting actual prosperity
of Luce, his enterprises. Sitting pretty are the boys.

LUCE . . . MARCHES ON!

Transmogrified by this success are the offices, personnel of
Time-Fortune. Last reliable report: *Time*, 308 employees;
Fortune, 103; Cinemarch, 58; Radiomarch, 10; *Architectural
Forum*, 40; *Life*, 47. In New York; total, 566. In Chicago,
mailing, editorial, mechanical employees, 216. Grand total
Timemployees on God's earth, 782. Average weekly recom-
pense for informing fellowman, $45.67802.

From first single office, Timen have come to bulge to
bursting six floors of spiked, shiny Chrysler Building, oc-

cupy 150 rooms, eat daily, many at famed Cloud Club, over 1,000 eggs, 500 cups of coffee, much bicarbonate of soda. Other offices: Cinemarch, 10th Avenue at 54th Street; Radiomarch, Columbia Broadcasting Building.

Ornamented with Yale, Harvard, Princeton diplomas, stuffed fish, terrestrial globes are offices of Luce & other headmen; bleak, uncarpeted the writer's dingy lair.

¶ Heir apparent to mantle of Luce is dapper, tennis-playing $35,000-a-year Roy Larsen, nimble in Radio- & Cinemarch, vice-president & second largest stockholder in Time, Inc. Stock income: $120,000.

¶ Looming behind him is burly, able, tumbledown Yaleman Ralph McAllister Ingersoll, former Fortuneditor, now general manager of all Timenterprises, descendant of 400-famed Ward McAllister. Littered his desk with pills, unguents, Kleenex, Socialite Ingersoll is *Time's* No. 1 hypochondriac, introduced ant palaces for study & emulation of employees, writes copious memoranda about filing systems, other trivia, seldom misses a Yale football game. His salary: $30,000; income from stock: $40,000.

¶ Early in life Timeditor John Stuart Martin lost his left arm in an accident. Unhandicapped he, resentful of sympathy, Martin played par golf at Princeton, is a crack shot with a rifle or shotgun, holds a telephone with no hands, using shoulder & chin, chews paperclips. First cousin of Cofounder Hadden, joined in second marriage to daughter of Cunard Tycoon Sir Ashley Sparks, Timartin is managing editor of newsmagazine, has been nimble in Cinemarch, other Timenterprises, makes $25,000 a year salary, gets from stock $60,000.

¶ $20,000 salary, $20,000 from stock gets shyest, least-known of all Timeditors, Harvardman John S. Billings, Jr., now under Luce in charge of revamped *Life,* once Washington correspondent for the Brooklyn *Eagle,* once National

Affairs Editor for *Time*. Yclept "most important man in shop" by Colleague Martin, Billings, brother of famed muralist Henry Billings, is naïve, solemn, absent-minded, once printed same story twice, wanted to print, as news, story of van Gogh's self-mutilation, drives to office in car with liveried chauffeur, likes Jones Beach.

¶ Fortuneditor Eric Hodgins is thin-haired, orbicular, no Big Three graduate. Formerly on *Redbook*, boy & girl informing *Youth's Companion*, Hodgins inherited Pill-Swallower Ingersoll's editorial job two years ago when latter was called to greater glory, higher usefulness, still writes much of content of magazine, is paid $15,000; from stock only $8,000.

¶ Doomed to strict anonymity are *Time-Fortune* staff writers, but generally known in spite of this are former *Times* bookritic John Chamberlain, Meistersinger Archibald MacLeish. Both out of sympathy with domineering business, both irked by stylistic restrictions, thorns to Luce as well as jewels they. Reward for lack of fame: Chamberlain, $10,000; MacLeish, $15,000; each, two months' vacation.

Brisk beyond belief are carryings-on these days in Luce's chromium tower. *Time*, marching on more militantly than ever, is a shambles on Sundays & Mondays, when week's news is teletyped to Chicago printing plant; *Fortune*, energetic, dignified, its offices smelling comfortably of cookies, is ever astir with such stupefying projects as sending the entire staff to Japan; new whoopsheet *Life* so deep in organization that staff breakfasts are held to choose from 6,000 submitted photographs the Nude of the Week; so harried perpetually all editors that even interoffice memoranda are couched in familiar Timestyle,* that an appoint-

---

* Sample Luce memorandum: "Let *Time's* editors next week put thought on the Japanese beetle. H. R. L."

ment to lunch with Editor Luce must be made three weeks in advance.

Caught up also in the whirlwind of progress are *Time*, *Fortune's* 19 maiden checkers. Bryn Mawr, Wellesley, Vassar graduates they, each is assigned to a staff writer, checks every word he writes, works hard & late, is barred by magazine's anti-feminine policy from editorial advancement.

COLD, BAGGY, TEMPERATE . . .

At work today, Luce is efficient, humorless, revered by colleagues; arrives always at 9:15, leaves at 6, carrying armfuls of work, talks jerkily, carefully, avoiding visitor's eye; stutters in conversation, never in speechmaking. In early days kept standing at Luce desk like butlers were writers while he praised or blamed; now most business is done by time-saving memoranda called "Luce's bulls." Prone he to wave aside pleasantries, social preliminaries, to get at once to the matter in hand. Once to interviewer who said, "I hope I'm not disturbing you," snapped Luce, "Well, you are." To ladies full of gentle misinformation he is brusque, contradictory, hostile; says that his only hobby is "conversing with somebody who knows something," argues still that "names make news," that he would not hesitate to print a scandal involving his best friend.

Because of his Chinese birth, constantly besieged is Luce by visiting Orientals; he is polite, forbearing, seethes secretly. Lunch, usually in a private room at the Cloud Club, is eaten quickly, little attention paid to the food, much to business. He drinks not at all at midday, sparingly at all times, takes sometimes champagne at dinner, an occasional cocktail at parties. Embarrassed perhaps by reputation for

unusual abstemiousness, he confesses proudly that he
smokes too much.

Serious, ambitious Yale standards are still reflected in
much of his conduct; in indiscriminate admiration for
bustling success, in strong regard for conventional morality,
in honest passion for accuracy; physically, in conservative,
baggy clothes, white shirts with buttoned-down collars,
solid-color ties. A budding joiner, in New York, Luce belongs to the Yale, Coffee House, Racquet & Tennis, Union
& Cloud Clubs; owns a box at the Metropolitan; is listed in
Who's Who & *Social Register.*

Colder, more certain, more dignified than in the early
days of the magazine, his prose style has grown less ebulli-
ent, resembles pontifical *Fortune* rather than chattering
Time. Before some important body he makes now at least
one speech a year, partly as a form of self-discipline, partly
because he feels that his position as head of a national insti-
tution demands it. His interests wider, he likes to travel,
meet & observe the Great. Five or six times in Europe, he
has observed many Great & Near Great. Of a twenty-min-
ute conversation with Duke of Windsor, then Prince of
Wales, says only "Very interesting." Returning from such
trips, he always provides staff members with 10 & 12-page
memoranda carefully explaining conditions.

Orated recently of conditions in this country: "Without
the aristocratic principle no society can endure. . . . What
slowly deadened our aristocratic sense was the expanding
frontier, but more the expanding machine. . . . But the
aristocratic principle persisted in the United States in our
fetish of comparative success. . . . We got a plutocracy
without any common sense of dignity and obligation.
Money became more and more the only mark of success,
but still we insisted that the rich man was no better than

the poor man—and the rich man accepted the verdict. And so let me make it plain, the triumph of the mass mind is nowhere more apparent than in the frustration of the upper classes." Also remarked in conversation: "Trouble is—great anti-social development—is the automobile trailer. Greatest failure of this country is that it hasn't provided good homes for its people. Trailer shows that."

MILESTONES

Good-naturedly amused by Luce tycoon ambitions was Lila Hotz, of Chicago, whom he married there on Dec. 22, 1923. In 1935, the father of two boys, Luce was divorced by her in Reno on Oct. 5. Married in Old Greenwich, Conn., without attendants, on Nov. 23, 1935, were Luce, Novelist-Playwright Clare Boothe Brokaw, described once by Anglo-aesthete Cecil Beaton as "most drenchingly beautiful," former wife of elderly Pantycoon George Tuttle Brokaw.

Two days before ceremony, "Abide with Me," by new, beautiful Mrs. Luce, was produced at the Ritz Theatre. Play dealt with young woman married to sadistic drunkard, was unfavorably reviewed by all newspaper critics.*

In a quandary was Bridegroom Luce when *Time's* own critic submitted a review suggesting play had some merit. Said he: "Show isn't that good. . . . Go back. . . . Write what you thought." Seven times, however, struggled the

---

* Of it said Richard Watts, blue-shirted, moon-faced *Tribune* dramappraiser:

"One almost forgave 'Abide with Me' its faults when its lovely playwright, who must have been crouched in the wings for a sprinter's start as the final curtain mercifully descended, heard a cry of 'author,' which was not audible in my vicinity, and arrived onstage to accept the audience's applause just as the actors, who had a head-start on her, were properly lined up and smoothed out to receive their customary adulation."

writer before achieving an acceptable compromise between criticism, tact.

A MILLION ROOMS, A THOUSAND BATHS . . .

Long accustomed to being entertained, entertaining, is Mrs. Luce, intimate of Mr. & Mrs. A. Coster Schermerhorn, Mrs. and Mrs. Bernard M. Baruch, Jock Whitney, glistening stage & literary stars. Many were invited last summer to 30-acre estate in Stamford to play tennis, croquet, swim; many, too, will come to 7,000-acre, $100,000 Luce plantation, near Charleston, S.C.; will sleep there in four stream-lined, prefabricated guest cottages. Given to first Mrs. Luce in divorce settlement, along with $500,000 in cash & securities, was French Manoir at Gladstone, N.J., where Luce once planned to raise Black Angus cows, to become gentleman farmer.

Described too modestly by him as "smallest apartment in River House," * duplex at 435 East 52nd Street occupied last winter by Luce contained 15 rooms, 5 baths, a lavatory; was leased furnished from Mrs. Bodrero Macy for $7,300 annually, contained many valuable French, English, Italian antiques, looked north and east on the river. In décor, Mrs. Luce prefers the modern; evasive is Luce. Says he: "Just like things convenient & sensible." Says also: "Whatever furniture or houses we buy in the future will be my wife's buying, not mine."

* Smallest apartment in River House has six rooms, one bath.

WHITHER, WHITHER?

Accused by many of totalitarian leanings, of soaring journalistic ambition, much & conflicting is the evidence on Luce political faith, future plans. By tradition a Tory, in 1928 he voted for Alfred E. Smith, in 1932 for Herbert Hoover, last year for Alfred M. Landon. Long at outs with William Randolph Hearst, it was rumored that a recent visit to California included a truce with ruthless, shifting publisher. Close friend for years of Thomas Lamont, Henry P. Davison, the late Dwight Morrow, it has been hinted that an official connection with the House of Morgan in the future is not impossible. Vehemently denies this Luce, denies any personal political ambition, admits only that he would like eventually to own a daily newspaper in New York.

Most persistent, most fantastic rumor, however, declares that Yaleman Luce already has a wistful eye on the White House. Reported this Chicago's *Ringmaster,* added: "A legally-minded friend . . . told him that his Chinese birth made him ineligible. Luce dashed to another lawyer to check. Relief! He was born of American parents and properly registered at the Consulate."

Whatever the facts in that matter, indicative of Luce consciousness of budding greatness, of responsibility to whole nation, was his report to *Time's* Board of Directors on March 19, 1936. Declaimed he: "The expansion of your company has brought it to a point beyond which it will cease to be even a big Small Business and become a small Big Business. . . . The problem of public relations also arises. *Time,* the Weekly Newsmagazine, has been, and still is, its own adequate apologist. Ditto, *Fortune.* But with a motion-picture journal, a nightly radio broadcast, and with four magazines, the public interpretation of your company's alleged viewpoint or viewpoints must be taken with great seriousness." Certainly to be taken with seriousness is Luce at thirty-nine, his fellowmen already informed up to their ears, the shadow of his enterprises long across the land, his future plans impossible to imagine, staggering to contemplate. Where it all will end, knows God!

Death in the Rumble Seat

(With the Usual Apologies to Ernest Hemingway)

Most people don't like the pedestrian part, and it is best not to look at that if you can help it. But if you can't help seeing them, long-legged and their faces white, and then the shock and the car lifting up a little on one side, then it is best to think of it as something very unimportant but beautiful and necessary artistically. It is unimportant because the people who are pedestrians are not very important, and if they were not being *cogido* by automobiles it would just be something else. And it is beautiful and necessary because, without the possibility of somebody getting *cogido*, driving a car would be just like anything else. It would be like reading "Thanatopsis," which is neither beautiful nor necessary, but hogwash. If you drive a car, and don't like the pedestrian part, then you are one of two kinds of people. Either you haven't very much vitality and you ought to do something about it, or else you are yellow and there is nothing to be done about it at all.

If you don't know anything about driving cars you are apt to think a driver is good just because he goes fast. This may be very exciting at first, but afterwards there is a bad taste in the mouth and the feeling of dishonesty. Ann Bender, the American, drove as fast on the Merrick Road as anybody I have ever seen, but when cars came the other way she always worked out of their terrain and over in the ditch so that you never had the hard, clean feeling of danger, but only bumping up and down in the ditch, and sometimes hitting your head on the top of the car. Good drivers go fast too, but it is always down the middle of the road, so that cars coming the other way are dominated, and have to go in the ditch themselves. There are a great many ways of getting the effect of danger, such as staying in the middle of the road till the last minute and then swerving out of the pure line, but they are all tricks, and afterwards you know they were tricks, and there is nothing left but disgust.

The cook: I am a little tired of cars, sir. Do you know any stories?

I know a great many stories, but I'm not sure that they're suitable.

The cook: The hell with that.

Then I will tell you the story about God and Adam and naming the animals. You see, God was very tired after he got through making the world. He felt good about it, but he was tired so he asked Adam if he'd mind thinking up names for the animals.

"What animals?" Adam said.

"Those," God said.

"Do they have to have names?" Adam said.

"You've got a name, haven't you?" God said.

I could see—

The cook: How do *you* get into this?

Some people always write in the first person, and if you do it's very hard to write any other way, even when it doesn't altogether fit into the context. If you want to hear this story, don't keep interrupting.

The cook: O.K.

I could see that Adam thought God was crazy, but he didn't say anything. He went over to where the animals were, and after a while he came back with the list of names.

"Here you are," he said.

God read the list, and nodded.

"They're pretty good," he said. "They're all pretty good except that last one."

"That's a good name," Adam said. "What's the matter with it?"

"What do you want to call it an elephant for?" God said.

Adam looked at God.

"It looks like an elephant to me," he said.

The cook: Well?

That's all.

The cook: It is a very strange story, sir.

It is a strange world, and if a man and woman love each other, that is strange too, and what is more, it always turns out badly.

In the golden age of car-driving, which was about 1910, the sense of impending disaster, which is a very lovely thing and almost nonexistent, was kept alive in a number of ways. For one thing, there was always real glass in the windshield so that if a driver hit anything, he was very definitely and beautifully *cogido*. The tires weren't much good either, and often they'd blow out before you'd gone ten miles. Really, the whole car was built that way. It was made not only so that it would precipitate accidents but so that when the accidents came it was honestly vulnerable, and it would fall apart, killing all the people with a passion that was very fine to watch. Then they began building the cars so that they would go much faster, but the glass and the tires were all made so that if anything happened it wasn't real danger, but only the false sense of it. You could do all kinds of things with the new cars, but it was no good because it was all planned in advance. Mickey Finn, the German, always worked very far into the other car's terrain so that the two cars always seemed to be one. Driving that way he often got the *faender,* or the clicking when two cars touch each other in passing, but because you knew that nothing was really at stake it was just an empty classicism, without any value because the insecurity was all gone and there was nothing left but a kind of mechanical agility. It is the same way when any art gets into its decadence. It is the same way about s-x—

The cook: I like it very much better when you talk about s-x, sir, and I wish you would do it more often.

I have talked a lot about s-x before, and now I thought I would talk about something else.

The cook: I think that is very unfortunate, sir, because you are at your best with s-x, but when you talk about automobiles you are just a nuisance.

Topless in Ilium

(Mr. Aldous Huxley Imagines a Tender Passage Between Helen and Paris in the Manner of "Antic Hay," "Point Counter Point," and "Eyeless in Gaza")

What a snout she had, he thought. Like a pig or, better, like some indecent marine slug. *Fulgur canaliculata.* That was it. The same obscene flaring nostrils, aimed at you like the twin barrels of a shotgun. He gave a little snort of pure disgust.

"I love you," he said.

"Oh, *love*," she murmured from some nether hell of waste and despair, and sketched him the anatomy of a smile. It would, he reflected, be pleasant to knock those celebrated teeth down her throat.

"Was this the face that launch'd a thousand ships, And burnt the topless towers. . . ."

It was possible, of course, that once she *had* been handsome, in her own degraded fashion. But that was before she had been mutilated by the Greeks. (What degree of sophistication, incidentally, is necessary before one can really appreciate the stigmata?) It was certainly before she had

24

begun to take naphtha. He felt only rage and humiliation that he loved her as he did, so that it would have been ecstasy to trip her up and sit on her.

"What about Menelaus?" he asked suddenly. It was, of course, supremely fitting that she should have a husband. It added a thin musk of evil to what otherwise might have been a simple and vulgar *liaison*. How degrading, he thought, to mate like the animals, without fear or remorse. It occurred to him that civilized love was rather like venison, best when it had gone a little bad, a little rotten. The sense of sin was a kind of *sauce maison,* rendering the whole sordid mess a little less nauseating, almost palatable to the connoisseur.

"Menelaus?" she said in her dead voice.

"Your husband," he explained with elaborate irony.

"Oh," she said and gave a little hoot of laughter. "The same as usual, I imagine. Poor dear."

He nodded. Menelaus had really behaved very badly. Quite hysterically, in fact. What limitless vulgarity always underlay the man of action! Even admitting that colonials were without any reasonable sense of proportion, the whole excursion had been absurd. All those ships and men! Quite as if he were setting out to discover a continent, and not simply to bring back a wife he had rather disliked in the first place. (It would certainly have required a more cultivated taste than Menelaus's to admire that ruined *chic,* that subtle ammonia of corruption.)

"I hear," she said indifferently, "that he's been inventing a horse."

"A what?"

"A wooden horse," she said from her perpetual deathbed. "He gets in it and they push him around. Such an inventive mind."

"But what on earth for?"

"I expect he'll have them push him in here," she said.
"He's really very much annoyed with you, you know."

Her nose wrinkled a little in delicious anticipation. This
bore and his apples! Some very interesting things would undoubtedly happen to Paris when the Greeks finally caught
him. Menelaus might not be much of a husband, but like
all his family he was clever with his hands. She remembered
those fascinating experiments with molten lead he had
made on his slaves.

"Oh," he said, "the old bourgeois prejudice against wearing horns. How unspeakably dreary."

And how childish and illogical. We are all maggots on
the same stupendous cheese, all intent on rooting out the
choicest nastiness, and love, of course, the choicest nastiness of all. Incredible that anyone could suppose it mattered
which slugs were mated with which.

"I wouldn't be surprised," said Helen pleasantly, "if he
began by cutting off your ears."

How ugly she was—her face a mask of malignance and
stupidity like those horrible little Nigerian primitives in
the museum at Mycenae. He reflected again on the bottom-
less degradation of his love for her, a passion based on his
loathing for her mind and body, on his own dark and secret
wish to destroy himself forever. He thought of the other
planets spinning clear in space, only the earth infected with
the disease of humanity, a surface putrescence so hideously
expressed in this woman beside him. He leaned over and
pulled her tawdry wig down over her eyes.

"Dearest," he whispered.

She gave her dreadful parody of a smile.

The Factory and the Attic

Small women in funny hats keep asking me how to tell a good short story from a bad one. For years, they complain, they have been reading such wholly disparate publications as *Scribner's* and the *Saturday Evening Post,* miserably unable to determine what is Art and what is Tripe. At the time they came to me most of these women had arrived at some arbitrary solution of their own. One pinched little thing admitted that she had come to the point of judging literature purely on the basis of its nuisance value: that is, a story must be regarded as important only if it bored her to the edge of madness. Another defined significant stories as those dealing with persons who would have been intolerable to her socially. (She was particularly impressed by one about a rural spinster with an unconquerable desire to go walking in the rain with no clothes on.) Still another reserved her approval for narratives in which nothing much ever seemed to happen. Curiously enough, this defeatist point of view was quite general; almost all the ladies assumed that literature, to be worthy of their admiration, must also make them unhappy. Unfortunately, I am not able to deny this theory altogether, since some moments of pain are inseparable from real culture, but it seems to me that any sound philosophy of criticism must go somewhat deeper. There are, in fact, almost infinite ramifications to be considered. Anxious to avoid the drain on my time

caused by these endless appeals, in this article I have prepared a few tests for separating the sheep of modern fiction from its gilded and elegant goats.

The first point to be considered in judging the merits of
any story is, of course, the plot, and here, for purposes of
comparison, I shall outline two which seem representative
of the best and worst in magazine prose. The first is called
"Even the Least of These, Thy Sparrows," and runs somewhat as follows:

Hector Le Boutillier, scion of an old Kentucky family, is
wounded at Belleau Wood while attempting to bring back
a wounded private, a colored man, from behind the German lines. When Hector stumbles into the trench with the
wounded man on his back, his comrades are horrified to
observe that his face has been almost entirely obliterated
by a burst of shrapnel. He is rushed at once to a base hospital, where he is placed under the care of a surgeon famous
for his work in plastic surgery. Unfortunately, the damage
wrought by the shell is so complete that the surgeon is unable to tell what Hector looked like before he was hit, and
obviously it would be absurd to equip him with a meaningless and irrelevant face made up out of the doctor's
head. The United States Medical Corps, however, rises to
the occasion and a cable is dispatched to the Le Boutilliers in America asking them for recent and characteristic
photographs of Hector. Through some error in the cable
office, Hector's name is transmitted as "Richard," which
chances to be the name of a ne'er-do-well younger brother,
who unknown to his family has deserted from the Allied
armies and become a German spy. It is his photograph
which reaches the surgeon, and when Hector leaves the
operating-room he is wearing Richard's face. The story
then leaps to the end of the war and to America, where the
Le Boutilliers' home town has been wiped out by a passing

earthquake, so that there is nobody to recognize Hector (even as Richard) upon his return. Before the war, however, Richard had become engaged to an old-fashioned girl who lived in the Greenwich Village section of New York, where she seems to have been a little out of her element. Richard's actual intentions toward her had been far from honorable, but the war started too soon, and he drew a blank.

Upon his return to America, Hector (in Richard's face) wanders around for a while trying to forget the loss of his rather extensive family, and eventually comes to the very city where the girl, whose name was Smyrna Phelps, is living. Finally, at a batik pull, they meet and Smyrna naturally supposes that Hector is Richard (on account of the face). She is so preposterously glad to see him that Hector, believing his brother dead, decides not to disillusion her. In a short time, too, he discovers that he has come to love her. They are married and are living quite happily in Montclair when the real Richard comes back to New York in search of Smyrna. Eventually he traces her to Montclair, and there is an extremely trying scene in which Richard accuses Hector of lifting both his face and his girl. At the end of it Hector promises to go away, leaving Smyrna to the real Richard, although she has discovered what a bounder he is. This looks pretty bad, but just as Hector is packing his bag to go away, a state trooper who had been in Richard's company abroad comes in and shoots him for being a German spy. This, of course, settles everything, and Smyrna contributes to the felicity of the moment by discovering that she is going to have a baby.

The other story, which can be summarized rather more briefly, is called "Meg" and the plot, disregarding some of its profounder psychological undertones, goes something like this:

At the age of fifteen Meg was seduced by the president

of the First National Bank, who was old enough not only to be her father, but also to make it seem like a pretty good trick. For some reason, doubtless professional, he elected to stage this idyll in a safe-deposit vault, and consequently Meg grew up with a horror of being shut up in anything. By the time she was sixteen, even houses had become intolerable to her, and she began to sleep out in the fields beyond the village. Eventually she gave up all contact with the villagers. Once a month she trudged into town for supplies, a bent and tragic figure, wrapped in an atrocity of rags, muttering endlessly to herself. She began to drink, too, and under its influence her behavior grew even more *outré;* she took to stopping young girls on the streets and warning them against bankers.

Inevitably this came to the ears of the matrons of the town, and at last (ironically enough, at the instigation of the banker's wife) Meg was arrested as a public nuisance and sentenced to a month in jail. She never served it. No sooner had the steel door of the cell closed behind her than Meg fell to the floor, dead. At the inquest the doctor said she died of fear. She thought they'd deposited her in a bank.

Although the discerning reader can have no real doubt about the comparative merits of these samples, it might be well to examine the technical considerations which are involved. By any enlightened standards it is apparent that "Even the Least of These, Thy Sparrows" belongs emphatically among the goats. We are struck at once by the author's basic insincerity—by his use of the most palpable literary tricks, and especially by his persistent overplay of coincidence. We are quite ready to accept one, and the mistake by which Hector was made to look like his brother seems both plausible and ingenious. From this point, however, we become involved in a welter of fortuitous circumstance. We are asked not only to believe that Hector's whole family was wiped out by an earthquake (in Kentucky, where they are extremely rare), that by pure chance he encountered his brother's fiancée in a city as large as New York, but also that Richard's old companion, the trooper, appeared at so critical a juncture of the story. In this connection, it seems to me that "Sparrows" exhibits another serious flaw in that, since both brothers looked precisely alike, it was just as probable that he would have shot one as the other.

Altogether we find that this story is an almost perfect example of commercial prose at its worst, written with an eye on the movies, and with no discernible relation to actual contemporary life.

"Meg," on the other hand, is a little gem of morbid psychology, moving with majestic inevitability from its tragic inception to its even more tragic dénouement. The setting is simple, even drab; the plot has none of the feverish activity, the insane complexity, which are so apparent in "Sparrows," and the protagonists, Meg and the banker, are not, as were Hector and Richard, actuated by any preposterous nobility or even more preposterous villainy. They are people very like you and me, and their behavior is doubtless what yours or mine would be if we were either a girl who had been enticed into a vault by a banker or a banker who had simultaneous access both to a girl and a vault.

For all these reasons it should be abundantly clear that "Sparrows" and "Meg" represent the poles of modern fiction. To be doubly sure, however, let us examine the styles in which they are written. First let us consider "Sparrows" —specifically the scene in which Hector relinquishes Smyrna to his brother. A few paragraphs will do:

Over the mantel there was a clock and to Hector it seemed that presently the ticking of the clock resolved itself into words. "'Vengeance is mine,' saith the Lord." This over and over until at last the bright hatred went out of his soul and he knew a curious peace. And again "Blessed are the meek, for they shall inherit the earth." And at last Hector turned from the window and it seemed to the two watching him that there was a light, lambent and unearthly, on his face. He put his hand on the doorknob and smiled at them.

"I am going," he said gently, "away."

And while they stood transfixed the door opened and closed and he was gone.

"Hector," cried Smyrna, but the room gave her back only the sound of her own voice and the slow and fatal ticking of the clock.

The passage from "Meg" describes her last journey from the hut in the fields to the village and goes as follows:

Meg walked slowly along the muddy road. It was hot and ragged children ran out of the farmhouses that bordered the road and threw stones at her. When one of the stones hit her Meg would turn around in the road, and the children would run screaming back into the houses, afraid of her tall, pale madness. Meg did not know they were stones. She thought they were half-dollars and that the children were bankers. Once she caught one of the children and broke its neck. That made her laugh.

"I guess that will learn you to get tough with me, Mr. James Waldemar," she said.

I see no reason for further comment. If any of my readers are still unable to distinguish between the produce of the factory and attic, with a clear conscience I leave them in Montclair, with Hector and Smyrna. The rest of you, imperturbably cultured, can follow me over the hill and down into despair and death with Meg.

Glorious Calvin

(A Critical Appreciation Many Years Later)

The comic art of Calvin Coolidge was a thing so subtle that it almost defied analysis, for, like all great actors, his was the technique of implication. In fact, in his ability to suggest frustration—the bitter futility of all living—by such small things as an eyebrow infinitesimally raised, an incomplete, embarrassed gesture, he was equalled only by the immortal Chaplin, only occasionally approached by Harry Langdon. As I write this it occurs to me to doubt whether this man, who was known and loved by millions of moviegoers, was essentially a comedian. There was more than a hint of tragedy in the shy little figure staring with solemn bafflement on an inexplicable world. There was a great pathos about him as he went awkwardly and unhappily through the gaudy antics which were so hilariously at variance with his appearance. This great sense of the comic value of paradox was never better illustrated than in the magnificent film in which, resplendent in buckskin and feathers, he was created a chieftain of the Blackfeet Indians. While tom-toms beat under a copper sky, naked red bodies circled in a furious dance about a tightmouthed little man with the edge of a stiff white collar showing at the neck of his costume and the toes of sturdy black boots

peeping out under the gay fringe at the bottom of his
trousers. His expression, which never varied throughout the
ceremony, suggested the faintly apprehensive geniality of
an elderly gentleman who has been dragooned into a game
of Post Office. The effect was irresistible.

This intelligent emphasis on contrast was present in all
Coolidge's camera work. I recall happily the film in which,
attired in a cowboy suit with "Cal" stenciled across the seat
of the trousers (a touch of genius, by the way), he made
timid overtures to a faintly derisive steer. Incidentally, an
adroit and characteristic touch was added to this picture
by a subtitle, reading "COOLIDGE IS AMUSED BY RODEO,"
which was immediately followed by a glimpse of the comedian, his back turned morosely on the rodeo, staring with
horrid dejection at nothing whatever.

Coolidge, ascetic in cap and gown, receiving a degree
from the president of a university; Coolidge, in yachting
costume, with a vague hint of nausea in his expression,
standing at the rail of the *Mayflower;* Coolidge, in overalls,
thriftly chopping kindling against the bitter Massachusetts
winter (the glittering nose of an enormous Packard appearing in a corner of this scene was a note of sheer and
beautiful idiocy); Coolidge, the fisherman; Coolidge, the
President of the United States—the man's comic sense was
unerring and his range apparently infinite.

In passing, it is perhaps worth noting that while, unlike
Chaplin, Coolidge varied the major details of his costume
with each part, the stiff collar was a constant item. With
an unfailing instinct for the incongruous, he chose it as the
inevitable label of the urban, the clerkly, the humdrum.
Infinitely more subtle than Chaplin's cane, derby, and
baggy trousers, it was at the same time far more effective.
To take a setting as strange and beautiful as the one used
in a picture he made in Georgia—bearded Spanish oaks,

oxcarts, the lovely keening of spirituals—and in an instant
reduce it to absurdity by the introduction of a stiff collar,
that was something very like genius.

While Coolidge depended upon simple incongruity for
most of his effects, when he did introduce gags they were
incomparable. I have in mind a bit, again in the Georgia
picture, in which the comedian entered surrounded by
secret-service men in business suits, uneasily raised a gun
to his shoulder and fired once into the air. A subtitle was
then flashed on the screen—"TRIBUTE TO A STEADY HAND AND
A CLEAR EYE"—and the next picture showed us two guides
shouldering a long pole, bowed under the weight of a deer,
two or three smaller animals which appeared to be raccoons,
and several wild ducks. The expression of the comedian's
face as he studied this exhibit—wild surmise succeeded by
a nervous and deprecating smile—I regard as one of the
screen's great comic achievements.

Unlike many cinema favorites, the introduction of the
talking picture held no terrors for Coolidge. His voice,
happily, was perfectly in keeping with the part he has
chosen to portray—dry, nasal, utterly without inflection.
The lines, which I am told he made up himself, were
miracles of brevity and did much to further the effect of
anticlimax upon which his art depended. Again in the
Georgia picture there was the moment when the comedian
rode onto the scene, seated upon an ancient wooden cart
drawn by oxen. His progress through the green tunnel
made by the overhanging trees was attended by the wail-
ing of spirituals, the cracking of whips, and the muffled
clump of the oxen's hooves. It was a moment of rare, almost
intolerable beauty. The cart stopped as it reached the fore-
front of the picture and the spirituals died away. There
was a sudden silence, which was broken by Coolidge's
companion, who addressed him in a tone of great defer-

ence upon a problem apparently of national importance.
. . . "What is your solution of that, Mr. President?"

The comedian smiled nervously, stared at the oxen, but did not reply. His companion tried again.

"What would you think of putting a tax on gasoline?"

This was obviously intended to be facetious, but the comedian considered it with perfect solemnity. At last his face brightened.

"Wal," he said, "I don't think I'd be in favor of that."

The spirituals rose again, and the cart drove on.

When Coolidge left the pictures, he was succeeded by Herbert Hoover, a comedian whose work displayed certain similarities. To the critical mind, however, it was thin and derivative, a self-conscious echo of his predecessor's magnificent technique. I doubt if we shall ever see the Master's like again.

Shad Ampersand

*(A Novel of Time and the Writer, Tentatively Based On
"Cass Timberlane," A Novel of Husbands and Wives)*

I

The city of Grand Revenant, in High Hope County and the
sovereign state of Nostalgia, has a population of 34,567,
according to the official census taker, a vast and bumbling
liar, receiver of puny bribes and secret high acolyte of the
poems of Algernon Charles Swinburne.

Grand Revenant is 49.6 miles from Zenith and 99.2 from
Gopher Prairie.

It was founded in 1903, a year that also saw the birth,
at Kitty Hawk, N. C., of a strange, boxlike contrivance
that held the bright seeds of death for Coventry and
Nagasaki and other proud cities, half the world away.

Its pioneer settler was old Cornelius Ampersand, a
prodigious seducer of Indians along the thundering marge
of Lake Prolix and on the cold, improbable trails that lead
from Baedeker and Larousse to Mount Thesaurus. Corn
was a He-Man, a Wowser, a High Anointed Member of the
Sacred and Splendiferous Tribe of Good Scouts, and if his
thin, despairing wife often wept alone in the night, nobody

37

knew—except perhaps her two or three hundred closest friends.

In the years since old Corn raped his last squaw (and how those golden girls would giggle in the dusk!), Grand Revenant had grown like an angry weed in the fertile soil of the prairie.

Factories came—Wilson & Fadiman, who ravaged the little, firm-breasted hills for copper for moot points; Trilling & Cowley, who made the smoothest, shiniest, most astoundingly complicated little instruments for determining tension and slack (it was hard to say what everybody did before it was possible to determine slack to one-ten-thousandth part of an inch); Mencken & Nathan, who manufactured Hortex and were said to have the seventh largest mangle in the state of Nostalgia.

Stores were born—the Mad Mode Mart, Avis Cormorant, prop. (Miss Cormorant was a nymphomaniac and, very discreetly, a German spy, but her chic was the despair of her rival, Elsie Drear, who was a virgin and an Episcopalian); Blitberg's Department Store which sold everything from needles to yachts, and if one or two salesgirls died each week from a strange and terrible disease called Dreiser's Botch, there was surely no kinder or merrier man in all Revenant than old Sam Blitberg; Dirge & Mouseman (Mrs. Mouseman, née Birdie Jump, was that object of almost inconceivable grandeur, a former inmate of the *Social Register*), where you could buy, for very little more than it would cost to build supernal beauty or to stamp out Yaws, rare stones of devious and bloody history.

Other noble monuments—the Revenant Museum of Art, which boasted a Modigliani and a Dali and a whole roomful of Grant Woods, but which was chiefly notable for its swimming pool which was as deep and blue as a lake; Revenant Junior High School, which regularly and gratifyingly beat the upstart team from East Hemingway in the annual marathon, and if very few of her graduates could tell you who wrote *Thanatopsis* or even *Mantrap,* they usually proved astonishingly nimble at selling not too aqueous real estate and beautifully shiny automobiles, which often ran quite well; and, always and most particularly, Mme. Moriarity's bowling parlors, where the nickering males of Revenant betook themselves for curious delights, which sometimes they even actually enjoyed.

Churches sprang up, to the glory of a Fat God, whose other names were Baal and Moloch and Ahriman and Progress and Rugged Individualism.

Hotels and restaurants—the Revenant Inn, which travellers had been known to compare favorably with the glittering Bellevue-Stratford in Philadelphia, but at which there was no room for the Indians whose doomed campfires had once glowed where now its flying towers mocked the sky; Doug's Hotburger, where the cop on the beat, a cold and melancholy man, dropped in nightly to sigh: "Geez, you take my wife. A good woman, I guess, but no get-up-and-go to her like some of these peppy society dames. And *talk!* Golly! One of these days maybe I'll have to shut the ole girl up." At six o'clock one bitter January morning, he did, very neatly and irrevocably, using the old .44 service revolver with which he had sworn to uphold the law; the Heyday Grille, where Doc Kennicott and George Babbitt and Sam Dodsworth and all the glorious he-male company of competent seducers (about once a year, Babbitt conducted a fumbling, inconclusive experiment with some derisive young woman in a canoe) and two-fisted drinkers (sometimes, uneasily, they had a cocktail before lunch) met every Friday to bumble cheerfully: "Well, I dunno what you other, uh, homo sapiensibuses think, but it strikes this not-so-humble observer that this lil ole burg is sure

goin' straight to the twenty-three skiddoos." Solemnly,
they agree that Grand Revenant could not compare in
splendor with Zenith and Gopher Prairie and Paris and New
York; secretly, they knew that she was strange and beautiful beyond all the other cities of the earth.

II

Shad Ampersand, old Corn's grandson, lived in a neat
$26,500 bungalow called Christmas Past, on Revenant
Heights, overlooking the brisk, aspiring town. He was a tall,
ramshackle hayrick of a man of fifty-six, copper red (a
testimony, it was whispered, to old Corn's prowess with the
squaws) and sad of eye, like a water spaniel or an early
Donatello. An admirer of loneliness and rye whiskey and
thin, hawk-vivid girls, who listened with vast politeness
while he explained such recondite matters as Arbitrary
Microcosm, Limited Frame of Reference, Elementary Symbolism, and Dated or Synthetic Idiom, about all of which
they knew precisely nothing and most enthusiastically
cared even less.

Sitting on his tiny porch on one of the brightest, briefest,
and most poignant of all October afternoons, Shad was very
weightily considering the profound mystery of Sex.

"I'm not one of these highbrow geezers like W. Somerset
Maugham or John Q. Galsworthy," he plondered heavily,
"and it sure gives me a pain in the ole bazookus to hear
some long-haired so-called intellectual claiming that love
and marriage and kiddies and everything a dumb ole
roughneck like me has come to hold most sacred is nothing
more nor less than something called the Biological Urge."

"Hey, you don't have to talk to *me* like that," said

Trenda Boneside sharply. "I'm not the Pulitzer Prize Committee."

She was a small, fierce kitten of a girl, who had lived for nineteen eager, sniffing years with her parents on a farm in Remnant, just across the state line.

"M? Nope. See what you mean," he said placatingly. She was a passionate white flame on a cigar-store lighter. He tried to imagine her cooking his breakfast. Tried and most conspicuously failed.

"No, you don't at all," she snapped at him, this brisk fox terrier of a girl. "You listen to me, Shad Ampersand. I'm not one of those old girls of yours—Carol or Leora or that awful Dodsworth woman, whatever *her* name was."

"Fran," he said humbly.

"Fran. Well, anyway, I'm not. Maybe that old hillbilly talk was all right for them, and even the *American Mercury*. But with me you can just talk like anybody else."

"M."

"That's another thing!" she cried furiously. "That 'M'! What the hell is that supposed to be? The name of a moving picture?"

"Gee, Tren," he sighed. "It's only an experiment in phonetics. You know, how to get something down the way it really sounds. As I was telling ole Doc Bongflap . . ."

Now she was really a tigress.

" 'Bongflap,' " she wailed. "I've known you for a long time, Shad Ampersand, and I've certainly heard some terrible names—Vergil Gunch and Roscoe Geake and Adelbert Shoop—but that's the worst ever. Nobody in the world was ever called Bongflap."

"Well, maybe not, but, drat it, when an author wants to suggest how a character . . ."

"I know all about that," she said, "and I know all about

Charles Dickens, too, and you both make me sick. My God, even *Tarkington* wouldn't call anybody Bongflap. Or Timberlane, either, for that matter. Timber*lane*. Timber*line*. Hansen and Chamberlain ought to be able to get that one, all right, but I think it stinks. I keep thinking it's Tamberlane or Timberleg."

"Aren't we getting a little off the subject, Tren?" he said mildly.

"I don't know. What *was* the subject?"

"Well, uh, love."

"Oh, *that*," she yawned. "What about it?"

"Well, uh," he fumbled. She was a laughing brook of a girl, cool, diamond-bright, a wanderer in secret loveliness. He dreamed of her in a gingham apron, cooking his breakfast. Golly! "Uh, I thought we might get married," he whinnied. It was so perhaps that Paris whispered to Helen before they came to the City of the Topless Towers, so the Roman gave his soul to Egypt's queen on the dreaming bosom of the Nile. She looked at him and suddenly her heart was in her eyes.

"Shad!" she trilled, and now she was a bell.

"Wife!" he clamored through their urgent kiss, and miraculously it was a word in nowise stained with use.

III

The little orange cat called Pox stretched languorously in Shad Ampersand's lap.

"I know you're lonely since your wife, Trenda, left you last November to join Blight Grimes, the polo player and nimble seducer, at his hotel in Chicago, Illinois," she mewed. She was a very fetching device of a cat, an explanatory butler at curtain rise in a Lonsdale comedy.

Shad scratched her ears and thought: I should have known all along about Tren and Blight. The time they went away together for a week back in March and Trenda said —oh, she was very innocent and airy about it!—that they'd just gone up to Alaska to look at polo ponies; the time I found them upstairs in bed and they said they were just lying down because their feet hurt. I must have been pretty credulous, he decided, and Pox blinked her copper eyes in sardonic agreement.

"You're damn right," she purred, "but now, of course, she has delirium tremens and this Grimes character isn't exactly the kind of man you can picture running up and down stairs with paraldehyde and strait jackets. There's a strange streak of cruelty in him."

He nodded, but he was thinking despairingly: I must have failed her somehow. Maybe I was wrong to want to keep her here in Christmas Past, pasting up scrapbooks for an old galoot like me—Blight, doggone his hide, was only forty-nine and lithe and puissant as a sword—when she ought to be running around with kids her own age, going to the movies and coming out with her head all full of stars and dreams (as a matter of fact, he knew she loathed the movies), having a soda with the Gang at Bleeck's and feeding nickels into the juke box for "Smiles" and "Margie," maybe even being kissed, in sweet and childish innocence, in the back seat of a Chevrolet.

"Pope Hartford," said Pox, who was also a mind-reader. "M?"

"Pope Hartford," repeated the cat irritably. "You might as well stick to the period. And while I think of it, you can lay off that 'M' with *me*, too."

Anyway, he had failed her, his lost and golden girl, and she was in Chicago with Blight. He looked at his watch. 11:46. Probably they were back from the theatre

now and up in their suite and Blight was slipping the little
silver-fox cape from her shoulders.

"His heart contracted," murmured Pox.

"M, uh, I mean what?"

"Don't keep making me say everything twice, for God's
sake. 'His heart contracted.' That goes in there somewhere.
In parentheses. After the second 'and,' I should say. It's
one of your mannerisms, though not a very fortunate one.
Also, you seem to have forgotten that she's on the sauce,
if you'll pardon the expression."

Trenda spifflicated, swizzled, tiddly. He knew it was
the truth, but the thought was a sharp agony, an unthinkable desecration, as if he saw the slender, terrible beauty
of the Samothrace deep in foul mud and marred with the
droppings of obscene and dreadful birds.

"I think you're overreaching yourself there," said Pox.
"Too many modifiers, and it's a pretty elaborate image.
After all, you aren't Henry James."

"Golly, Pox—"

"Ah, the hell with it. Let it go. It's your stream of consciousness, thank God, not mine."

In his despair, his cold, unutterable loss, Shad Ampersand began to think of all the world, and Pox looked at
him sharply for a moment and then hopped off his lap
and left the room. Shad thought: Marriage. A man and a
woman—him and Tren, Romeo and Juliet, Philemon and
Baucis, Ruth and, and, drat it, who *was* that guy—anyway,
they fell in love—oh, Tren, sweet, we *must* have been in
love the night we read "Gideon Planish" until the stars
went out!—and they promised to love, honor, and obey—
golly, the most beautiful words in the English language,
except, of course, maybe some parts of Shakespeare—till
death you did part. But then something happened. One
day they woke up and the magic was gone. (He and Tren

were having breakfast, Homogenized Virtex and Spookies, and suddenly, appallingly, she cried, "Shad! I'm going away with Blight! Right this minute! He's going to take me to London, Paris, Berlin—Gee, I've always wanted to see the Taj Mahal and all those cute little Androgynes or whatever you call 'em—and we're going to take along a sleeping bag, you know, like in that Hemingway book I read some of, and camp right out on the biggest darn ole Alp we can find." He had burbled, "Gee, that sounds mighty interesting, Tren. Yes, sir. Like to take a little trip sometime myself," but the Spookies were ashes in his mouth.) Anyway, it always ended—either in the hideous, clinging slime of the divorce court, or else—and this was unutterably worse—in the terrible, icy vacuum of indifference, the final, shameful acceptance of infidelity. ("You ought to get yourself a girl, Shad," she had told him one night; as usual, she was sitting on Blight's lap, knitting a new-fangled sock. "Why don't you call up Avis Cormorant? *There's* a cheerful little giver for you. Or maybe one of those Piutes you say old Corn was always talking about." He had almost struck her then.) It was this, this modern cynicism, this flat denial of marriage, not the Communists or the Fascists or the Technocrats or even the hot-eyed disciples of Fourier and Adam Smith, that was destroying America. In the ultimate scheme of things, the continuing marriage of Tren and Shad Ampersand, or, if you chose, of plain Helen and Robert Lynd, was more important than—

"Hey," said Pox, putting his head around the door, "I wouldn't disturb you, except you didn't seem to be getting anywhere in particular with that editorial. Anyway, she's back."

"Who?" spurted Shad, though his heart obliteratingly knew.

"Who the hell did you think?" said Pox scornfully.
"Little Round Heels. With a hangover I could swing on
by my tail."

She came in then, with a glad, unsteady rush, a broken
cry, into his waiting arms, and if she was damaged, if she
was no longer the bright, imperious child his dreams had
known, but something harder, wiser, and infinitely sad,
he had no eyes to see.

"Tren, baby!" he whispered fiercely in her hair.

"Shad!" she breathed, and gave him the ruined glory
of her smile. After all, she thought, stroking the remembered kindness of his cheek, you always have to figure
that the old horror is practically indestructible, there
ought to be plenty of books still batting around in him for
all the endless years to come.

"Nice going, sister," murmured Pox, and most discreetly
shut the door.

The Education of Henry Apley

(A Brief Grapple with the Boston Legend After Reading the Complete Works of Mr. J. P. Marquand on the Subject)

I

Grindle Point was always best in the fall. If I knew how to write, I could tell how the old river went dreaming by in the sun and how the copper beeches marched down to its bank in strict and orderly procession. Sometimes in the morning, before the mist had burned away, the trees looked like silver ghosts and there were diamonds in the grass on the lawn. Time itself seemed to hang suspended in that clear, level light, so it was easy to believe that all the people who had once lived there were there still and always would be. As I've said, however, I am not a writer, and all I know is that I am part of Grindle Point. It is where I belong.

I shall never forget the day I came back to it after the war. My father was in his study, reading the *Transcript* and eating an apple, as he always did in the late afternoon.

"Hello," he said. "Kill any Germans?"

"Eight or nine," I said. "Nothing to amount to much."

"I suppose not," he said. "Naturally you were decorated?"

"Well, yes," I said. I hadn't meant to tell anybody about the medal, because there is nothing worse than showing off. I only hoped he wouldn't mention it to the servants.

47

"You look older," he said. "Probably time you were think-ing of getting married."

"I don't know," I said. "I've never been much good at that kind of thing."

"An awkward business," said my father. "Going off that way with a comparatively strange woman."

I could see he was embarrassed. He wanted to tell me something, but it was hard because we had never talked together very freely.

"A damned awkward business," he repeated irritably. "They ought to have told you about it at Harvard. I suppose it's customary these days to assume that a gentleman knows about these things instinctively, but sometimes he doesn't."

"Yes, sir," I said.

"All a man can do is try to play the game," he said. "It won't be easy, especially with your training, but the Apleys have always got through it somehow. With me it was always something one owed to Harvard. A matter of loyalty."

I could understand that. Harvard had made me what I was, and the least I could do in return was to make a certain amount of effort.

"I'll do my best, sir," I said.

Just the same, I wasn't happy when I got up to my old room and started unpacking my bag. Outside my window the river lay opalescent in the twilight, but for a moment I saw it as a dark and relentless torrent bearing me on into the unknowable future, and I shuddered. I didn't want to get married; I just wanted to go back to Harvard.

II

I was bringing George Hill's trunk up from the cellar. It was pretty heavy, and I put it down for a minute outside the library door. I didn't mean to listen, of course, but I couldn't help hearing them inside.

"We've got to be careful," said Jane. "He may be feeble-minded, but he isn't blind."

George laughed. "He went to Harvard, didn't he?" he said.

I came in and put the trunk down. My wife was sitting on George's lap. She looked tired, and I felt guilty. It was probably an imposition to ask her to entertain George, because after all he was my guest.

"Who went to Harvard?" I asked idiotically.

"Oh, my God," said Jane.

"Rutherford B. Hayes," said George. "He was the typical Harvard man—dense but energetic."

George often talked that way, probably because he had gone to school at St. Paul's in Garden City instead of the right one. Afterward, of course, he'd run sixty yards against Yale with a broken neck, and he'd made Hedgehog and the Scapula Club, but he never seemed to feel the same way about Harvard as the rest of us.

"Listen, clumsy," said Jane. "How about getting on with that trunk?"

"Well," I said, "I thought I might just sit down here with you two for a minute and have a drink. My feet hurt."

"Never mind about your feet," said Jane. "You get that trunk out in the car. George and I have to start right away if we're going to get to New York before it's dark."

"You're going to New York?" I asked. "You and George?"

"Just for the week-end," said George. "You don't mind, do you?"

"Of course not," I said, "but some people might think it was a little odd. You know how it is in Boston."

"My God," said Jane, "I think he's jealous!"

"Of old George?" That made me laugh. I knew a lot of

things had changed since I was at Harvard, but of course there were a lot of other things that never changed. I hadn't quite liked George's remark about Rutherford B. Hayes, who, incidentally, had only gone to the law school, but he was my best friend and I knew he was a gentleman. He might be wrong about some things, but he'd be right about the important ones, and that was what really mattered.

They came out while I was still strapping the trunk onto the car, and climbed into the front seat. George started the motor.

"Good-bye," I said. "Have a good time."

"Good-bye, darling," said Jane. "Don't forget to put the cat out."

It was like Jane to think about the cat, even when she was tired and upset. I smiled as I watched the car dropping out of sight down the drive. Things often work out a lot better than you have any business to hope they will.

Eva's Deathbed Revisited

(The following play is an account of a nightmare experienced by a man who went to a play by Mr. Maxwell Anderson and then went home and tried to get to sleep by rereading Uncle Tom's Cabin. *Most of the speeches are supposed to be in blank verse, so the actors' voices should be imagined as swooping around a good deal, rhythmically, like the cars on a roller coaster. How to raise Little Eva up and get her out the window is a hard technical problem, but it ought to be attempted because this business was particularly effective in the dream. The whole thing probably needs some kind of banjo accompaniment.)*

LITTLE EVA *(who is not going to last much longer)*: What says it by the clock, by that shrewd handyman of Time there on the wall?

ST. CLARE *(her father)*: Four-forty-one. Four-forty-one or two.

LITTLE EVA: So dark for such a time! So dark a time regardless of the clock, when honest men must suffer for their skins—the accidental difference in the shape and stain of that which gives us color. Father!

ST. CLARE: Eva, dear?

LITTLE EVA: What is it, please, that makes some black, some white? You, white; Tom, black; and all the world divided thus in two?

ST. CLARE: You are unwell.

LITTLE EVA: Unwell? No, *well!* I'm going home. To God!

ST. CLARE: To God? And where is God, or what?

LITTLE EVA (*with tender amusement*): He is no thing, I think, that you would know. No wheel, no gear, no formula, no strict pragmatic pattern or design that you can study from a book. "What's God?" God's love; God's Uncle Tom, or Mr. Lincoln, or a daisy in a field.

ST. CLARE: She's fading fast! The fever in her blood gives rise to thoughts like these. Oh, Tom! Oh, Uncle Tom!

UNCLE TOM (*entering left and removing a stovepipe hat*): Yassuh, boss. I'se comin'.

ST. CLARE: She's dying, Tom!

UNCLE TOM: Dyin'? Whut is death? De faulty chemistry ob our po' flesh may melt. De atoms change aroun'. De earth git back to earth. De *soul* don' nebba die!

LITTLE EVA (*expiring fast*): God bless you, Tom! This rough, untutored mind has its own metaphysic. The lore of jungle priests, the atavistic sense of secrets lost before our time, survive, I think, in this poor woolly pate.

UNCLE TOM: Dat's right, Miss Eva. De beat ob Congo drums ain't lost; it's runnin' in ma blood. *Ah* ain't forgot de black man's lore!

ST. CLARE: But Tom is still a slave.

LITTLE EVA: All that will pass. Machines now building in the North will change the face of this unhappy land, this rich, agrarian South. Steel hands that move by steam will pluck our cotton, and the slave, without his useful function in the scheme, will vanish from our fields.

UNCLE TOM: We all be free? To wuk, to lub, to *vote?*

LITTLE EVA: The vote can't come at first. The subtle rot,

the slow decay of slavery, has bit too deep. The black must *earn* the franchise, prove that he can grasp the awful concept of the state. *Then* he may vote—the half made whole, the shackled serf made free, prepared for life as I'm prepared for—

ST. CLARE: Ah, don't say that! Don't say the word! I cannot let you go!

LITTLE EVA (*beginning to levitate*): But go I must. Already I can hear the sweet and muted humming of the stars, already see God's infinite plantation.

ST. CLARE: Oh, no!

UNCLE TOM: Whut it look like up dah, chile?

LITTLE EVA (*about halfway up to the ceiling*): Oh, fair! Oh, very fair! The work of many hands well done by one machine; no tangled laws to bind bright, imperious wings; the people free to love and pray; no hunger, hate, or sickness of the flesh.

UNCLE TOM: Whut form ob government dey got, Missy?

LITTLE EVA (*heading out of the window*): The best of each we know. The strong and wise are still in charge, but without hardship to the weak. The brighter angels near the throne use their position but to serve those farther off. It is a blend of all the sweetest dreams men dream—Democracy well ordered and controlled, the Total State where all decrees are just, a Soviet where men still own the land.

UNCLE TOM: I'se scared dat ain't goin' to wuk so good, Miss Eva.

LITTLE EVA: It will! Just pray for faith, poor Tom! Dear Father, pray! The time will come, I know, when both of you, alike in pigment and design, will join me in the sky. Goodbye. My weary day on earth at last is done. I'm going home!

(*She floats skillfully out of the window, but can be heard dimly offstage for a minute or two. She seems to be explaining something to God.*)

ST. CLARE: She's gone. She's in a better place now, Uncle Tom.

UNCLE TOM (*to himself*): Don' *soun'* like bettah place to me. Not wid dat little Eva dah. (*He has been facing the wall, head bowed. Now he turns around. There is an automatic in his hand.*) Git up yo' dukes, St. Clah! Long I disliked bofe you an' she. I woulda brought her down jus' now, a-tumblin' off dat ceilin' like a grouse, but dey was but one shot in dis here gun. I'se saved dat shot for you. Why plug de daid when you kin plug de quick?

ST. CLARE (*with his hands partly raised*): Why, what's the matter, Tom? What secret sickness festers in your soul, what wrong that only lead can right?

UNCLE TOM: You don' know dat? Yo' think I'se fooled by al dem purty words dat don' quite rhyme, but run in neat and calculated rhythm, again' de colored man? Dis Little Eva like to change mah skin an' pull de racial kink from out mah hair. She gone to Heben talkin' mighty big, 'bout woolly pates an' pigments an' designs, but still Ah got *you* lef'. *Keep up dem han's, St. Clah!*

(*St. Clare, however, has managed to drop his hand and get at his own gun. They both fire at once, and both fall to the ground, fatally wounded.*)

ST. CLARE: You've got me, Tom! This boil and tumult in my breast, this chill, this fading light, this deadly damp can mean one thing: I'm done. Why is it, Tom? Why is it I must die?

TOM: You was her paw. Ain't dat enough?

ST. CLARE (*thoughtfully, after a long pause*): Enough, and more, I think.

UNCLE TOM (*raising himself on one elbow*): Whut dat you say?

ST. CLARE: I say that you were right. To be the author of

that yellow hair, that tinkling voice, those blank geranium eyes is cause enough for any man to die.

UNCLE TOM: *Whut dat you say?*

ST. CLARE: I loathed her, too, the empty-headed brat. The half-chewed thought, the sanctimonious smile, the pat, inane abstraction—all that she thought was borrowed from bad books, all that she loved was Little Eva's voice. She was the queen of bores. I die content, now she belongs to God.

UNCLE TOM: I'se wronged you, Massa.

ST. CLARE: And *I've* wronged you, a sad and mortal wrong, but most *she* wronged us both. Dear Tom, give me your hand.

UNCLE TOM: An' you take mine, an' hol' it fast an' strong, until we come to that fair place where Little Eva ain't.

(*They die and go to Hell together, hand in hand and smiling. A red, lovely, and infernal light plays on the stage as the curtain falls.*)

Shakespeare, Here's Your Hat

(A New Play by Mr. William Saroyan, in Book Form, with the Customary Prefatory Notes by the Author)

I

This play is a masterpiece. It is young, gusty, comical, tragic, beautiful, heroic, and as real as a slaughterhouse or some dame fixing her hair. It could only have been written in America, by an Armenian boy who is an artist and a lover and a dreamer. All at once. All mixed up. It could only have been written by Saroyan.

Other people write plays, but they are no good. I go to them and I sit there and think, "My God, this is lousy! It was written by a man in an English suit of clothes who makes fifty thousand dollars a year, but it is not alive. It is dead. It stinks." A man making fifty thousand dollars a year doesn't write about Life; he writes about other people who make fifty thousand dollars a year; he writes about a bunch of rich corpses and, generally speaking, he is a rich corpse himself. Not me, though. Not Saroyan. This play is lyric and simple and alive. It says just exactly what it means. When the boy in this play dynamites his grandmother because he needs some money to get gin, that is something real. When he puts a nickel in the piano for music, that is real, too. When he

56

meets the society girl and says, "How's chances, sister?" and
she answers, "O.K., Mac," that is a real, lovely, and heart-
breaking thing.

In the plays about the rich corpses, it takes three acts and
about sixty thousand dollars' worth of scenery to get around
to a beautiful and natural request like that, and half the
time nothing comes of it, either.

II

I am a warm, rich, and passionate human being and very
few things are too much for me. Not even drama criticism.
When a man writes in a newspaper or a magazine that he
doesn't understand this play or is bored by it, that is all right
with me. It is hard to imagine anybody not liking something
that is as eloquent and native and true as a child running
after a butterfly or a colored man scratching himself, but I
do not get sore. I am just sorry for the crazy bastard.

III

The following are excerpts from some of the reviews published in the New York press:

RICHARD WATTS, JR., Herald Tribune: *It is a darling play
. . . but we must not ignore the Chinese.*

BROOKS ATKINSON, Times: *Lit with the same ineluctable
fire that once informed the witches and the cauldron on the
heath.*

JOHN MASON BROWN, Post: *Challenges the best of Aris-
tophanes, Gogol, Pirandello, Racine, and the Song of Solo-
mon.*

BURTON RASCOE, World-Telegram: *Either Saroyan is
crazy . . . or I am. A child has done this horrid thing.*

I V

This play was written in an hour and a half with a quill pen
I generally keep in a little bowl of bird shot. For a man like
me, an original, talented, profound, sensitive, and humorous
Armenian, a typewriter is an artificial barrier standing between the living brain and the clean paper. It is not for me,
as the airbrush was not for Michelangelo and the adding
machine was not for Euclid.

At that time I was working in Hollywood, where all authors use typewriters. "The greatest play in the world is
right there on those keys, if you can only figure out how to
hit them in the right order," one of them said to me. He was
a man who made forty, fifty, a hundred thousand dollars a
year, and he went around with a falcon on his wrist. I would
rather use the quill pen. Me, personally.

V

Generally speaking, the American theatre is the aspirin of
the middle classes. People go to a play because they want to
get in out of the rain. Or because they have a date with
some mouse in it later on. Or just because they happen to
know the press agent and don't have to pay. It is not that
way with me. I go because I love Life. That is an important
statement and I want to repeat it: *William Saroyan loves
Life*.

In the theatre today, except in this play of mine, what
you see is not Life. It is a drawing-room compromise with
Life arrived at by a man who has never had to sleep in a silo
or eat birch bark or trap mice to make himself a hat or any
of the other brave, haunting, and sometimes foolish things

people do when they don't happen to have been born on
Park Avenue or in Newport, Rhode Island.

The cure for the American theatre is more plays like this
one. More plays by Saroyan.

THE TIME OF *WHOSE* LIFE?

(*A dormitory at Groton, just before vespers. Three of the
boys—Jones Minor, Ferris Major, and Tilden Elliott III—
are changing from their rugger togs into their vespers togs.
They are breathless and wondering, enchanted with a sweet
world that also holds things like ginger beer and scones and
Esquire* magazine. *Ferguson Nicholson, the housemaster, a
tall, thin man, noble because of the pain in his heart, is sitting in one corner, reading* Variety *and drinking a dry Martini. In another corner an old graduate, mad and very dirty,
is throwing cards into a hat. A scrubwoman comes in. A lifetime of toil, including six years with the Shuberts, has not
quenched her brimming and precious spirit.*)

SCRUBWOMAN (*compassionate, supernatural; the Earth
Mother*): How about sweeping up around here, gents? Get
some of the fug out of the joint.

JONES MINOR: Sweep. You won't sweep the torture and
despair of Life from the heart with a broom. . . .

FERRIS MAJOR: Or the beauty of it either.

OLD GRADUATE (*lost in his eternal dream of the past*): Dissolute and damned. Both the student body and the faculty.

HOUSEMASTER: Elliott.

ELLIOTT: Yes, sir?

HOUSEMASTER: Go down to the Greek's and get me two
ham sandwiches and a billiard ball.

ELLIOTT (*uneasily*): What for?

HOUSEMASTER (*watching the scrubwoman; fascinated by*

*the unique, all-female, and mysterious experiences once en-
joyed somewhere in the world by this scrubwoman*): Ham
on white. British mustard.

ELLIOTT (*still puzzled, but going out dutifully*): A cue
ball?

HOUSEMASTER: No, the red one. (*To the scrubwoman;
waving the cocktail-shaker*) Martini?

SCRUBWOMAN: No thanks, pal. The Head don't like us to
drink on duty.

HOUSEMASTER: You're missing a lot. *I'm* always drunk. The
days and nights are whittling me away, and—(*He breaks off
as the Headmaster, a quiet, grave man, carrying a bridle,
comes into the cubicle.*) Were you looking for something,
sir?

HEADMASTER (*genially*): Ah, Nicholson. Fried again, I see.
(*With a change of mood, sternly*) Ferris Major!

FERRIS MAJOR (*springing up, dynamic, translated*): Sir?

HEADMASTER: Is there a polo pony in this room?

FERRIS MAJOR: A what, sir?

HEADMASTER (*going to a closet, opening it, and discovering a polo pony*): As I thought. You know the rules, I believe, Ferris. No polo ponies or young women in dorm after
four o'clock.

FERRIS MAJOR (*in a low voice, accepting his doom*): Yes,
sir.

HEADMASTER: This means a birching, of course. (*He goes
out, leading the polo pony; fatal, inexorable, the Scourge of
God.*)

OLD GRADUATE (*throwing the ace of spades at the hat*):
Dissolute and damned. Both the student body and the faculty.

HOUSEMASTER (*still preoccupied by the scrubwoman; the
strange, illicit, by-gone adventures of the scrubwoman*): I
drink to your unconquerable spirit, Mrs. Le Bogan.

SCRUBWOMAN: My name ain't Mrs. Le Bogan.

HOUSEMASTER: Then Guinevere or Héloïse. In any case, I drink. To your ancient sins, Faustine.

SCRUBWOMAN: Listen, what the hell are you talking about?

HOUSEMASTER (*wearily*): I don't know. What do any of us talk about? Love. Happiness. Towering injustice everywhere. The game with St. Paul's. (*Furiously, draining the Martini*) How the hell do I know? What do *you* talk about?

SCRUBWOMAN (*sly, roguish, Salome, old but not regenerate*): Jeez, I dunno, Mister. Harry K. Thaw. The time we burned up the city of Chicago. Shooting Garfield. All like that.

HOUSEMASTER: Life! The terror and the wonder and the beauty of it! (*Gathering momentum*) Life! *Life!* LIFE!

(*As he goes on, Elliott re-enters with the sandwiches and the billiard ball; the scrubwoman wrings out her mop and starts to wipe up the floor; the old graduate opens another pack of cards and begins throwing them at the hat; Jones Minor and Ferris Major gather up their hymnals and prayer books, the polo pony trots in backward through the door and re-enters the closet. Life has come full circle.*)

OLD GRADUATE (*sombre, triumphant; his opinion of everything borne out*): Dissolute and damned. Both the student body and the faculty.

(*From the courtyard the bell for vespers sounds, very wonderful and sad. The curtain falls.*)

To a Little Girl at Christmas

(How a famous question might be answered if it were asked today and Mr. Westbrook Pegler happened to be writing editorials for the "Sun")

You're damn right there is a Santa Claus, Virginia. He lives down the road a piece from me, and my name for him is Comrade Jelly Belly, after a poem composed about him once by an admiring fellow-traveller now happily under the sod.

In a manner of speaking, this Jelly Belly is in the distributing end of the toy business, and I guess the story of how that came about has its points for the social historian. Mr. Claus is understandably a reticent man, but the facts would seem to be that he was born quite a while back in the Red Hook section under the appetizing moniker of Sammy Klein. His mother was employed in a celebrated bucket of blood known as the Haymarket, also in what you might call the distributing end, and his father was any one of a number of slick operators, though the weight of evidence would seem to point to Police Lieutenant Becker of fragrant memory. How his mother happened to name him Sammy Klein is not known to this deponent, but there is a suspicion that she got it off the front of a clothing store she was in the habit of looting.

It is not my way to speak ill of the dead, Virginia, but you'd have to go a long way to find a scurvier pair than the two who spawned the tot we're discussing.

In his youth, Jelly Belly did a short stretch of military service with the Hudson Dusters and the Dead Rabbits, two pinko front organizations of the period, and then passed on to the less perilous profession of rolling lushes in the subway. According to surviving court records, an operative in this classification, variously known as Sid Kline, Saul ("Fingers") Klem, and K. Stein, was arrested no less than thirty-seven times between 1908 and 1916, and stored in the poky for periods ranging from ninety days up. This was presumably Santa Claus.

So much, Virginia, for our hero's boyhood. In 1917, as you probably remember, a sick college professor in the White House ranted us into what he called a war to make the world safe for democracy, and Jelly Belly had one of the first numbers they pulled out of the bowl. This, however, was one rap he knew how to beat, and young Klein sat out World War I in a hospital for the criminally insane, having prudently assaulted a six-year-old girl on the very day his draft board invited him to call. He was pardoned in 1919 at the special request of the Assistant Secretary of the Navy, whose name happened to be Franklin Delano Roosevelt, and who even then displayed a strong affinity for the unbalanced.

It was at this time that Jelly Belly changed his name to Santa Claus, partly to escape from his too vivacious past and partly because he had just become a full member of the Communist Party and needed an alias with a sanctimonious flavor. His affiliation with the toy business began soon after that. When F.D.R. sprung Jelly Belly, or Santa Claus, from the loonybin, he went to work for the New York *Times* as a bushwhacker in the circulation department, his job being to mess up delivery boys from the rival *Herald*. This was naturally an employment highly to his taste, but when one boy died as the result of his attentions, it seemed sagacious to move on. It was in this manner that he came to F. A. O. Schwarz, where they made him first a shipping clerk and then the driver of a truck. The rest of the story—the prearranged hijackings that proved profitable enough to set Santa Claus up in the toy business for himself, the deals with Henry Agard Wallace, Felix Frankfurter, and his old friend Roosevelt that permitted him to pick the taxpayer's pocket to the tune of about eighty million dollars a year—is too complicated and dirty for a lady of your tender years. The important fact is that there *is* a Santa Claus, Virginia—a fat old party, with nasty habits and a dirty white beard, who, for reasons best known to himself, likes to go around either wholly undressed or else in an ill-fitting red suit.

Today, Jelly Belly enjoys what is sometimes called the odor of sanctity, being generally regarded as a hell of a fellow by little children, soft-headed women, and the kind of deep thinkers who openly profess their opposition to the sterilization of all Communists. My own information is somewhat different. Jelly Belly gets around even more than Eleanor the Great, and I can't speak for his activities in other parts of the country. In my neighborhood, however, it is a matter of common knowledge that the burglary rate never fails to hit its peak at Christmas. No one has ever been caught for any of these misdemeanors, but the evidence in each case is always the same—a few shoddy toys in a stocking on the mantelpiece, and a mink coat or a pearl necklace missing from the hostess's effects. One victim I know said she wouldn't mind so much if the toys were any good, but they are just the cheap, tasteless junk that crooked labor unions have been turning out ever since the Great Brain decided to sell out his country to the lazy and incompetent.

I could go on for a long time telling you about Jelly Belly, Virginia. I could tell you, for instance, how the gross old slattern who passes herself off as his housekeeper would be described in less respectable pages than these by quite another word. Or I could tell you how he is a member of the Westchester Commuters Association, the National Association of Dahlia Growers, the Society for Improving the Condition of the Poor, and any number of other thinly disguised Communist organizations. Or I could even tell you with what drooling pleasure he beats his eight undersized reindeer, whose cruel whip sores I have seen with my own eyes. But these are probably not good things for a little girl to know. Youth is a time for innocent dreams and illusions, Virginia, and I don't believe I could live comfortably with myself if I destroyed yours. Yes, Virginia, there is a Santa Claus. There is old Jelly Belly.

On a Darkling Plain

(Two ladies from very different magazines, conceivably The Saturday Evening Post *and* The New Yorker, *clash by noon)*

Madge Farraday stepped through the door of the restaurant and into the foyer outside the dining room. The wind in the street had unfurled its banners in her cheeks, and a few flakes of snow still glistened in the flung-back mane of hair, which it would have been very dangerous indeed to call red. There were little permanent crinkles of laughter around her blue eyes, and her generous mouth held its own mutinous hint of merriment—at the world, at life, at herself. She was dressed in a dark-blue jump-along that clung to her slender body in just the proper places; her small hat was an expensive absurdity; and her tiny shoes and the feet in them seemed made for dancing. Young, you felt, was the word for this girl. She was radiantly, triumphantly young—like a tree, a bird, the proud figurehead of a Viking ship. She was, as a matter of fact, twenty-three, and almost everything lay before her, including this lunch with Bob Contrapine, who was young, too, and had a funny twisted grin that might come to mean a lot—too much, perhaps, if you weren't careful.

Lunch at Gorza's. She looked around appreciatively. There could hardly be a more satisfactory place for what she felt they had to say to one another. The discreetly uniformed attendants, the sombrely luxurious furnishings, the proprietor who might well have been a grand duke in disguise, the waiting diners who so inevitably belonged in this atmosphere of security and sophistication. Her eye paused briefly on a beautiful woman sitting in a chair against the wall.

Mrs. Flexner touched the bell on the table beside her. The proprietor came over, and she pointed to her glass.
"You wanna *more* drink, Miz Flesner?" he said.
"Yes. I wanna more drink," she said. "Get it."
"O.K., O.K. But I dunno . . ."
"Get it," she said.
She was twenty-two. Her face was pale and discontented, and one shoulder was two or three inches higher than the other. When she danced, she crouched down a little to lower her skirt because her ankles were rather thick, and she held her partner tightly around the waist because there was always time for that. Her coat would have to do another year, unless this lunch worked out. She looked around the waiting room. A fine dump. Every tart in New York winds up in Gorza's, she thought. Look at that redheaded tramp that just came in. Look at me. A waiter went by and she could see his calves swelling against the worn cloth of his uniform. The man she was meeting had no calves, or much of anything else. Well, there would always be waiters, though, of course, the problem of a tip . . . Mrs. Flexner remembered her teeth and did not smile.

Madge Farraday stopped a little breathlessly beside the empty chair. "Excuse me," she said in her clear young voice, "but is this seat taken?"

"Mmm," said Mrs. Flexner.

"Then you won't mind if I sit down?" said Madge Farraday. Her eyes sparkled as she sank into the welcoming upholstery. She had the grace of a healthy young animal. "What a day!" she said, throwing back her hair. "Oh, that snow! I can still feel it against my face!"

"Filthy," said Mrs. Flexner. "Do you see that wop anywhere?"

Madge glanced at the lovely face beside her with amusement. "Wop?" she asked.

Mrs. Flexner was spared the trouble of answering, because the proprietor arrived at that moment with a glass on a tray.

"Jus' thisa one, Miz Flesner," he said. "I tell you that, please. I don' wan' no trouble."

"He don' wan' no trouble," Mrs. Flexner said to Madge Farraday.

Madge gave a little tinkle of laughter. She looked very young and appealing. After all, she didn't meet Bob Contrapine at Gorza's every day of her life. "I'd like a glass of sherry, please," she said. "Some nice, sweet sherry."

"Christ," said Mrs. Flexner.

The proprietor left, and Madge smiled at her companion. "I suppose you're waiting for somebody?" she said shyly.

"Yes," said Mrs. Flexner. She felt a little better after the second Martini. This is quite a babe, she thought. I wonder what she knows about waiters.

"So am I," said Madge Farraday. She was a little intimidated by the other's cold perfection, but she went on resolutely, "My young man. Or at least I *hope* he's my young man."

"Your husband?" said Mrs. Flexner. She thought briefly of her own husband. Dr. Brown says alcoholism is really

a disease. Leprosy is also a disease, but you don't necessarily pick them to go bumming around with.

"Well, not yet," said Madge Farraday, blushing a little.
"He's only a v.p. in charge of consumer desecration right
now, but I guess they think pretty highly of him. I know
I do. That nice, funny smile."

"How are his calves?" said Mrs. Flexner.

"What?"

"Nothing," said Mrs. Flexner. "I was thinking about
something else. Waiter!"

It was the proprietor, however, who came over to their
chairs.

"Please, Miz Flesner," he said. "What I ask you, eh?"

"I want a Martini," said Mrs. Flexner very distinctly.
"Or do you want me to crumple up this joint?"

"Please, Miz Flesner. I don' wan' to have to call—"

"Try it," she said. "Just try it is all I say. A *double*
Martini. And you'd better bring this young lady some more
of that Lavoris."

"Sherry," said Madge Farraday, whose eyes were a little
brighter from the unaccustomed wine.

"Lavoris," said Mrs. Flexner. "All right, beat it."

The proprietor withdrew, and for a moment the ladies
sat in silence. At last Madge spoke. She looked like a little
girl trying to seem grown up at her first party.

"And yours," she said. "Tell me about yours."

"What do you want to know?" said Mrs. Flexner.

"What's he like? What does he do? What are your
plans? Oh, I want to know *everything!*"

"Well," said Mrs. Flexner. "Everything" was a fairly
large order when it came to Dillon Flexner. The combination of Yale and then that long fall from the windmill at

Sconset accounted for a good deal, but it left some things
to be explained. It still astonished her to remember her
husband setting out those muskrat traps for the children.
Seriously and intently fastening on the bait and pulling
back the jaws. Disappointment with life took odd forms.
As a matter of fact, if he hadn't been so dismayingly plain,
she might have found his total irresponsibility rather at-
tractive. Boyish. The beatings, of course, were nothing,
and the girls . . . Well, as far as the girls were concerned,
they must have been rather amused. God knows, she had
been. At least, at first. No, when you came to Dillon, there
wasn't much to say. "Everything" was actually just about
the same as nothing. As for this other one—the one that
was coming . . . "I don't know," she said. "He's tall."

"Oh, so is mine!" cried Madge Farraday. She remembered that so well, and the kind eyes, and the big
hands that looked clumsy but weren't really. She often
wondered what went on in that head of his, under that
funny, untidy hair. He never said much when they were
together, but the way he looked at her said all she wanted
to know. Oh, she could see him now. A shadow fell across
the little table in front of her and she looked up, and there,
amazingly, miraculously, he stood. Tall and somehow shin-
ing.

"Bob!" she cried, and her heart was in her eyes. "You've
come at last!"

Mrs. Flexner looked up, too.

"Hello, Robert," she said. "It's about time. I was just
about to start calling the hospitals."

Zulu, Watch the Snakes

Spring came very late that year (though well and truly in the end), and beyond the fields and the men working in the fields you could see Laredo or Dallas, diminishing and dancing in the sun. I have put down that sentence for reasons of my own—to remind myself that I was once attentive to popular literary accents and prepared to rearrange them for purposes of my own. It has, however, almost nothing to do with anything that is to follow and I suggest you forget it.

Anyway, on the afternoon I want to write about, my eighteen-year-old sister Zulu and I were lying out behind one of the barns, watching the copperheads stirring back to life in the hot sun, and talking just a little out of our depth, as I suppose children always will.

"You noticed anything in particular about the writing that's been going on this year?" she asked.

"No," I said. "I don't read much."

At the moment, Zulu is in her final year at Lawrenceville. First, she was in Perry Ross House, where most of the Laredo girls go; then she spent two years at Woodhull; and now she's a director of Upper, which is pretty good if you're a Texas girl in a big Eastern school. She is editor of the *Lawrence;* president of Periwig; and last spring she got a minor "L" in Track. Anyone from Laredo can tell

71

you that's pretty good, especially if you live out north on Townsend Street, which is about the same as living up on Riverside Drive in New York. Townsend Street girls usually wind up at either Peddie or Admiral Farragut, and then go on to Colgate or Rutgers. You can tell that about them just as surely as you can that their clothes will come from Peck & Peck and they'll be meeting people under the clock at the Biltmore. Zulu's young men, of course, take her to the Colony, and she buys most of her clothes in Paris.

"I've just been reading some kind of a novel called 'Cash McCall,' by a boy called Cameron Hawley," she said.

"You have?" There were a couple of big snakes warming up right beside my ankle, but they weren't ready yet.

"It's a pretty complicated book," she said, "but the point seems to be that you can gyp the government out of a couple of million dollars and still get the girl. It all seems to be a matter of adjusting your tax base, or some damn thing. All I really got out of it was that if you've got any sense, an eight-dollar lunch only really costs you forty cents."

"Why bother your pretty head?" I said, watching the snakes.

"Well, it is apparently some kind of a trend. This fawning regard for big business. The interesting thing, or anyway the least *uninteresting* thing, about this book is the idea that practically everything can be charged off to capital gains, including women. You understand any of this?"

"No," I said.

"Neither do I. There is also depreciation. Suppose you happen to have an apartment carved out of living rock . . ."

"What?"

"That's out of the book. I forget the details, but this

man has chopped himself out a very fancy little establishment in the side of a mountain, and he flies the girl there in his private plane."

"Zulu," I said, "for God's sake, watch the snakes."

"*You* watch them," she said. "The point is that this would appear to be a pleasure trip. Or at any rate hardly a business one, since this girl hasn't got more than two hundred thousand dollars to her name, and even that is tied up in an irrevocable trust."

The reason Zulu was called Zulu was that, even as a baby, she was very dark and bushy and warlike. Once she got started, you had about as much chance of stopping her as a Mack truck. It used to amuse my father.

"Well, anyway," she said, "this plane cost a quarter of a million dollars in the first place and God knows how much to keep up. Normally, it would seem like a rather expensive method of getting girls off to yourself. However, we live in strange times, and if you know the ropes, nothing really costs anything."

It had cost us around ten thousand dollars to send Zulu to Lawrenceville for four years, not counting her clothes and allowance, and lately it had begun to seem to me that it might be a mistake.

"This plane," she said, "used for what I think we can only describe as a facetious purpose, apparently came right off his income tax. Gasoline, wear and tear on the motors and presumably the upholstery, obsolescence of equipment—the works. All deductible. You see what I mean?"

"You sure you've got this straight?"

"It's near enough," she said. "What I object to is that everybody keeps going on about the amazing *style* of this man's operations. The girl is particularly impressed. First,

the two-motored plane—a remodelled DC-6, I think—then
the house in the cliff, then, as I remember it, a very elaborate lunch with all the proper wines, and then, of course
—well, *l'amour*. Magnificent. And all, as I think I've explained, really working out to about five cents on the dollar. Disgusting, if you ask me."

"Don't take it so hard," I said. "It's only a book."

"I can't help it," she said. "I get sore. Who wouldn't?
One way or another, most girls have to go out with quite
a bunch of pinheads. It's a nuisance, but up to now there's
always been the consolation for me that I was a pretty
expensive proposition. I have put up with the little beasts,
but I've always been able to think that I was putting
quite a dent in them financially. It seemed to me I had a
kind of moral or social function. When I got through with
an eager young seducer, he was usually lucky if he had
fifteen cents to get home in a bus. It was certainly quite
a while before he was in shape to badger any more girls.
I suppose I thought of myself as the great deterrent."

"That's a very spiritual point of view, Zulu," I said.
"Sometimes you surprise me."

She ignored me and laughed bitterly. "The great deterrent," she said. "That's what I thought. I thought, when
I get through there is going to be a trail of bankrupts
from Boston to Key West, and the Atlantic Seaboard
will be a much cleaner, better place to live. I felt very
proud and virtuous and happy. And then along came this
damn book, and *now* what am I supposed to think?"

"The snakes," I said. "Watch out for the snakes. They're
really warming up."

"I am beyond snakes. You see, don't you, that it's all
lost, wasted, spoiled? What's left for me now? If a girl
works out an evening carefully—taxis, dinner, theatre tick-
ets, a night club afterward—she ought to be able to stick

a man for at least two hundred dollars. It used to enchant me. I was very innocent. I thought two hundred dollars was two hundred dollars. I know better now. With any kind of reasonable tax advice, it won't run to ten per cent of that. A lousy twenty bucks. Who is going to be deterred by *that?* I have never been so humiliated in my life. How do you suppose it feels to know that a bunch of bums and half-wits have been deducting you for entertainment and then laughing their disgusting heads off about it in every bar in town? I tell you quite frankly there have been times these last couple of weeks when I wished I were dead."

"You will be," I said, "if one of those things bites you."

"See if I care," said Zulu, but it was clear that her spirit was broken, and in a little while we got up and started walking home in the sun.

SOME MATTERS OF FACT

Big Nemo

I

A lady who loves him said once that Alexander Woollcott has eight hundred intimate friends. This may easily be true, because he leads a social existence that might have seemed exhausting to Catherine of Russia; it is also true that there is scarcely one of the eight hundred who has not spoken of him derisively. Edna Ferber, even before her first passion for him had cooled into loathing and he in turn had stopped dedicating his books to her, remarked that she was getting damn sick of this New Jersey Nero who mistook his pinafore for a toga. It was Miss Ferber, too, who, being asked by a frantic bookworm if Mr. Woollcott didn't seem exactly like a character out of Dickens, replied generously that he often seemed to her like *two* characters out of Dickens, both from the same book. This was "The Old Curiosity Shop," and the pair of whom Miss Ferber thought when she was reluctantly obliged to look at Mr. Woollcott were Little Nell and Quilp. Charles Brackett, a devoted admirer, described him in one of his novels as "a competent old horror with a style that combined clear treacle and pure black bile," while Harpo Marx spoke of his idol considered sheerly as an artist. "He is just a big dreamer," said Mr. Marx, "with a good sense of double-entry bookkeeping." Elsie Janis's mother, struggling to define the effect that Mr. Woollcott has on people who aren't altogether used to him, said that in many ways he was like a fine old olive, and S. N. Behrman, who twice permitted him to play himself on the stage, caused one of his heroines to express herself crossly. "Oh, Sig, Sig," she cried, "if you'd been a woman, what a bitch you would have made!" Back in 1921, George Jean Nathan wrote a scurrilous article about him in the *Smart Set* entitled "The Seidlitz Powder of Times Square," and once, Howard Dietz, afflicted by prose more beautiful than he could bear, called him Louisa M. Woollcott, thus speaking for thousands who had also been troubled without ever quite knowing what was the matter with them. These tributes for the most part have come from the more articulate of the eight hundred. The rest have usually contented themselves with describing him simply and passionately as a monster, or at the very least as a man of absurdly mixed ancestry.

The caricaturists have also been severe, which is probably ungrateful of them, for Mr. Woollcott is a persistently obliging model, one wartime associate on the *Stars and Stripes*, the A.E.F. weekly newspaper, even hinting that he was by no means above using his sergeant's chevrons to *compel* gifted privates to draw pictures of him. His face, of course, could not have been more helpfully designed for their purposes. Florence Atwater, one of Booth Tarkington's darkly observant little girls, once came close to his total effect, although at the time she was speaking of her grandfather's cook. "Her *face* is sort of small," she said, wrestling with the inexpressible, "but the other parts of her head are terribly wide." Mr. Woollcott's small features occupy the front part of a head which is at least wider than most. He has a rather beaked nose and a tight mouth and a negligible mustache, all closely grouped. His eyes are made strange and fierce by thick glasses. A clever child could easily draw him and, as a matter of fact, many have, although usually under the impression that they were turning out owls. The caricaturists, of course, have made the most of this resemblance, as well as of a body which suggests the anatomy of St. Nicholas in "The Night Before Christmas." A gallery of Woollcott portraits would include the work of almost every considerable black-and-white artist in the country and, while all the pictures would be very different, in some mysterious fashion they would all look precisely like Mr. Woollcott and all, naturally, rather like owls.

The average man might be embarrassed at finding himself the focus of quite so much hilarity and be inclined to swing on somebody. Mr. Woollcott, however, loves it, and often shakes with laughter when he comes on an especially damaging sample. The fact is that insult is a casual demonstration of regard with him, as it is with most of his friends. "Hello, repulsive" is a tender greeting under his roof and goodbye is said as sweetly. "I find you are beginning to disgust me, puss," the great man will say as his bedtime approaches. "How about getting the hell out of here?"

As far as his friends have been able to tell, in fact, the old fascinator is actually enraged only by two forms of misbehavior. He finds it very hard to forgive any man or woman who, through forgetfulness, drunkenness, or even simple disinclination, breaks an engagement with him, thus upsetting a social program as delicately assembled as a little watch; and he is furious with humorists who try to discredit his favorite philanthropies.

As long ago as 1926, growing rich through his dubious employment as a critic for the late Frank Munsey, he moved from the hovel which he shared with three penniless adventurers on West Forty-seventh Street and went to live at the Hotel des Artistes. These premises offered many advantages, including a remarkable chef, and Mr. Woollcott began to spread out socially, his little dinners becoming the talk of his circle, many of whom lived almost entirely on ham sandwiches in the back room at Tony's. Everything at des Artistes was arranged with extraordinary care—the chef advised long beforehand what to cook and the instant when it must leap, brown and lovely, from the dumbwaiter. The guests were selected as carefully as the roast and expected to turn up as promptly. Informal people sometimes found so much ceremony oppressive, and, while admiring Mr. Woollcott for his other qualities, considered him a little peremptory as a host.

One man, born with a horror of having to be anywhere at any particular time, successfully dodged his fate for two weeks only to be pinned down at last for dinner a week from Tuesday. As his time drew near, despair overcame him and the afternoon of the great day found him in a speakeasy, nervously drinking Scotch. He was with friends and finally one of them, a Mr. Connelly, was persuaded to call up Mr. Woollcott and explain that his guest had been delayed.

"Dishere Mr. Smiff's body servant," said Mr. Connelly upon being connected with his party. "He say he cain't—"

The noise that came from the receiver was like the crackle of summer lightning, and after a while Mr. Connelly hung up and went back to his table.

"Well, I fixed it up all right," he said airily. "You don't have to go."

They went instead to the Algonquin and had been sitting in the lobby for some time, bothering nobody, when the door revolved to admit an object both fashionable and alarming. It was Mr. Woollcott in evening clothes. He was wearing a broad-brimmed black hat and a flowing cape, carrying a heavy, silver-headed cane, and on the whole he looked very much like Dracula. Afterward it developed that, having sent back the dinner (he was on a diet of toast and orange juice himself), he was now merely looking for someone to replace the unspeakable Smith as his guest at Walter Hampden's performance of "Caponsacchi." At the time, however, the guilty crew thought he had tracked them down and probably meant to do something nasty with the cane. His eye, in fact, did light on the little group and for a moment his face was contorted with pique, but instead of assassinating them, he whirled and flung out of the hotel, spinning the door so furiously that two little old ladies, standing near it, bowed in the wind.

The humorists were not content to let it go at that. Smith, encouraged by his associate demons, sent him a telegram which read, "If anybody asks you where I was last night will you say I was with you?" At first, on receiving this, Mr. Woollcott was somewhat mollified, having a pleasant sense of being mixed up in some kind of dirty work. Learning that it was merely an extension of the original insult, however, and that Smith had, in fact, been seen that night innocently amusing himself with friends at Hubert's Flea Circus, he came close to apoplexy and wrote a letter so vitriolic and unusual that it became a sort of museum piece and was ultimately acquired by a rich collector for twenty-five dollars. It is noteworthy that in moments of actual fury Mr. Woollcott has no use for the fancy epithet; his style then is simple and austere, almost Biblical. This valuable letter said what he wished to say in the bleakest terms. "I find," it began, "that you are a distinctly third-rate person."

In spite of many discouragements—for other people have

also objected to having their lives so arbitrarily arranged
—his schedule remains elaborate. His itinerary is always
laid out at least a month in advance, and his calendar,
when he is in New York, is as precisely calculated as a
dentist's.

Mr. Woollcott's enthusiasms are often apt to seem a little
arbitrary, too. Critically, for instance, he was able to dismiss "The Children's Hour" as "gauche, implausible, and
untidy," and "Strange Interlude" as an " 'Abie's Irish Rose'
of the pseudo-intelligentsia," while finding in Mr. James
Hilton a talent "as warming to the heart and nourishing to
the spirit as any I can remember" and in Little Orvie, certainly one of Mr. Tarkington's glummer inspirations, a
creation in many ways superior to Penrod. The truth is
probably that he prefers to dig up his own crusades, finding
no especial satisfaction in getting excited about something
that excites everybody else. So, while most commentators
have been busy with anti-Fascist demonstrations, labor
disputes, and other community activities, Mr. Woollcott
has found his own causes and stood up for them, vocal but
alone. The Seeing Eye, which, thanks to him, probably
needs no further identification, has received in print and
on the air more publicity than has ever been given to any
other organization dedicated to so special a purpose, and
Hamilton College, which graduated him and of which he is
a trustee, has also come into its just reward. He has not
even neglected the Several Marx Brothers, an outfit which,
from time to time, he appears to believe he invented himself. Journalistically, all this has been sound and profitable,
since there are many people who feel that they have
heard more than enough about the state of the world. It
has also called forth a certain amount of criticism, a few
serious thinkers being of the opinion that Mr. Woollcott's

interests are rather peripheral, to put it mildly. There
have even been moments of embarrassment when his pro-
tégés have backfired on him.

There was, for instance, the story of Sergeant Quirt,
which is probably as good a name for him as any. The
saga of the Sergeant, who picked up his title as a member
of the American Expeditionary Force, is practically endless.
A literary though virile sort of man, he once worked for a
newspaper syndicate, and there he was in the habit of returning a manuscript to its anxious author with a letter
saying that it wasn't *quite* right, but that with a little professional advice, he was sure, it could be made to do. There
was, now he happened to think of it, a literary agency that
specialized in just that sort of thing and, if the author cared
to send his manuscript to them, he felt confident that—for
a small fee, of course—they could tell him what repairs
were necessary. The literary agency, it turned out, was the
Sergeant masquerading as a post-office box, and he made
a very nice little thing out of it until something slipped up
and he was fired. After that he caused a temporary confusion in the publishing world by setting up a McClure
Syndicate to compete with the real McClure Syndicate
simply by going into business with a man whose name
happened to be McClure. A pretty ingenious fellow all
around was Sergeant Quirt.

Mr. Woollcott and the Sergeant had worked together on
the *Stars and Stripes,* where they shared heroic experiences
and a strong bond grew up between them. Back in this
country, the friendship persisted and Mr. Woollcott invited
his buddy to come and live in his apartment. The Sergeant
had not yet affiliated himself with the newspaper syndicate,
or indeed with any other employer, and he was without
visible means of support. Mr. Woollcott's kindness provided
him with a roof and meals, of course, but the Sergeant

wanted other things from life, including a little pocket money. His host had gone to Europe, leaving him alone in the apartment, so he turned to other friends of his army days. He was successful with them, so successful, in fact, that he made up his mind that he could afford to travel. Action always followed closely on decision with the Sergeant, and presently, handsomely dressed and equipped with fine luggage, he was on his way to the Coast in a bus. He rode in peace, busy, no doubt, with his innocent plans, until the bus reached a more or less desolate portion of the Western plains. Here an embarrassing thing happened. A pair of state troopers, appearing from nowhere, drew up beside the bus and announced grimly that they were looking for an escaped convict. Even as they spoke, a pale man in one of the front seats leaped to his feet and through an open window. Before the troopers could get clear of their roadster, Sergeant Quirt was in action. He, too, leaped through the window and took off across the desert. The convict ran fast, but virtue lent wings to Quirt and he brought the man down not a hundred yards from the highway. When Quirt came back with his catch, the troopers were grateful and admiring.

"It was nothing," said the Sergeant.

The officers soon departed, taking with them the convict and a suitcase he claimed to be his. The bus rolled on, with Quirt the object of much favorable comment. It had not gone many miles, however, before the same patrol car appeared beside it again and ordered the driver to stop. One of the troopers got out and stood in the highway. He was holding up a suitcase and he looked even more menacing than before.

"All right," he said, "*now* I want to know who in hell belongs to this bag."

Sergeant Quirt took one look at it and sighed.

"I do," he said.

"You?" said the trooper incredulously, recognizing the recent hero.

"Yes," said Quirt.

"O.K., buddy," said the trooper, though still doubtful. "Then I guess you better come along."

Quirt went, for he knew when he was licked, and he also knew that the suitcase, which fate had malignantly mixed up with the convict's, contained about as fine a set of plates for counterfeiting traveller's checks as you could buy east of the Alleghenies, as well as a neat bundle of Southern Pacific pay checks which he had turned out from time to time on a little press he happened to have kicking around the house.

When this news finally reached Mr. Woollcott, he was embarrassed. It was too bad, he cried; it was obviously just some innocent misunderstanding. In proof of all this, he would personally redeem every dollar's worth of false checks that could be shown to have originated with his virtuous friend. He even had his lawyer make an announcement to that effect, and this was a mistake, because several thousand dollars' worth of pay checks which had been issued by the Sergeant on previous business trips to the West were now joyfully presented for payment. Such a sum being somewhat beyond his means at the time, Mr. Woollcott was obliged to retract his offer and leave the Sergeant to the mercy of the State of California, which apparently had the strongest claim on him, although Oregon and Nevada were mildly interested, too. Mr. Woollcott, in fact, withdrew from the whole matter after arranging with the warden of San Quentin to get the Sergeant a set of false teeth, his own being in shocking condition.

Things like that hurt, because there can be little question that Mr. Woollcott is one of the most sentimental men alive in spite of his prickly exterior. At fifty-two, the world to him is still a strange and glamorous place, with all its values heightened and transposed as the appearance of a landscape is dramatized when it comes out in Technicolor. Mr. Woollcott's world isn't perhaps very much like anybody else's, but certainly he is happy there. It is a little remarkable that he should be so invincibly romantic and especially that he should feel such an overwhelming affection for the past, because his impressionable years were spent in what would appear to be more or less discouraging places.

He was born in what had once been the *phalanstère* or head house of a Socialistic community near Red Bank, N.J. This settlement, commonly known as Phalanx, was an experiment in coöperative living, based on the writings of Albert Brisbane, Arthur's father. It was akin to Brook Farm and, though less celebrated, it was more successful. In 1855, however, it blew up—largely because none of the disciples cared to act as garbage collector—and Woollcott's grandfather, who happened to be president at the time, came into possession of the enormous eighty-five-room building which his descendant remembers as a "shabby, rambling caravansary, bleak as a skull." In 1887, when little Alexander was born, there were fourteen other grandchildren infesting this barracks and the chances are that he would have grown up quite happily there if it hadn't been for some aching discontent with life that lay at the back of his father's mind. Walter Woollcott, who came to America from England when he was thirteen, was at various times and rather apathetically a lawyer, an accountant, a government clerk, and a Stock Exchange member. He also seems to have been one of the most accomplished escapists in history. Once, in Germantown, he went to bed and stayed there two years although there was nothing in particular the matter with him; most of the time he had to be on the move, hoping that in each new town he would find the power and glory that had just eluded him in the last. In the course of his marriage, accompanied by his docile though bewildered family, he turned up as a resident of such assorted places as Raleigh, Washington, Omaha, Fort Union, Pittsburgh, and Manchester (England).

In November, 1889, he took his brood to Kansas City, Mo. A lady who taught little Aleck when he was in the Second Grade there reports on him favorably:

As a very young boy, Aleck was very frail-looking, with delicate features, blond hair, and the finest, keenest, intellectual face I have ever seen on such a young lad. His vocabulary, then as now, was marvellous. He was a constant reader—in fact, he read everything he could find in the family library, supplemented by first-class reading matter, such as *St. Nicholas*, the *Youth's Companion*, etc. Small and slender as he was, he held his own with the larger boys. I can see him now, walking with his chest out and trying to look strong and manly. He thirsted for knowledge and I realized even then that he would go far.

A surviving photograph, taken at this period, bears her out. It shows a frail, intent infant who, although as cute as a bug's ear, in the beautiful old phrase, exhibits nevertheless strong traces of that devouring curiosity which has brought the mature Woollcott far indeed from Kansas City.

The child played one of the Vinard children in a "Trilby" tableau given at the Coates Opera House, and Puck in the days when Mrs. Roswell Martin Field, a sister-in-law of Eugene Field, used to "do" Shakespeare in the Woollcott doorway while the audience looked on from the street. He sent his first composition, "The Adventures of a Shopping Bag," to the Kansas City *Star*, which rejected it impassively; he got his first complimentary seats to the theatre from Roswell Field. He was notable chiefly in the neighborhood, however, because when hurt, strong and manly though he might be, he would set up such an unbearably doleful cry that adults could be relied upon to pacify him with nickels. It got to be a practice among the larger boys to toss the little intellectual off the veranda onto his head and then, when he had wept and subsequently collected his nickel, to take it away from him.

In 1895, Walter Woollcott found that the Holy Grail was not in Kansas City and he moved his wife and five children (there were three other sons and a daughter, all older than the constant reader) back to Phalanx. They stayed there about a year and Aleck went to school. Then, for the mysterious search was never ended, they went to Philadelphia, where he finished his primary education and entered Central High School in the class of 1905. Woollcott was living by himself now, his father having wandered away again, this time alone, breaking up the family group forever. Aleck supported himself by reviewing books and doing similar odd and menial jobs for the *Evening Telegraph* and the *Record*. He won a gold medal for writing an essay and sold it, cash in his little damp hand being at the moment even more important than glory. Beyond the discovery, however, that he could turn a phrase with the next man, he didn't get much out of Central High School. He had met a nephew of Elihu Root's who had been to Hamilton College, at Clinton, N.Y., and, impressed by this man's worldly manner, young Woollcott decided to go there too.

Hamilton is a small college and in its student body of two hundred Alexander Humphreys Woollcott '09 was pretty conspicuous, having a busy little finger in practically everything except athletics, which he loathed. He was editor of the monthly magazine; he founded and directed the dramatic club and acted female parts in its productions; he did monologues with the glee club; he even drank a little from time to time, preferring absinthe because of its sinister reputation. He was rather bizarre in appearance, for he habitually wore corduroy trousers and a turtle-necked sweater and topped them off with a jubilant red fez, and he was already firmly prankish, fellow-members of Theta Delta Chi recalling that in "rushing season" he was accustomed to get himself up even more repulsively than usual and go and sit on the steps of rival fraternities as a horrible example of what the prospective brothers might expect to find inside. Above everything else, however, he was a scholar (he made Phi Beta Kappa in his junior year) and his chief concern was writing.

Of what he wrote, only one curious fragment has survived. It is called "The Precipice: A Story of Bohemia" and the action takes place at a New Year's Eve party in the Philadelphia equivalent of a Greenwich Village studio. Nana, the heroine, it seems, is not exactly beautiful, but she has other charms which Woollcott '09 is too delicate to specify. She is a virtuous girl, though given to swilling Benedictine, but unfortunately she is infatuated with one Bonny, a cad who operates from hansom cabs.

In the course of the party, this louse, a married man, arranges to come back and meet her after the others have all gone.

"We'll see the old year out together," he says, brimming with lechery.

"That will be joyous," says Nana, who has already been at the Benedictine.

He leaves, and Nana, alone at last, really goes to work on

the bottle. She is, in fact, flat on her back, lighting matches and muttering away to herself about "playing with fire" when a messenger comes in with a package and an explanatory letter for her. The letter is from a man called Morton K. Enderby and Nana is in no shape to cope with that, but the package contains her mother's picture and *its* effect is very gratifying indeed.

"The great grey eyes looked at her reproachfully, accusingly, and the girl cowered. She turned quickly and her glance fell on the tabouret with its litter of cigarette ashes, and in the mess her glass with the dregs of the Benedictine staining its sides. The sight sickened her. There was a tremendous revulsion of feeling in her soul; a shattering of the illusions of the past few weeks. The fair lights of Bohemia were calcium; the gayeties tinsel; the beauties tawdry."

Nana was sober as an owl when she heard Bonny's footsteps on the stairs. He was singing a questionable song and it was clear that he thought everything was in the bag. He was too optimistic.

"For a moment she saw his figure outlined against the light: then . . . she was flying down the dark stairway, one hand nervously feeling the banister as she ran, the other pressing the picture to her bosom. The little slippered feet sped along the streaming pavements, the crimson figure passed swiftly out of the great swinging circle of the creaking arc light and she was swallowed up in the darkness.

" 'Just in time, mother,' she whispered. 'Just in time.' "

This excruciating piece of prose was actually bought by a magazine called *The Black Cat*, which paid twelve dollars for it, and it also won a twenty-five-dollar prize for the best piece of undergraduate writing of that year.

When the day came for Woollcott to leave Hamilton, he went sadly, for he had loved it. Furthermore, he had a nervous distaste for the world beyond the campus and for a while he dreamed of a cloistered life as principal of a high school. He even went to Hudson, N.Y., where he had heard a vacancy existed, but when he found that he would be expected to preserve discipline by violence if necessary and was shown a group of students any one of whom could have dissected him singlehanded, he abandoned the project as impracticable. He came instead to New York and went to work as a fifteen-dollar-a-week clerk in the Chemical National Bank, adding and subtracting, dreaming of the horrible day when he would be promoted to teller. Samuel Hopkins Adams, a trustee of Hamilton and, in fact, the man who had put up the prize won by "The Precipice," rescued him from finance by informing Carr Van Anda of the *Times* that a *Wunderkind* had come to town, a journalistic prodigy who would eclipse even the great Frank Ward O'Malley. This, it turned out, wasn't strictly true. There could be no question that the *Times'* new man could write very nicely, though in a strangely lacy and intricate fashion, but as a reporter he was exasperating. He wasn't exactly hostile to facts, but he was apathetic about them, and he liked a story to be neatly assembled in one place—a good cornerstone-laying, for instance—and not spread out untidily all over hell so that a man had to run himself ragged trying to get it together.

He was assigned to the sinking of the *Titanic*, the Equitable fire, the Rosenthal case, and even what might be called the aesthete's angle of one World Series, but his heart wasn't in it. Neither, apparently, was the *Times'*, for in 1914, after Woollcott had expressed his discontent by having a nervous breakdown, Van Anda made him dramatic critic. The reasons for this appointment are obscure. Detractors say it was a choice of getting young Woollcott off news or turning the paper into a weekly (the *Times* was beaten daily on the Rosenthal story before Mr. Woollcott retired in favor of a more curious and mobile man); admirers, on the other hand, claim that the management considered it wasteful to confine the most ornamental prose in New York to routine journalism. The subject of the whole controversy says modestly that *he* thinks it was only because Mr. Van Anda imagined that his employee looked like Thackeray.

It wasn't much of a job anyway. The *Times* was inclined to be haughty about the drama and considered reviews of it just barely fit to print. The column occupied a modest position and its author was paid sixty dollars a week. Nevertheless, Mr. Woollcott felt that at last he had come into his own, and when he was barred from all the Shubert theatres for wickedly denouncing almost everything he saw in them, it gave him an almost intolerable sense of power.

When he was first chosen, he wrote his mother and told her the magnificent news, but she wasn't especially impressed.

"*I* should think it would be very narrowing," she wrote back.

II

Alexander Woollcott, erstwhile dramatic critic for the *Times*, now risen to the estate of private in the United States Medical Corps, embarked for France on July 11, 1917, but his transport was rammed and sunk by the liner Panama halfway down New York Harbor. Mr. Woollcott, who didn't even get his feet wet, was extricated and put back on shore.

A week after this anticlimax he sailed again, and this time, in spite of a skirmish with two U-boats off Belle Isle, he reached St.-Nazaire. From there he was sent to Base Hospital No. 8, in the village of Savenay in the Loire-Inférieure. For six rather exasperating months he lingered in Savenay, performing duties which would unquestionably have amused a great many actors back in New York if they could have seen him.

While he was engaged in this embarrassing fashion, the *Stars and Stripes,* the weekly newspaper of the A.E.F., had been started in a crowded little office on the Rue Ste.-Anne in Paris. In those early days it was badly understaffed—the first few issues, in fact, were almost entirely written by one man—and soon the editor began to look around for American journalists in other branches of the service. When he telegraphed Savenay to ask if there was any reasonable objection to transforming one Alexander Woollcott from an orderly into a reporter, the colonel in charge of the hospital was on duty elsewhere and the message was given to his adjutant to deal with in his absence. This agreeable man called Woollcott—he was Sergeant Woollcott by now—into his office and allowed him to cook up his own answer.

"Sergeant Alexander Woollcott has done magnificent work here," wrote Sergeant Woollcott after a moment's thought, "but can be spared."

Woollcott the reporter for the *Stars and Stripes* wasn't really very different from Woollcott the dramatic critic for the *Times.* The war appeared to him in the light of an enormous and essentially rather good-natured melodrama, and he wrote about the men in the trenches with the same romantic intensity that he had once reserved for Mrs. Fiske. The atmosphere in the office on the Rue Ste.-Anne, and later in the one on the Rue des Italiens, was also not unlike that he had known in New York. His colleagues were rude men who preferred on the whole witnessing the confusion of one of their superior officers to any catastrophe that might overtake the Germans. Most of them were what might be called old-fashioned newspapermen, with a childish contempt for high-class prose, and when the former dramatic critic for the New York *Times* proudly reported for duty, their behavior must have been a little irritating. One of them, in fact, a barbarian who had worked on almost every paper in the United States, laughed so insanely that he had to be helped out of the room.

To some extent they got used to Sergeant Woollcott after a while and even came to respect him for the way he was able to adjust himself to a life that was wildly foreign to his nature, but he never stopped entertaining them. Woollcott was probably the most heavily burdened war correspondent in history, being festooned on his tours of the front with a collection of binoculars, cameras, gas masks, canteens, and other spare parts that would have weighed down Richard Harding Davis. In spite of all this fancy equipment, he always looked dismally non-military. Once he was dining in Paris with another member of the staff who had done no more than button up his blouse in honor of the occasion. A young lady who was with them studied Mr. Woollcott anxiously for a long time but clearly could identify him with nothing in her previous military experience. At last she gave him up and turned to her other companion.

"But you," she said timidly, "*you're* in the Army, aren't you?"

On another occasion he was with Elsie Janis and her mother when the news came that the draft age had been extended to take in men of forty-five.

"Goodness, Aleck," said both ladies as one woman, "that means *you'll* have to go, doesn't it?"

Altogether his appearance was so exotic that A. A. Wallgren, who drew a comic strip for the *Stars and Stripes* and usually employed his colleagues as models, liked to show Sergeant Woollcott carrying a single lovely rose. General Pershing, in fact, was probably the only man in the A.E.F. who ever mistook Mr. Woollcott for a soldier. This was long after the Armistice, on a day when several members of the editorial staff had just got their discharges and the only occasion on which Pershing ever visited the office. Sergeant Woollcott, still in uniform, was presented to the Commander in Chief together with the information that he had that day, after twenty-two months of service, at last become a civilian.

"Well, well," said the General, amid a stunned silence, "he doesn't look much like a civilian to *me*."

The old sergeant still likes to quote this inexplicable compliment along with another he received from the New Orleans *Times-Picayune*. In a review of one of Mr. Woollcott's books, this paper published an unusually hideous photograph of the artist. The caption under it, however, was what would have confounded every man who ever worked on the *Stars and Stripes*. "Soldier-Author," it said.

Even though the A.E.F.'s correspondent didn't look especially warlike, he saw a lot of the battlefield. He had a sort of roving commission from the paper and spent most of his time up close to the front lines, sending his dispatches back to Paris by courier. It is the general impression that Mr. Woollcott was imperturbable under fire, although one cynical man who knew him at the time has his own explanation.

"I thought he was a hero myself," says this small spirit, "until I found out he had something the matter with his eyes. Hell, he could get right up on top of a town without even knowing it was under fire."

Myopic or not, Woollcott occasionally found himself within range of the cannon, and witnesses say that it was a moving and pitiful sight to see him trying to get down on his stomach when he heard the scream of an approaching shell. Other men dropped where they were, but Mr. Woollcott weighed close to two hundred pounds exclusive of hardware and his descent was gradual and majestic, like a slowly kneeling camel. Even when he had got safely down, he was still far from flat, and it is one of the miracles of the war that he came through it unperforated. Unwieldy as he was, however, he was a conscientious reporter. There were even those who felt he was *too* conscientious, their number including one cross-grained sergeant who was bringing his platoon back from a tour of duty in the front-line trenches when he was accosted by Mr. Woollcott in his best New York *Times* manner.

"Sergeant," he said crisply, "I'm from the *Stars and Stripes,* and I'd like you to tell me exactly—"

"You go to hell, Willie," said the sergeant.

The *Stars and Stripes,* which had built up a weekly circulation of 550,000 and returned to the government a net profit of $700,000 in a little less than a year and a half, went out of existence on June 13, 1919. Things had been pretty dull in the seven months following the Armistice, and Mr. Woollcott was glad to get back to his job on the *Times.*

In retrospect it is not very easy to evaluate him as a dramatic critic. He had enthusiasm, an honest love for the theatre, and a gift for the neat and deadly phrase. On the other hand, he was sentimental, partisan, and maddeningly positive about everything even before he had been a critic long enough to know much about anything. His style, which could be lucid and witty, could also be muddled and frantic, and reading him in this mood often made subscribers feel as if his hot breath was actually on their necks. The short space of writing time allowed by a morning paper, of course, had a lot to do with that, for the Woollcott style, pouring too richly from his heart, needed a great deal of skimming and straining before it was fit for public consumption. He was aware of this himself and once, when an admiring lady asked him how he ever wrote so much in such a short time—most of his reviews were turned out in less than an hour—he answered her reasonably.

"If I had twice as much time, my blossom," he said, "my pieces would probably be half as long."

The case against him was not too temperately stated by George Jean Nathan, then writing about the theatre for *Smart Set*. Mr. Nathan's performance had a fascination of its own, because in calling his rival unbearably dogmatic he exhibited the same quality in an even stronger degree, and in commenting on a style that seemed to him lush and juvenile he employed one that was tangled, multilingual, and indecently burdened with learned reference. It was not unlike Lady Godiva reproaching September Morn for not having enough clothes on, but it was not without some justice, either.

Mr. Nathan began by questioning some of the Woollcott judgments, which seemed to him rather in the nature of valentines. It struck him, for instance, as a little excitable to write the following about a fetching but by no means extraordinary young actress: "This most beguiling rôle . . . is played to incredible perfection by Lotus Robb, the April charm of whose delicate performance seemed . . . a thing which only lyric verse could adequately describe." Mr. Nathan was also pained to hear Jacob Ben-Ami, a strolling player of the period, described as a matchless world

genius and *his* performance as so supernatural in every way that "some of us would crawl on our hands and knees to see it." So much indeed did this bonbon upset the little pundit that without half trying he reeled off the names of Arbatoff, Teliakovsky, Dalmatoff, Glagolin, Massalitinoff, Adelheim, Katchaloff, Moskvin, and Uraloff as a few of those who might be employed to teach this Ben-Ami the rudiments of acting. Alice Delysia, for whom Mr. Woollcott also entertained a respectful yen, provoked a similar outburst from Mr. Nathan, who this time listed no less than fifteen little-known French music-hall comediennes who were in every way her superior.

While Mencken's partner disapproved of much that Woollcott said, it was the *way* he said it that really made his head hurt.

"This style," he wrote sombrely, "is the particular bouquet I invite you to sniff. . . . It never strikes a mean; it is either a gravy bomb, a bursting gladiolus, a palpitating missa cantata, an attack of psychic hydrophobia, or a Roman denunciation, unequivocal, oracular, flat and final. . . . A style, in brief, that is purely emotional, and without a trace of the cool reflectiveness and contagious common sense suitable to criticism."

It is sometimes felt in the theatrical world, however, that nothing can possibly be half as bad as George Jean Nathan says it is, and certainly Mr. Woollcott had many passionate admirers. They conceded his faults—even his best friends were apt to murmur "Ben-Ami" in a thoughtful way whenever he turned up with a new world genius—but insisted that in spite of them his pieces had a life that was missing from those of his more austere competitors. There was an excitement, a quality of shared experience, of having been there and seen it yourself, which you couldn't get from anyone else.

There must have been something in what they said, because in 1922 the late Frank Munsey offered him the critic's
job on his *Herald*. Like almost every newspaperman in
New York, Mr. Woollcott loathed Munsey, but the *Times*,
which had started him at $60 a week and now paid him
$100, indicated clearly that it considered this figure more
than ample for a man who had nothing more exhausting to
do than inspect actors. Munsey offered him $15,000 a year,
and in October, 1922, Mr. Woollcott went to work down
the river. He stayed with Munsey nearly three years—on the
Herald until it was sold to the *Tribune*, and then on the
Sun. It was an unrewarding experience, for the *Herald* and
the *Sun* were spiritless affairs, run by a clammy, ruthless
man whose heart was really in the delicatessen business.

In 1925, Heywood Broun, succumbing to a combination
of claustrophobia and a desire to rearrange the solar system,
resigned as dramatic critic of the *World*, and Woollcott
was chosen to succeed him. The pay was the same as it
had been on the *Sun*, but the surroundings were vastly
different. Financially the *World* was already sickening for
its last illness, but editorially it was the most provocative
paper in New York. The celebrated "opposite-editorial
page," which was worshipfully read at almost every up-
and-coming breakfast table, was a sort of five-ring circus.
F.P.A. was doing the Conning Tower; Broun, though no
longer a critic, was still writing It Seems to Me, Laurence
Stallings and Samuel Chotzinoff dealt with books and
music, respectively, and now Woollcott had come to do the
theatre. On the day that the new dramatic critic went to
work, it undoubtedly seemed to *him* that he could remain
in the Pulitzer Building happily forever.

Ever since he came back from the war, Mr. Woollcott's
social life had been expanding in a very satisfactory way.

Before that, to most people he had just been a man who wrote dramatic criticism for the *Times* and signed to it a name that always looked like a typographical error. Now he began to emerge as a metropolitan character and a member of the group which firmly took charge of humor in America throughout the nineteen-twenties and early thirties.

They were a remarkable gang, however you look at them, and they have left us many legends, of which the most durable are the Round Table at the Algonquin Hotel, the Thanatopsis Literary and Inside Straight Club, the back room at the West Side Tony's, and, conceivably, Herbert Bayard Swope. Franklin P. Adams was their official biographer, and it was a rare Saturday when his Pepys' Diary failed to mention A. Woollcott, H. Broun, G. Kaufman, M. Connelly, D. Parker, D. Stewart, I. Berlin, R. Sherwood, H. Dietz, E. Ferber, H. Swope, D. Taylor, F. Sullivan, N. McMein, C. MacArthur, R. Crouse, and one or more of the interminable Marx Brothers. This was the nucleus of the group, the permanent acting company. Others attached themselves to it briefly from time to time. Noel Coward and Beatrice Lillie belonged when they were in town and so did the Lunts; Thornton Wilder and S. N. Behrman, coming into glory rather later than the others, were more or less honorary members, and even Jed Harris sometimes hung around because in that dim yesterday several people were actually speaking to him.

Because of a certain patriarchal though not entirely benevolent aspect and a superior talent for abuse, Mr. Woollcott gradually became a sort of spiritual focus for the rest. It was he who played the parlor games of the period—Anagrams, Adverbs, Categories, Murder, and a dozen others—with the fiercest relish; it was he who won or lost at cards with the noisiest rejoicing and the blackest hate;

it might even be said that it was he who, writing about his friends in almost every publication extant, earned against fairly stiff competition the title of the noblest logroller of them all. As a matter of fact, it was logrolling of a singularly high-minded and disinterested sort, for Mr. Woollcott, in his romantic way, had no doubt that he was entirely surrounded by genius, and every bouquet came from his heart. Nor was his generosity confined to print. He was passionately and even almost intrusively concerned with the private lives of all his acquaintances, and when catastrophe visited them, as it much too frequently did, he was usually the first to hear about it and his response was invariable. Dorothy Parker, who is not always so mellow, wrote an article about him in *Vanity Fair* in which she said, "He does more kindness than anyone I have ever known; and I have learned that not from him but from the people who have experienced it."

In 1920, the average age of the members of the Thanatopsis-Algonquin axis was somewhere around twenty-eight, and with one or two exceptions they were comparatively unknown. The next ten years, however, brought extraordinary wealth and celebrity to most of them. Kaufman and Connelly wrote "Dulcy" in 1921 and worked together on such successes as "To the Ladies," "Merton of the Movies," and "Beggar on Horseback" until they split up, in 1926, after which Connelly wrote "The Wisdom Tooth" and "The Green Pastures" alone, and Kaufman collaborated with many people, among them Edna Ferber ("The Royal Family"), Ring Lardner ("June Moon"), and Moss Hart ("Once in a Lifetime"). MacArthur wrote "Lulu Belle" with Edward Sheldon in 1926 and "The Front Page" in 1928 with Ben Hecht, the latter to the considerable profit of Jed Harris, who had already produced "Broadway" and "Coquette."

In the same period, Howard Dietz, until 1924 a not
especially humble press agent, helped to turn out two
"Little Shows" and "Three's a Crowd." Behrman wrote
"The Second Man" and adapted "Serena Blandish"; Sherwood came out with "The Road to Rome," "The Queen's
Husband," and "Waterloo Bridge;" and Donald Ogden
Stewart, after an initial success with "A Parody Outline of
History" and three or four other books, wrote and acted in
a profitable little play called "Rebound." The ladies were
busy too, with Edna Ferber turning out "So Big" and "Show
Boat," Dorothy Parker picking up a reputation as the most
murderous book critic of her time while herself producing
two books of verse and one of short stories, and Neysa
McMein becoming recognized as about the best pastel
artist in the business.

It was an exciting and gratifying time for everybody, but
its very magnificence spelled the end of the Algonquin
group as a local phenomenon. Hollywood got some of
them and others moved to Connecticut, partly to escape the
New York state income tax and partly under the sad old
delusion that a man can write far more rapidly and beautifully while raising his own vegetables. Those who didn't
move away were by now temperamentally unfit for the old
close association, since there is nothing more enervating to
the artist than the daily society of a lot of people who are
just as famous as he is. The new conscience, born of dark
doings abroad, also had some bearing on it. Mr. Woollcott's
friends, who had no political convictions worth mentioning
in 1920, began to think rather intensely and presently occupied conflicting positions ranging all the way from
mild liberalism to the ultimate hammer and sickle.

They grew apart, meeting only occasionally and usually
by accident. While they no longer knew one another intimately, however, almost all of them kept in pretty close

touch with Mr. Woollcott. His apartment at 450 East
Fifty-second Street, which Dorothy Parker in a spasm of
rascality had named Wit's End, was a comfortable, untidy
garret looking down on the East River, and long after the
Round Table and the Thanatopsis Club were dead it was
still a hangout for whatever members of the old mob happened to be in town. Sunday breakfast there lasted practically all day, with Mr. Woollcott, in rumpled pajamas and
an ancient, rather horrible dressing gown, receiving his
guests from a throne in one corner with an air that would
have done credit to Queen Victoria.

"You kept thinking you ought to kiss his God damn hand,"
said one man who should never have been admitted to
polite society in the first place and never was again.

Games of chance in which a careless gambler could
easily lose four or five hundred dollars at a sitting went
on day and night, and when that palled, they played
croquet, at which most of them were ferociously expert,
either on the green in Central Park or out at Herbert
Swope's house in Sands Point.

It is hard to tell just exactly when Mr. Woollcott worked
in the midst of all this revelry, but he did. He wrote his
daily reviews and erudite pieces for the Sunday theatre
section, which, incidentally, he and George Kaufman elevated from a press agents' clearing house to its present
handsome and literary state. He even found time to turn
out casual belles-lettres for many magazines. He was
aided in all this by a succession of secretaries—intense,
rather fragile young men, who protected their master from
the vulgar public as reverently as if he had been a fine old
tapestry. It is pleasant to report that most of them have
passed on to artistic careers of their own, one man, indeed,
now being known to millions as a gossip columnist on the
Daily News, while another is visible nightly to thousands

as a mandolin-player in "The American Way." The rest of
Mr. Woollcott's domestic staff consisted of one dapper and
mysterious young Negro, who had, to the best of anyone's
knowledge, no other name than Junior. He was an im-
aginative man, given to inventing dramatic and unlikely
pasts for himself, and he has gone down slightly to history
for a comforting remark he made to Jed Harris, who, or so
it seemed to Junior, was unduly conscious of his racial
heritage.

"You take me now, sir," said Junior. "Why, my own
grandfather was a Jew."

With the close of the theatre season in the spring, Mr.
Woollcott always left town. For a few years he experi-
mented with houses on Long Island and in Westchester,
but they were never very satisfactory. He dreamed of
something more remote and inaccessible, a communal Eden
—the theories of Brook Farm and Phalanx have never been
far from his heart—free from the sights and sounds and
disgusting little faces that haunted him in Times Square.
In 1920 he found it in Neshobe, a seven-acre, beautifully
wooded island in Lake Bomoseen, Vermont.

Neshobe was bought from its original owners about
thirty years ago by a lawyer named Enos Booth, who built
a small cottage there as a headquarters for hunting and
fishing trips. Mr. Booth was apparently a simple man himself, but he had literary friends and just after the war a
few of them began to come up for weekends. That wound
up the hunting and fishing, but it also sent the island off
on its career as the most relentlessly playful resort in New
England. It wasn't long after the first artists came to Neshobe before the place was overrun with them. Eventually
Mr. Booth decided to turn the island into a club and then,

shortly after having made his contribution to American art and letters, he passed quietly from the scene.

In addition to Mr. Booth, the early members were Woollcott, Alice Duer Miller, Harpo Marx, Neysa McMein, Raymond Ives, George Kaufman, Dorothy Parker, Marc Connelly, and Charles MacArthur, and all but the last three, who turned out to be languid about their dues, now belong. The dues, still in force, were probably reasonable enough, all things considered. There was an initiation fee of $1,250, an annual charge of $150, and another charge of $7.50 for every day spent on the island. While the membership was restricted to ten, there were beds for sixteen and guests could be brought provided that their sponsors paid $7.50 a head for them and also that they were acceptable mentally to everybody. A young lady who went up there explained this matter clearly though rather forbiddingly in an article she subsequently wrote for a magazine. "There is no pat way to sum up the perfect guest on the island," she said. "Individuality and vitality of thought, quick wit, charm, and proficiency at games are desirable qualifications. . . . But if a guest can qualify simply as an engaging companion, he needs no additional social talents. For, contrary to rumor, talk on the island is not entirely badinage; it is anything and everything, as rich and unflagging a mixture as ever stemmed from an assortment of active, alert, and challenging minds. Sooner or later an opportunity to chime in comes to everyone who is there, but it is better to say nothing than to say something badly. Pleasant as they may be personally, bores are never tolerated."

She didn't explain what happens to the bores, and it is best perhaps just not to think about it.

In the beginning the island was actually coöperative,

but by now it is half owned and almost wholly buffaloed by
Mr. Woollcott. It is he who, grimly impatient for the
games to begin, routs the rich, challenging minds up at
seven-thirty every morning to go for a swim in the cold
lake; it is he who, from morning to midnight, drives them
ruthlessly from the lake to the croquet ground to the back-
gammon table; he who a year ago removed himself grandly
from the community shack and built a fine stone house
all his own, with marble baths and an open fire in every
bedroom. The other members visit the island intermittently
between May and October, but Mr. Woollcott spends almost all the summer there and even goes up alone in the
dead of winter, crossing dangerously from the mainland
on the ice. He loves Neshobe as proudly and jealously as
young Bonaparte loved Corsica.

The island is a perpetual source of wonder to the simple
Vermont natives who circumnavigate it cautiously in mo-
torboats and observe the inmates, who are frequently to
be seen lying like seals along the rocky shore. The general
opinion apparently is that Neshobe is a sort of Hollywood
nudist camp, and this leads to odd confusions. Thornton
Wilder has been mistaken for Jack Benny, and MacArthur,
sun-bathing in the nude, was once pleased to hear himself
identified as Irving Berlin and sang "All Alone" loud and
clear in gratitude. A few years ago, Mr. Woollcott himself,
inadequately wrapped in a dressing gown and wearing a
limp, enormous straw hat, was reading one day on the dock
when a boatload of sightseers drifted by. Their voices
came to him quite plainly over the water.

"Who on earth is *that?*" he heard one lady cry in startled
and even rather horrified tones.

"I'm not sure," said another voice doubtfully, "but I
think it's Marie Dressler."

Mr. Woollcott resigned from the *World* at the end of the 1928 theatre season. For a long time the physical discomfort and mental anguish of writing daily theatrical criticism had been wearing him down. He was not as thin as he once was, and the after-theatre congestion in Times Square was driving him crazy. He wrote his pieces in a little office in the Hotel Continental, where breathless couriers snatched the completed pages out of his typewriter and delivered them to a telegrapher. In the end even this got too hard, especially as the *World,* in a desperate effort to beat the other papers to the street, kept advancing his deadline until, unless Mr. Woollcott left before the curtain went down, he often had no more than twenty minutes to turn out his copy. It was not only nerve-racking to work under such pressure; he also felt that there was something vaguely absurd in making such a commotion about plays that nine times out of ten were of no conceivable interest to anybody.

"It was like engaging Balto to rush a relief supply of macaroons to Nome," he says, obviously pleased with the metaphor.

He also felt in a dim way that perhaps he had got to be a dramatic critic too young. He still loved the theatre better than anything else, but somehow he couldn't imagine being a critic for fifteen or twenty years more. It was too long a time just to keep on doing the same thing. The prospect appalled him.

"A man can't take the job of his life at twenty-seven," he said once, trying to explain the almost panic restlessness he felt.

III

With his resignation as dramatic critic for the *World* in May, 1928, Alexander Woollcott entered the present phase of his career, a period of great, though rather jumbled activity. During the next ten years he was to be, often simultaneously, a Broadway star, a playwright, a contributor to the magazines, a radio performer, a moving-picture actor, a lecturer, an anthologist, a stock-market operator, and an advertising-copy writer for tobacco, whiskey, and fast automobiles. He was forty-one years old, and Walter Pitkin might well have used him for a frontispiece.

He had left the *World* because of the wear and tear on his nervous system caused by the demands of daily journalism. Looking around for something that would give him time to arrange his thoughts in a decent and leisurely fashion, his eye fell on the magazines and by February, 1929, he was writing for them busily. Here, for the first time, he was able to deal with the things, unconnected with the theatre, which had been cluttering up his mind for years. He still paid an occasional fragrant tribute to Mrs. Fiske, Chaplin, and the Marx Brothers, of course, for these names write themselves almost automatically on his typewriter, but for the most part he dealt with his experiences in the larger world. The past played a considerable part in all this—memories of his early days in Phalanx, N.J., Kansas City, and Philadelphia; anecdotes about Hamilton College and the A.E.F.—but he covered the present, too, writing winsomely about the celebrated people he knows all over the world. Sometimes he spoke chillingly of murder and sometimes he published even more gruesome collections of Americana. He told about the books he liked and the ones he loathed, the games he played, the restaurants he ate in, and once he even described, though in rather evasive terms, his impressions of the Soviet Union. It was a remarkable potpourri and it was served with remarkable elegance. Newspaper deadlines had been hard on his style, but now it came into its own, a sort of heavenly compound of Dickens and Chesterton with perhaps a little earthly leaven of Booth Tarkington and even hellish prophecies here and there of Lucius Beebe, whose intolerably flossy column wasn't to make its appearance for nearly five years.

As other men fear and hate the dentist's drill, Mr. Woollcott is tortured by an unbalanced sentence. Adverbs and adverbial phrases ("oddly enough" is his favorite) and tender apostrophes to the reader ("my blossom," "puss," "my little dears") are judiciously inserted until the magic equilibrium is achieved. His mind is intricate and circuitous and thoughts often emerge from it in an arrangement of subordinate clauses that would have satisfied Henry James. Woollcott is romantic, and this can express itself in a tropic violence of description. He is in love with the dear past, and it lives again in his prose in words like "wraprascal," "gaffer," "tippet," and "minx." At its best, all this can have an admirable effect, charming the reader's ear and conveying the author's own emotion vividly to his mind; at its infrequent worst, when Mr. Woollcott is betrayed by his too easily accessible heart, it suggests to some extent the tormented prose of a sophomore writing to his girl.

Mr. Woollcott's relations with his various editors were amiable for the most part. He was prompt with his copy, which was typed with never a misspelling or an erasure on long sheets of delicately tinted paper, and he was agreeably reliable when it came to facts. The difficulties that arose were usually temperamental, resulting from a curious

paradox in Mr. Woollcott's character. Although the innocent vulgarities of the advertising business horrified him
—a product called Didy Panties almost did him in—he
had a lingerie salesman's fondness for smoking-car
anecdotes, the lower the better. About once a month a
specimen would turn up which would usually not only be
unprintable in any magazine not intended exclusively for
the United States Marines but would also be drearily
familiar to all worldly editors. Its removal from his copy
was always the signal for a fierce battle, with Mr. Woollcott passing from blank astonishment that anyone could be
virginal enough to object to such a pretty story, then to a
vehement lecture on the subject of taste, and finally to the
cold tendering of his resignation. On several occasions,
when some editor had as usual proved adamant, he actually
did resign and had to be won back with humble telephone
calls and ardent letters. These lovers' quarrels turned up
periodically and while they brought two or three editors
close to nervous collapse, Mr. Woollcott enjoyed them
thoroughly. Up in his topless tower on the East River, he
sometimes felt as controversial and desirable as Helen of
Troy.

On the morning of October 19, 1929, Mr. Woollcott was
reasonably well off. He and his friends knew gifted people
in Wall Street and with this professional assistance, or
perhaps in spite of it, they had all done very nicely in the
market. It was reflected in their lives. They spoke in the
proud, mysterious language of finance, and they moved
their poker game from the Algonquin to the Colony, where
the check for refreshments was usually more than anybody had made in a week when the Thanatopsis Club
began. Almost everybody bought a little place in the country. Like so much wealth of the period, however, their

profits were entirely a matter of bookkeeping, and when the American dream abruptly turned into a nightmare, most of them were seriously damaged. In two days Mr. Woollcott had dropped more than $200,000. He was playing croquet out on Long Island when his broker telephoned to say that he was finally undone. Mrs. George S. Kaufman, who was playing with him and had herself had a fairly painful lesson in the folklore of capitalism, says that he came back to the croquet ground and finished his game without batting an eye.

Later he was even able to describe his broker genially as a man who could run your fortune into a shoestring, but in spite of this unearthly detachment his losses had been annoying. His income from his magazine writing was somewhere around $30,000 a year, but he had strong obligations to his family and to other people—he was putting a Vermont boy through Hamilton, for one thing—and his scale of living, with the New York apartment and the island in Lake Bomoseen, was not especially modest. Mr. Woollcott admires money as much as the next man and now, especially, a little extra would come in handy. He had been approached by the radio from time to time, but he had never paid much attention. In fact, he had never willingly listened to a broadcast in his life and regarded the unpleasant sounds he occasionally heard in his friends' houses as no more than childish attempts to upset him when he was concentrating on the cards. This, however, was no time to be proud, and by the end of October he had succumbed, going on the air one Sunday night in a fifteen-minute sustaining program called "The Town Crier." There wasn't a great deal of money in that, but by the following September he was being sponsored by the Gruen Watchmakers Guild and appearing two nights a week. At this time he also took over a sustaining program in which he

reviewed books under the prettily whimsical title of The
Early Bookworm, a choice which was more or less per-
plexing in view of the fact that he had once expressed
horrified disgust upon learning that Mrs. Isabel Paterson
of the *Herald Tribune* had decided to call *her* column
"Turns with a Bookworm." He was off the air from March,
1931, until September, 1933, when he came back again as
The Town Crier and was handsomely sponsored, first by
the Cream of Wheat Company and then by Liggett &
Myers, for whom he spoke admiringly of Granger Cut
Plug. For a while he was being paid $3,500 a broadcast,
which is probably not much as radio salaries go, but is
not, on the other hand, just hay, puss.

Mr. Woollcott came to like the radio, there being something about projecting himself into several million parlors
at the same time which answered the special requirements
of his spirit, and although his programs were a little ad-
vanced for the Amos 'n' Andy public, he was successful and
popular. Like his magazine articles, his broadcasts covered
a great deal of ground, touching on books and the theatre,
furnishing affectionate bulletins about his friends, and
carrying on his perpetual crusades for the Seeing Eye and
Hamilton College. He was, if anything, more emotional
than he was in print, and finally this led to one of the most
maddening experiences of his life.

On the day following an especially rich performance, he
was going over his fan mail when he came upon a letter
written on ruled paper in a hand that shook a little but was
fine and legible still—an old-fashioned hand, with curlicues.
The letter bore no address and it was unsigned, but nevertheless there was something about it that afflicted its recip-
ient with the same romantic melancholy he felt whenever
he thought about Mrs. Fiske.

His correspondents, it appeared from the text, were two

old ladies, sisters, and they lived somewhere near Albany. They didn't care to be more specific than that because they were afraid that Mr. Woollcott might want to help them and they couldn't take charity from anybody. The fact remained, however, that they had little left in life except their radio, to which they listened every night when the dishes were washed and the chores all done. They liked a lot of things they heard, but they thought Mr. W. was about the *best* thing in the world. He had no idea what comfort he'd brought into their lives, and for their part they didn't know what they'd do without him as they went down into the Valley of the Shadow. There was indeed a scriptural tone all through the letter, as might have been expected from two ladies whose only consolation, at least until The Town Crier came along, had presumably been Holy Writ.

Mr. Woollcott had photostatic copies made of the letter and sent them around to his friends, declaring that this was the greatest tribute he'd ever received. He also serenaded the sisters on the air, having the studio orchestra play what he felt sure must be their favorite tunes—the old simple songs, things like "Home, Sweet Home" and "Way Down Upon the Swanee River." These serenades, incidentally, had already gone out from The Town Crier to many people, among them ex-Justice Oliver Wendell Holmes, who died three days later, causing Charles MacArthur, a Baptist faun, to send Mr. Woollcott a brief wire. "One," it said pleasantly. Anyway, more letters came from the sisters and at last one that announced that the elder of them had died, died happily and confident of her salvation at the very moment he went off the air. It was a lot to ask, said the survivor, but next week, if he could spare the time, would Mr. Woollcott mind reading the Twenty-third Psalm over the radio. It would be a sort of requiem. Mind indeed!

The next week, with a catch in his throat, Mr. Woollcott read the Twenty-third Psalm. It was a great emotional performance, judged by any standards. "He was right in the groove that night," says a musical friend admiringly.

Nothing was heard then for a week or two, but finally a letter came in another, younger hand. Both sisters were dead now, it said, and the last one had also died with gratitude to Alexander Woollcott in her heart. The sisters were gone, but their memory plagued him. He was determined to find out who they had been, where and how they had lived, anything at all about them. He exhausted all the possibilities, even sending an agent up to explore the country around Albany to see if anybody remembered two old ladies who had lived alone. A Catholic priest had been named in one of the letters—the only actual clue—but he proved as elusive as his parishioners and nothing came of him, either. Mr. Woollcott spent almost as much as he made from his broadcasts trying to beat the sisters out of the bush, but it was no good. Apparently they had left behind them no relatives, no graves, and, what was most curious of all, no death certificates.

Some of Mr. Woollcott's friends, who may have heard a little too much about the sisters while they were alive, began to ask if they had ever lived at all. Mightn't it be just a little joke? How else could you account for this strange vanishment? The case was never publicly proved one way or the other, but people who ought to know said that the weird sisters and their letters were in actual fact the work of a brooding author whose book Mr. Woollcott had dismissed too arrogantly as tripe. They knew this miserable man, they said, and had even listened to his shameless confession. Mr. Woollcott found it hard to accept this explanation. In spite of all the evidence, he couldn't believe that any human heart could be black enough for such villainy. Nor can he even now.

Mr. Woollcott still appears on occasional guest programs, although he hasn't had a regular hour of his own since July, 1937. A few weeks ago, as The Town Crier, he spoke over WEAF in behalf of political refugees (this was a triumph for him, since once he had resigned in disgust because they wouldn't let him criticize dictatorships), and more recently he might have been heard praising—of all things—the Hamilton College Choir. Some time ago he was on the Information Please Hour when it embarrassingly developed that, although Dickens is one of his most widely advertised enthusiasms, he had never finished reading "Bleak House," and the behavior of his colleagues on this occasion was so exasperating to him that one listener reported that he was the only man she had ever heard who could pout quite unmistakably over the air.

His career in the theatre began about the same time as his first venture on the radio. During the summer of 1929, he had been collaborating with George S. Kaufman on "The Channel Road," an adaptation of de Maupassant's "Boule de Suif," and it was put on at the Plymouth Theatre in the fall of that year. The critics, who may not have been precisely laying for Mr. Woollcott but certainly hadn't been weaving any garlands for him either, jumped it with glad little cries. It was a wordy, shapeless, amateurish piece, they said, and suggested that Mr. Woollcott go back to his fancywork. This vigorous reception was enough to discourage him until the fall of 1933, when, again in collaboration with Mr. Kaufman, he turned up with a pathological study in murder called "The Dark Tower." This was a little better, but not much. In spite of an unusual amount of villainy, it was a rather static play and the sight of Miss Margalo Gillmore wandering through most of it in a hypnotic trance seemed to have a rather stupefying effect on the audiences.

The reason for both these failures probably lay in a curious relationship between the authors. Mr. Kaufman, usually an acute and practical judge of scripts, with strong opinions of his own, was a helpless admirer of Mr. Woollcott's prose, which seemed to him to have a grace and felicity not entirely of this world. He had occasional misgivings about how some of the more elegantly sculptured lines would sound when offered on the stage as the casual speech of human beings, but his modest heart told him that this was Art and therefore not to be tampered with by the likes of him. The result was that Mr. Woollcott was played as written, and was presently playing largely to empty seats. The budding playwright's own opinion of both these ventures can be guessed at from his paragraph in *Who's Who,* which lists all his other occupations but says nothing to suggest that he ever wrote a play in his life.

His acting, of course, was something else. On November 9, 1931, Mr. Woollcott made his first appearance as a child actor of forty-five in S. N. Behrman's "Brief Moment." He opened before a first-night audience made up largely of his dearest friends, most of whom hoped, in an amiable way, that he would stink. They were disappointed. Woollcott, who spent the evening lolling around on a sofa and insulting people, was barely distinguishable from the Woollcott they knew in private life. Since this was just what Mr. Behrman had in mind, the performance, while not precisely acting, had to be regarded as adequate. The *Times'* Mr. Atkinson, clinging desperately to ancient standards, said that for Mr. Woollcott "acting consists in speaking rather more deliberately than he does in the aisles and lobbies" and added that he not only dislocated the couch on which he sprawled but also to a certain extent the play itself. This, however, can be dismissed as the remark of a classicist. Languidly horizontal, beautifully plump, and talking in that strangely precise voice, which still has sharp overtones of Kansas City, Mr. Woollcott was the hit of the show and it was he rather than Miss Francine Larrimore, or even the author, who was responsible for the fact that it ran for thirteen weeks. His second appearance on the stage, in Mr. Behrman's "Wine of Choice" last winter, was a very similar performance, but since he had a lot more to do and was even asked to move around a little, it was not quite so successful. As an occasional choral effect he is admirable, but as a featured exhibit he can grow monotonous.

In spite of the fact that Mr. Woollcott's technique on the stage involved no more than playing himself, he took his acting pretty seriously. Once, during the run of "Brief Moment," he happened to see a special matinée of a play starring his old friends the Lunts, and its effect was immediately perceptible in his own next performance. Miss Larrimore, coming off after the first act, complained bitterly to Mr. Behrman. "He just lies there and mutters, Sam," she said. "I can't hear a damn word he says."

Tactfully questioned by Mr. Behrman, who asked him if he was unwell, Woollcott dissolved the mystery.

"I see everything now," he said. "I've been working too hard. God, you ought to see Alfred. Never raises his voice. It's marvellous."

He was also given to experimenting on his own hook and often came to Mr. Behrman or Guthrie McClintic, who directed him, for approval.

"Did you notice me in the second scene tonight?"

"You were swell, Aleck," they would say politely.

"I know, but that business with the cigarette, where I

look at Larrimore and *then* light it instead of the way we had it before?"

"Sure. That's swell."

"I thought it kind of pointed the whole thing up myself," he would say with satisfaction.

These improvisations had a somewhat disturbing effect on the rest of the cast, who were never completely sure what Mr. Woollcott was liable to do next, and they were also handicapped by the fact that his performance moved at a tempo of its own which hadn't very much to do with anything else that was going on on the stage. It was in "Wine of Choice," however, that he startled them most. Somebody had given him a Spanish cape, a spectacular thing, richly lined with crimson silk. It was, his false friend said, exactly what was needed to give his part a little extra touch of color and romance. Mr. Woollcott, who is no man to resist beauty, wore the cape in the out-of-town tryouts and would undoubtedly have done so on Broadway if his colleagues hadn't protested in a body. Not only was he a vehement spot of color, they said, reducing the rest of them to pale ghosts; he was even bad for their nerves.

"Every time he comes on I think, 'Good God, it's Bela Lugosi,'" said the pretty ingénue rather wildly.

Mr. Behrman was chosen to express their discontent, and when he explained that the cape was disturbing everybody terribly, Mr. Woollcott gave up, although he still wore it around town and was frequently mistaken for an advertisement.

In spite of his dreamy passion for the theatre, he never lost his practical financial sense. At one time, when "Brief Moment" wasn't doing especially well, the whole cast was asked to take a twenty-five-per-cent cut, and, though sadly, they all at last agreed—all, that is, except Mr. Woollcott. It had been his contention from the beginning that he was miserably underpaid, and the proposal that he take even less infuriated him. Not only did he refuse to take the cut; he demanded a raise and a substantial one, too. He threatened to resign and he had them there, because there was no question by this time that it was the prospect of seeing Woollcott plain that got people into the theatre. His salary, which had been $400 a week, was nearly doubled, which was more than could be said for his popularity with the rest of the company.

All his financial affairs, as a matter of fact, have gone nicely in the ten years since the crash wiped him out. His income from the radio varied widely, but it seems likely that he collected at least $200,000 for the four years he was on the air; his magazine work brought in about $125,-000; and as an actor and playwright he must have made $50,000, including his percentage from the sale of "The Dark Tower" to the movies. "While Rome Burns," published in 1934, sold an amazing total of 290,000 copies and his royalties from that were $70,000, while the two "Woollcott Readers," issued in 1935 and 1937, although they didn't approach that figure, made together between $15,000 and $20,000.

These were his main sources of income, of course, but other tidy sums kept dropping in his lap. In 1935, for instance, he played himself for a brief, profitable moment with Noel Coward in a moving picture called "The Scoundrel," and, in 1934, he had made a short for R.K.O. about spelling games; out-of-town ladies were always delighted to hear him lecture, since he was known to be personally acquainted with all the bright, disreputable people in the world; and in his spare time he had drummed up a very satisfactory little trade in commercial endorsements (Woollcott collapsed bonelessly on the back seat of a Chrysler, Woollcott urging all his friends in a rather peremptory form letter to give him a bottle of Seagram's whiskey for Christmas, Woollcott in full color and waving a bell, saying Granger Cut Plug is good for you). His ten-year total was certainly well over $700,000, and while an income of $70,000 a year, about thirty per cent of which went to the tax-collectors and perhaps another ten to agents, isn't money in the Hollywood sense, it was doing all right for a man who on the whole had managed to devote his talent only to things that really interested him.

Mr. Woollcott's life, while unquestionably ideal for him, sometimes makes morbid observers think of a spider in its web. Recently, whenever he hasn't been hibernating up on Lake Bomoseen, he has been living at the Gotham Hotel in a suite that has the same untidy but expensive air that clings about him personally. His friends drop in obediently when he sends for them, and he loots and insults them over the card table with the best nature in the world. He is also high-handed with the employees of the hotel, who have learned rather painfully that the usual rules don't apply to the old eccentric in 9B. The other day, for instance, the clerk at the desk telephoned him to say that Miss Ina Claire was downstairs.

"All right, send her up," said Mr. Woollcott.

"I can't, sir," said the clerk nervously. "She has a dog."

"Either Miss Claire's dog comes up or I'm coming down," said Mr. Woollcott, and added gently, "I'm in my pajamas."

Miss Claire's dog came up.

Although he is fascinated by other people's domestic arrangements, Mr. Woollcott has never come very close to getting married himself. He has admired many ladies and once his engagement was considerately announced for him by the tabloids, but the idea of a little woman sashaying around the house has never really appealed to him. He is, however, a terrific matchmaker—nothing delights him quite so much as throwing his startled acquaintances into one another's arms—and he is strongly attached to children. His four nieces, the daughters of his brother William, who lives in Baltimore, are proudly exhibited and handsomely entertained when they come to town, and he is godfather to many of his friends' children. He is always flattered when anybody asks him to take on these spiritual responsibilities, although not as flattered as he was last year when Harpo Marx, who once inserted a "Duer" in his own name as a tribute to a lady he adored, decided to call his adopted son William Woollcott Marx.

At the moment Mr. Woollcott's plans are a little vague. Sometime in May, if not before, he will go up to his island and, dressed in a few disgusting rags, spend the summer knocking croquet balls around and thinking up new ways to badger the other inmates. If he feels like it and there is still peace anywhere in the world, he may even decide to go travelling again, as he used to do whenever his friends' personalities got to seem more than he could bear. As a world traveller, he has covered a great deal of ground, skipping breathlessly from the polite and ancient splendors of Knole in Kent (where he was embarrassed to learn that he had spoken rudely of Lady Sackville when she was an American actress), to the Riviera (where Frank Harris, decaying in obscurity, tried to sell him an armful of books), and even turning up in Moscow (where the peasants were impressed by his royal stomach and Mme. Litvinoff asked him severely if, as an employee of *The New Yorker,* he wouldn't please find out why she hadn't been getting her magazine).

Mr. Woollcott likes to travel, but somehow he always comes back a little sooner than he had planned. He doesn't actually believe his friends are incapable of conducting their lives in his absence, but on the other hand they are peculiar and helpless people, and he feels happier when he is around where he can keep an eye on them.

Just now Mr. Woollcott's writing is confined largely to the stupendous correspondence he always carries on—a deluge of affectionate or indignant or blasphemous but always stylishly written bulletins that many of his friends are thriftily storing up for posterity. In a day when most letters aren't much more than hastily expanded telegrams, they are unique, and his correspondents are grateful to him—grateful, that is, except once in a while when they are apt to be a little startled by Mr. Woollcott's intricate sense of humor. When Beatrice Kaufman, for instance, gave her celebrated friend as a reference to the school in which she was entering her daughter, she received from him what for an uneasy moment she actually believed was a carbon copy of the letter he had sent the headmistress. "I implore you," it began, "to accept this unfortunate child and remove her from her shocking environment," and went on from there to describe the orgies which took place nightly in the Kaufman household. S. N. Behrman was also momentarily taken aback when he got a carbon of the letter to a real-estate agent in which Mr. Woollcott remarked that he was astonished to learn that the company was even remotely considering accepting as a tenant such a notorious drunkard, bankrupt, and general moral leper as his miserable friend Behrman. Mr. Woollcott's correspondents undergo another small strain because he seldom puts his own name to his letters, preferring to sign them "Richard Whitney" or "Charles Hanson Towne" or sometimes, fondly, just "The Prince Chap."

When he starts writing professionally again, he will probably go back to contributing to the magazines, for it is in them he finds the audience that suits him best. However, the theatre and the movies and the radio are always there waiting for him, and television, of course, is just around the corner. At the back of his mind, he has a rather vague but entirely magnificent project for writing a definitive biography of the late Oliver Wendell Holmes, whom he considers the greatest American of our time. He may get around to doing that. It doesn't really matter what he does. He will almost certainly be successful at it, but his greatest success will always lie, as it did when he was an actor, in his tireless, eloquent, and extraordinarily diverse performance of the character called Alexander Woollcott, a man whose influence and importance can be attributed only in part to the work he has actually done. "He is predisposed to like people and things, in the order named," Dorothy Parker wrote of him once, "and that is his gift from Heaven and his career."

Lady of the Cats

Since 1919, Miss Rita Ross has done her best to rid the city of half a million homeless cats which the S.P.C.A. estimates roam its streets. Almost singlehanded, during that period she has turned over more than two hundred tons of cats to the Society for painless destruction. Like the Post Office ideal, Miss Ross is deterred neither by snow, nor rain, nor heat, nor gloom of night on her round of deadly mercy. On Sundays and holidays, blown along by the high March wind or baked by August, in buildings rotten and sagging, through streets that crawl and smell, almost always among people who are hostile or derisive, she has followed her incomprehensible star. It is a bad day when she gets only six cats; it is a good one when she gets sixteen. Once, when the S.P.C.A. recklessly provided her with one of its wagons and a driver, she bagged fifteen hundred. She has the peculiar reputation of being able to move off under her own weight in cats.

Miss Ross, though a furious and indomitable woman, is also a small one. She is five feet two and a quarter inches tall, and without equipment she weighs only a hundred and one pounds. Her face is shrewd, her glance penetrating, with a sort of birdlike fixity, her manner self-possessed and bouncy. She talks a good deal—coyly about her cats, sardonically about the enemies she has routed on a thousand battlefields. She is around thirty-seven years old.

Every morning at seven-thirty she leaves her home, a small stucco one-family house in the Bay Ridge section of Brooklyn, and takes the subway to the east end of Brooklyn Bridge. Here she alights and proceeds on foot over the bridge, gathering in cats as she goes. She works an average of fourteen hours a day, and she always keeps herself in first-class condition. Once, when a gang of hoodlums tried to deprive her of forty cats, she routed them decisively, wielding an ashcan with murderous effect.

Of the agility which makes a seven-foot billboard only a negligible obstacle in her course, she says, "I studied acrobatic dancing when I was a chorus girl and that comes in handy in climbing. I can beat any man in the S.P.C.A. up a tree except Johnny Joule of the Brooklyn Shelter. He used to be a tree pruner for the Park Department and he is wonderful at getting up a tree."

This is no empty boast. Once Miss Ross was interrupted in her customary work on the third floor of a deserted Harlem tenement by a man who came in quietly and locked the door behind him. His manner was menacing and Miss Ross did not stop to question him about his intentions. She dissolved an untidy situation by scrambling through the transom.

Miss Ross's clothes are nondescript except for an enormous cone-shaped hat, which she wears to keep cobwebs and plaster out of her hair. Her equipment is bizarre. She carries more impedimenta than the average Red Cap: a big, homemade wire trap of the cage type, an animal case, and a good-sized market basket. The trap may contain as many as ten swearing cats, the animal case up to six more. In the market basket are tins of canned salmon, catnip, tin pie plates, a can opener, a flashlight, a police whistle, a ball of twine, and five burlap sacks, used to contain an occasional overflow from the trap and the animal case. Laden with these unusual devices and proceeding at an effortless lope that eats up the miles, Miss Ross is an arresting figure. She is even more so when a vague but cheerful impulse leads her to dye her black hair red, or to wear a yellow wig.

Cat-catching on the grand scale leaves little time for other interests. Miss Ross has none of the accepted vices. She neither smokes nor drinks and if she had her choice, she says emphatically, she would rather kiss a cat than the best man who ever walked on two feet.

While Miss Ross is unquestionably the champion cat woman, there are lesser ones, and occasionally she is accompanied by a Miss Marion Kane. Miss Kane is about thirty-three, short, Celtic, and a ferocious hitter with either hand. When she and Miss Ross roam the streets of Harlem at night, prudent residents take cover, for both ladies have hasty dispositions and would not hesitate to engage an army. Most of the time, however, Miss Ross prefers to hunt alone, having, like so many gifted people, a distaste for collaboration.

Her usual hunting grounds are the bleaker, poorer parts of town. There she operates with matchless precision and technique, as relentlessly as doom. Every day she speaks to about a hundred people on the street, asking them to be on the lookout for stray cats and to communicate with her by mail when they hear of any. One ally, who modestly prefers to be known only as "The Lady from Grantwood, N.J.," scarcely allows a day to pass without providing Miss Ross with the address of at least one underprivileged cat. Miss Ross carries the answers to these requests in her bag and they dictate roughly her course for the day. In addition, she cuts out bankruptcy notices from the papers, because small-store failures almost always result in homeless or locked-in cats. The greater part of her success, however, can be laid to simple vigilance. She penetrates sewers, elevator shafts, and cellars, and climbs to roof tops. She investigates freight yards, abattoirs, bridges, and cemeteries. She never passes a deserted building without making cat sounds, and it is a hard and cynical cat that can resist Miss Ross when she mews. She never allows any animal to be maltreated in her wide and various wanderings and can be almost as indignant about a horse whose teeth aren't clean as she can about one that is being beaten. While Miss Ross has room in her heart for the entire animal kingdom, she focusses principally on cats because she thinks they are victims of prejudice and bigotry.

"A dog has a million friends to a cat's one," she says. "Why, even *snakes* are sometimes praised!"

In a typical working day Miss Ross frequently covers between twenty-five and thirty miles, running like a flame through the Bronx, Brooklyn, Manhattan, and nearer New Jersey, stopping only reluctantly for food. In restaurants and lunchrooms her mystifying burden often arouses comment, but she is not embarrassed.

"They're just a little nervous," she says, referring to the ghostly heave and bounce of the containers at her feet.

The people among whom Miss Ross works always regard her with amazement and sometimes even with consternation, a lady so oddly possessed being a little upsetting to the simple-minded. Once, accompanied by an admiring representative of this magazine, she entered a building at 447 Lexington Avenue to call for a cat. The building was being renovated and the only occupant was a moody Negro in spectacles, hoeing mortar in a tub. Miss Ross told him she had come for the cat.

"Whut cat?" he said. "I don't know of no cat."

"Listen," said Miss Ross, and she gave her celebrated cry. They listened, and from a dark tunnel in the rear of

the basement there came an answering cry, soft and dolor-
ous.

"Why you want that cat?" asked the colored man, nervously.

Miss Ross did not reply directly. She had put on her bee-
hive hat and prepared a mess of salmon on a tin plate. She
paused at the mouth of the aperture and looked at the
colored man.

"I don't suppose you noticed whether it was a boy or
girl?" she asked.

"No'm," he replied. "I don' recollect."

"Well," said Miss Ross, and disappeared, mewing softly.

When she came out, blurred with cobwebs, she was carrying a thin, exasperated cat which she thrust into her
basket, already the prison of three others. Leaving the
building, she spoke once more to the colored man, who had
retreated behind a barrel of lime.

"If you see any more kitties, you be nice and play with
them, won't you?" she said.

The uneasiness inspired by Miss Ross is by no means
confined to the humble. There is no way of telling what the
cats themselves think about her, though their gratitude is
probably mixed with other emotions, but the S.P.C.A., that
enlightened body of humanitarians, speaks of her with horror. The day in 1926 when she brought in fifteen hundred
cats is still remembered as the darkest point in the Society's
history, although Miss Ross dismisses her stupendous feat
lightly. She had spotted colonies of cats around town too
large to be handled by a lady on foot—there were eighty-
seven in the basement of one deserted tenement—and she
had dreamed of the day when she would be able to deal
with them wholesale. The Society's wagon and driver gave
her her glorious opportunity and she seized it fiercely.

From dawn until deep night, driven furiously from the Battery to the Bronx, delivering fifty, sixty, a hundred cats at a clip to the stupefied officials, she accomplished the miraculous. The wagon and driver were withdrawn soon afterward. Miss Ross, disappointed but by no means daunted, went back to patrolling the streets on foot, and even with this handicap continued to tax the Society's facilities. She still does. Sydney Coleman, vice-president of the Society and not essentially a robust man, has barred his door against her in a pitiable effort to save his reason. The Society itself would like to have her restrained legally before it is engulfed in a living wave of cats. This, however, would mean a court suit and such an advertisement might easily be bad for the Society. Kindly people, unaware of the real nature of the crisis, would take Miss Ross's side; contributions would drop off. Last year an unofficial hearing was arranged before Magistrate Louis Brodsky in West Side Court. The judge told Miss Ross that the Society had a legal right to refuse cats in such staggering abundance. Miss Ross, with a ringing eloquence that made the representatives of the Society shudder, cried that it had no *moral* right before God or man to close its doors to sick or suffering animals. Magistrate Brodsky, a sanguine man, said in conclusion that he was satisfied that no further trouble would come up between Miss Ross and the Society. Miss Ross continued to use the Society's five borough shelters to deposit her cats.

The charge has arisen—and the Society would probably give its handsomest medal to the man who can prove it—that Miss Ross is indiscriminate in her choice of cats, that in the fever of the chase she has abducted cats whose home lives were by no means insupportable. One fall, a few years ago, the West End Fruit Market, the New Yorker Delicatessen Store, Schwartz Brothers Fruit Store, and other establishments on the upper West Side missed their cats after Miss Ross had passed that way, conceivably on a broomstick; but whether she had anything to do with these disappearances has never been proved. To accusations of this kind Miss Ross has a firm, invariable answer. Three kinds of cats are safe from her—well-fed cats, altered cats, and nursing mothers. The first two imply ownership, the third maternity. No one can say with certainty that she has ever violated this rule.

If nobody calls for them within forty-eight hours, the cats Miss Ross brings in to the S.P.C.A. are placed in a lethal chamber and asphyxiated in fifteen seconds. That her love is deadly, her artful miaou a siren song, does not concern Miss Ross too much. The stray cat in New York, she feels, can look forward only to a life of great suffering and anxiety, a lonely and miserable end. The alternative is euthanasia and, since he cannot make the choice himself, she does so for him, merciful beyond pity or regret. Estimating that Miss Ross has seduced an average of ten cats a day for nineteen years, she has nearly seventy thousand souls on her conscience. They weigh lightly.

"It's a better death than most humans get," she says.

The police have also met Miss Ross, and they look on her with distaste mixed with a sort of stunned respect. She knows that any citizen has a right to use a patrolman's box to call the station house, and that a reported felony will bring two patrol cars; a murder, five. Several times when she has felt that things were getting a little out of hand, Miss Ross has not hesitated to shout murder.

Innocent patrolmen have occasionally made the mistake of summoning Miss Ross to court and charging her with disorderly conduct. Not one of them has done so twice. She has an imposing courtroom presence and an astonishing legal vocabulary, so her accusers are often dismayed to learn that in the eyes of the law they have been either brutal or incompetent or both. She has even been known to bring departmental charges against patrolmen who have tried to thwart her in one way or another, and this has made the force wary, since such a charge remains on a man's record, proved or not. There are officers in New York who would not arrest Miss Ross if they caught her setting off a bomb.

Thoughtful policemen, in fact, have concluded that the best way to deal with Miss Ross is to do what she says, even if it involves situations not found in the Manual. Once she commandeered two patrolmen from the Borough Park Station in Brooklyn and took them to a deserted bakery which, she said, contained two cats. This was true. The cats were plainly visible and painfully emaciated but, as the policemen discovered when they had forced their way in, Miss Ross had forgotten to mention that they were also insane. In their delirium they mistook their rescuers for aggressors and leapt furiously about the bakery. They were marvellously light from hunger and strain and for the better part of an hour they kept their freedom while Miss Ross and the patrolmen, all heavily floured, toiled irritably after them among the barrels. At last superior physical condition triumphed and the cats were captured and turned over to their nemesis. Miss Ross can be appreciative when the occasion seems to call for it. She wrote a letter of commendation to the Police Commissioner himself.

Probably the most striking example of the influence Miss Ross has with the police occurred some time ago in the Williamsburg section of Brooklyn. She was chased into the subway by a gang of boys trying to rescue a rather unwieldy dog which she had been given by one of their mothers and now carried under her arm. It was her plan to conceal the dog in the ladies' room until the excitement blew over, but she was thwarted by an officious guard. Undaunted, Miss Ross reversed her field, ran up another flight of stairs, and swung down the street to a stationery store. Once inside, to the owner's amazement she slammed the door and locked it.

"Don't open that door," she said sharply as he came from behind the counter.

"But Madam, this is a place of business."

"Don't open that door," repeated Miss Ross, and gave him the dog to hold. While he held the dog uncertainly, she went to the telephone and put in a murder call. Inside thirty seconds, five radio patrol cars, commanded by a Sergeant Kelly of the Canarsie Station, had rushed to the scene. The police dispersed the crowd, and Miss Ross emerged triumphantly with the dog.

"I demand protection against these ruffians," she said, and rode majestically in Sergeant Kelly's car to the nearest police station, where she left an order for an S.P.C.A. truck to come and pick up the dog. Then, as calmly as if such stirring things happened every day, she went out cat-gathering.

Miss Ross met Sergeant Kelly just the other day in the subway.

"Remember all that excitement in the stationery store, Rita?" he asked genially.

In spite of the truce which she has forced upon the Police Department, Miss Ross is still a familiar figure in the magistrates' courts. At least six times a year she appears against people who have maltreated animals or else have insulted her or hampered her in the performance of her duty. She is merciless with those who abuse animals. She has succeeded in having countless five-dollar fines imposed on tradesmen who beat their horses, and one Negro janitor who was convicted of burning cats alive in his furnace was sentenced to six months in jail. She has never lost a case, though sometimes the penalties have seemed to her soft and foolish beyond belief.

"My pet dislike is judges who are lenient in cruelty cases," she says, and probably only their judicial robes have saved many magistrates from the more tangible weight of her displeasure.

With those who harass her personally, she is more moderate, though no less effective. All she wants is an apology, and her courtroom manner is lucid, demure, and undoubtedly maddening to her opponents. Last summer Miss Ross summoned an Irene Mara before Magistrate Nicholas Pinto in Coney Island Court. This woman, aided and abetted by her mother, had used uncivil language in attempting to restrain Miss Ross from making off with a brood of cats. Unkind words had led to blows and in the end the embattled ladies had been separated by several patrolmen. A certain disarray in Mrs. Mara's appearance suggested that Miss Ross had had all the better of the skirmish. Nevertheless, the judge, influenced by the deceptive meekness in Miss Ross's manner, ruled that she was entitled to an apology.

"Me apologize to *her!*" cried Mrs. Mara incredulously, and started to flounce out of the courtroom. The judge had her brought back and, after a stern lecture, the apology was given.

"He called me a lady," Miss Ross says merrily, recalling this scene. " 'You apologize to this lady,' he said. Me, a lady!"

Before the stray cats of the city so relentlessly took possession of her life, Rita Ross gave every promise of a successful career on the stage. Born Marion Garcewich, in the section of Harlem just north of 110th Street, she was the daughter of the German-Jewish proprietor of a gents' furnishing store. She attended Public School 170 in that neighborhood and eventually was graduated. In her teens, her family moved to Brooklyn. For a while she was a salesgirl for Loft's, and afterward a model for Galen Perrett, a commercial artist, from whose studio at 51 West Tenth Street her likeness emerged as the radiant face in the Bel-Ton Powder advertisements, displayed throughout the transportation systems of the city. In 1919 she got a job as a chorus girl in a road company of "So Long, Letty."

Unfortunately for her career, it was at this time that she fell under the influence of her private daemon. Foreshadowing that remarkable pedestrianism which was later to wear down strong men, Miss Garcewich (now, for theatrical purposes, Rita Ross) used to walk across Brooklyn Bridge every day on her way to work in Manhattan. The cats of the lower East Side, degraded and mournful, attracted her strongly, and she got to picking up one or two of them and taking them to an S.P.C.A. shelter on her way uptown.

It is hard to say how this merciful habit gradually became a compulsion. It appears that one cat simply led to another. Miss Ross herself has no explanation of it except in vague, humanitarian terms. It is only clear that from a lady who could, on the whole, take a cat or leave it alone, she was suddenly translated into the most prodigious catcatcher of our time. As her obsession grew, her other interests inevitably suffered. She was no less fetching as a chorus girl, of course, but she became a little embarrassing as an associate. In Salt Lake City, she rescued an alley cat from a vivisectionist by beating him severely over the head with her handbag. In Indianapolis, where she had gone with "The Spice of 1922" company, she was dismissed for picking up a dirty white poodle and installing it in her dressing room.

By 1926, when she was playing in "The Song of the Flame" in Chicago, her peculiarities were so generally recognized that she was warned by the management not to bring any animals into the theatre. She wrestled heroically with temptation, but the habit had her in an iron grip. One night she smuggled in two shivering kittens and hid them in shoebags below her mirror in the general dressing room. The cats, numb and grateful, remained as they were during the first number. When, however, the chorus girls came back after the second number, clawed costumes covered the floor and the wardrobe mistress panted after two hilarious cats. Miss Ross returned to New York. She remained on the stage during the run and tour of Hope Hampton's "My Princess" in 1927, but her heart wasn't in it. When it closed, she retired to devote all her time to her cats.

"I'm not sorry I stopped the stage," she says. "This work is much more interesting. You never know what's going to happen."

She realizes that a professional cat-catcher cannot hope to be as immaculate as Mrs. Harrison Williams, and occasionally this causes her mild distress. Last summer she passed Arthur Hammerstein in Greenwich Village. Miss Ross was in full regalia and the producer looked firmly at something else.

"My, was I embarrassed! I just slunk past."

On the whole, though, she has never regretted her choice. The average chorus girl, she feels, is at least as peculiar as she is, and not in the direction of good works, either.

Miss Ross now lives with her widowed mother, a brother, two sisters, and a nephew, all of whom regard their relative's habit of sleeping in a room crawling with cats as merely odd. These cats are transient, being ones that she has picked up too late at night to turn over to the S.P.C.A. She maintains only one cat of her own, a deaf, toothless antique named Tibby-Wibby Simpson Ross, the gift of an amiable colored woman Miss Ross met on Lenox Avenue. In addition to the usual handicaps of age, Tibby-Wibby has another, of an embarrassing nature.

"He'll never be a daddy," Miss Ross explains delicately.

Miss Ross is given her room and some of her meals by her family, and, since she is a vegetarian and a light eater anyway, the others don't cost much. Money for her clothes, her cat-trapping equipment, and the rest of her needs comes from well-wishers. She is supported at the moment by two anonymous ladies—one in Brooklyn and one in Manhattan—who send her a total of fifteen dollars a week in care of *Variety*, which still nervously handles her mail. At various times during her career, Miss Ross's patronesses have changed, but she has always been able to find ladies, generally prominent supporters of the S.P.C.A., who were anxious to continue her good, though unusual, work. Occasionally there are windfalls from antivivisectionists or people whom she has helped to rid of a plague of cats. In all, she receives about nine hundred dollars a year, which is ample for a woman who up to now has never even been able to find time to go to a talking picture.

Singular things have happened in the course of her career. Once, when she was rearranging her cats in a ladies' room in an "L" station, a habit she has when pressed for time, another passenger, alarmed by strange, thin cries from an adjoining booth, told the ticket agent that a child had just been born, and was barely restrained from sending for an ambulance. Again, in the old New York Hospital at Fifteenth Street and Sixth Avenue, Miss Ross was forced by a series of improbable circumstances to pursue a cat up from the basement and under a bed in the psychopathic ward. Doctors and nurses, coming in to find what they imagined to be a fully dressed patient down on her hands and knees mewing, tried to get her undressed and back into bed. Things looked fairly black until somebody discovered that there actually *was* a cat under the bed. Miss Ross, however, kept her poise.

As a matter of fact, she says she has been really at a loss only once. That was when a dozen of her cats escaped three summers ago while she was riding on the Third Avenue "L." Miss Ross was sitting quietly with her eyes closed, bothering no man. Suddenly, for some unexplained reason, the lid of her animal case flew open. A stream of cats, long pent and indignant, emerged and, with Miss Ross anxiously after them, leaped and gambolled down the aisle, springing over and upon the agitated passengers. When the train stopped, the cats, Miss Ross, and most of the passengers got off in a hurried flux. The passengers milled unhappily around on the platform. The cats, with Miss Ross pursuing the main body, scampered down both stairways. Baffled by their unfamiliar surroundings in the street, the cats darted perilously about in the traffic while Miss Ross sifted after them, like an image in an old moving picture cranked up to dizzy speed. In the end she got them all, but for once the situation threatened to be a little beyond her.

"I can tell you I blushed," she says, describing a vehicular chaos which must have compared very favorably with that immediately following the Wall Street explosion.

The future, like the past and present, holds for Miss Ross only a continuation of her singular crusade. The half-million cats still loose on the streets are a challenge to her genius and she cannot rest until the last one is trapped and riding to its doom. Even at her present spectacular rate, it is the work of a lifetime. She approaches it without misgiving.

St. George and the Dragnet

In a great many ways, Thomas Edmund Dewey is an impressive Presidential candidate. He was born in a typical American town (Owosso, Mich., pop., 14,496) and he came of sound American stock (the hero of Manila Bay was his grandfather's third cousin). In his virtuous youth, he belonged to the Boy Scouts, sang in the choir, and peddled the *Saturday Evening Post*, winning a bicycle. At one time he spent the summer working as a hired hand on a farm, and at another he learned to set type on his father's newspaper. He went to the local public schools and was never late or absent a day in his life. After he was graduated from the University of Michigan and had taken his LL.B. at Columbia, he was admitted to the bar, and presently emerged, at the age of thirty-three, as a fighting prosecutor and the terror of the underworld.

Obviously all this is in the most acceptable tradition—the saga of a more virile and melodious Coolidge, without the snobbish taint of Amherst or the sad comedy of the electric horse. Fortunate as he was in this personal background, however, he was even more fortunate in the times that produced him. Whatever else it accomplished, prohibition got the world ready for the coming of Dewey. The intense melodrama of the twenties accustomed people to the idea of an aristocracy of crime, to a superheated vision of

140

America ruled by an outlaw nobility of vast and incalculable powers. Beer barons and vice lords were a dime a dozen; almost every thug was at least a king. In New York, there were kings of vice, poultry, dope, fur, policy, and artichokes, to mention a few, and each of them commanded a band of desperadoes capable of dealing with the United States Marines. It was wonderful. Even more wonderful were the names that some of these monsters and their mates obligingly bore. In addition to such celebrated figures as Lucky, Waxey, Dixie, Legs, and Lepke, there were Spasm Ison, Cokey Flo Brown, Stone-Faced Peggy, Jenny the Factory, Crazy Moe, Abadaba, Gashouse Lil, Six-Bits, and Blue Jaw Magoon.

From almost the beginning of his political career, Dewey tangled with this demoniac royalty, and he made the most of it. If the voters were already inclined to believe that they were taking part in a moving picture, he did little to disillusion them. His private and public conversation always emphasized the menace of the underworld, omnipresent, almost omnipotent, crouched for a leap. "What do *you* know about the Unione Siciliana?" he asked a startled interviewer, and when it turned out that the man knew almost nothing, he described the fate of a prominent writer who offered to sell *Liberty* a story about its machinations and was shot down like a dog for his pains. "Never been in the papers!" whispered the District Attorney, rolling his eyes wildly. "No indictment. A terrific business! If you had seen men blanch as I have at its mere mention—its mere *mention* —you would know what terror it holds." He was no less alarming when addressing millions. "He has a Japanese butler," he said over the radio, referring to the king of something or other, "who—serves—him—well." He has prosecuted few cases in which he was unable to suggest that there were nameless forces at work, and this has sometimes irritated his critics. "No matter if it was only rolling a lush," said one of them in his homely way, "Dewey could always make it look wonderful on the record."

While there are many things in favor of the District Attorney, almost an equal number oppose him. Physically, he is not majestic, or even especially bizarre, which is probably the next best bet. He is five feet eight and a half inches tall and he weighs a hundred and fifty-seven pounds stripped. His teeth, with centre gaps in both the upper and lower sets, are his most unfortunate feature; his eyes, next to the mustache and the voice, his most arresting. These are brown, with small irises surrounded by a relatively immense area of white, and Dewey has a habit of rotating them furiously to punctuate and emphasize his speech, expressing horror and surprise by shooting them upward, cunning by sliding them from side to side behind narrowed lids. At climactic moments, he can pop them, almost audibly. Lloyd Paul Stryker, who has had less occasion to admire them than most, says that they are the only piercing brown eyes he has ever seen.

Dewey has a jutting jaw, high cheekbones, a slightly bulbous nose, and thick eyebrows. His face, on the whole, has a compressed appearance, as though someone had squeezed his head in a vise. His suits are custom-made but uninteresting, and always seem a little too tight for him, although the Merchant Tailors and Designers Association of America chose him this year as one of the twenty-five best-dressed men in America. Altogether—smallish, neat, and dark—he looks like a Wall Street clerk on his way to work; unlike the late and magnificent Harding, he is a hard man to imagine in a toga.

Dewey is also unfortunate in the fact that people too close to him are usually either entertained by his super-cinema technique or else irritated by his proud, peculiar ways. One crisp hostess has said, "You have to know Mr. Dewey very well in order to dislike him," and the reporters in the Criminal Courts Building usually speak of him lightly as The Boy Scout or, more simply, just The Boy. One man, who frequently boycotts Dewey's press conferences for ten days at a stretch, explains his absence airily. "You got to rap The Boy on the knuckles once in a while," he says.

Lawyers, politicians, and others whose careers are directly affected by Dewey's activities are apt to be more portentous. An attorney for the Civil Liberties Union has compared him with Mayor Hague, though conceding Dewey a good deal more class, and a Republican leader, noting the candidate's petulant behavior at a Party dinner, observed gloomily to Mr. Kenneth Simpson that they seemed to have a problem child on their hands. He has been accused of bullying hostile witnesses and coddling favorable ones, demanding exorbitant bail, wire-tapping, condoning the use of perjured testimony, and even (in the case of Dixie Davis, who was allowed to leave the Tombs some eighty or ninety times in the course of three months to go up to a lady's apartment and change his shirt) of conniving at adultery. In this case, Dewey's answer was frank, if not precisely responsive or even in the best possible taste. "Well, gentlemen," he told the jury, "if Davis did not have . . . desires, he wouldn't be human . . ."

Some hecklers even go to the length of complaining that the leading contributors to the Dewey campaign fund represent more wealth and special interest than seem quite consistent with his notorious enthusiasm for the underprivileged. Among these well-heeled angels are, it is claimed, Ruth Hanna McCormick Simms, a President-maker by inheritance and a Dewey Cabinet member by inclination; John Foster Dulles, a senior partner in the law firm of Sullivan & Cromwell, counsel to some of the biggest corporations in the country, including the North American Company, International Nickel, and Brown Brothers Harriman (Mr. Dulles might turn up as Secretary of State); Roger W. Straus, vice-chairman of the board of the American Smelting & Refining Company, who might land an ambassadorship; Artemus L. Gates, president of the New York Trust Company; S. Sloan Colt, president of the Bankers Trust Company; Robert H. Thayer, who has Standard Oil connections; and Francis Dwight Bartow, vice-president of J. P. Morgan & Co. Up to now, it is estimated that they have been largely responsible for raising between $250,000 and $300,000 for private Pullman cars, publicity, rental on campaign headquarters, and all the other expenses necessary in presenting a candidate appetizingly to the public.

Dewey's most serious handicap, however, is the fact that he was born as recently as March 24, 1902. It is difficult for a great many people to think seriously of a candidate who was sixteen years old at the end of the World War, ten when the Titanic went down, six when William Howard Taft entered the White House, and thirty-one before he could buy a drink legally at any bar in the United States. If he happened to be elected, Dewey, of course, would be the youngest President in history, four years younger than Theodore Roosevelt, thirty years younger than William Henry Harrison, and about sixteen years below the average age of his predecessors at the time of their inauguration. Mrs. Dewey, who will be thirty-eight on February 7, 1941, would not, however, be the youngest First Lady—Dolly Madison was thirty-six when she entered the White House and Mrs. Cleveland was a tot of twenty-two.

Critics, in an attempt to make these cold figures a little more picturesque, have pointed out that he is only eight months older than Lucius Beebe, the fashionable pamphleteer, and seven weeks younger than Colonel Charles A. Lindbergh, the aviator—two national phenomena who, although of almost equal prominence, are not generally regarded as quite ready for the Presidency. Dewey's detractors also like to quote Secretary Ickes' comment that the District Attorney of New York had finally thrown his diaper in the ring.

Beyond a slight and comprehensible annoyance, it is doubtful if the candidate pays much attention to these brickbats. Nobody believes that Thomas E. Dewey is better qualified to be President of the United States than Thomas E. Dewey. Last fall many Republican heavyweights were asked to sign a resolution which read in part:

Convinced that he possesses above all other leaders in the country today the ability, temperament, training and ideals which the next President of the United States must have, we have determined to coöperate in the movement to elect Thomas E. Dewey President in 1940.

This movement has in every sense originated with the people themselves. Mr. Dewey's record has inspired new efforts on behalf of good government throughout the country. It has evoked a spontaneous demand everywhere for his election to the Presidency. In him the people see a new hope for a better America.

He has experienced judgment on public questions. He has vigor, executive ability, sincerity and devotion to duty. All these qualities have been proved by exceptional performance in the public service.

New York will be a pivotal state in the 1940 national elections. We are convinced Mr. Dewey will carry not only New York but also the country at large next year against any opponent. . . . We extend to all citizens a cordial invitation to join us.

According to the best authorities, this document was not only circulated by the candidate, who would whip it out of his pocket like an automatic when he had his victim cornered, but was also written by the man of experienced judgment himself.

This version, picturing Mr. Dewey drafting himself almost singlehanded, differs a little from the District Attorney's own account of what went on. Shortly after his defeat by Governor Lehman, he says, "they" began to badger him to run for the Presidency. Dr. Gallup made a few soundings and discovered that he was far ahead of all other Republican Presidential possibilities. "It looks like I'm in for it," Dewey recalls saying to himself rather ruefully at the time. "If that many people want me elected, it is my duty to give them a chance." He held out for a while, but when the procession of supplicants began to clog the halls of his office, he saw that it was no good; he shouldered the cross.

The cold fact seems to be that Dewey became the nominal choice of the New York Republican Party for one of those reasons which make practical politics such a fascinating study for the layman. For years the New York delegation had gone to the national convention with its members hopelessly split, some favoring this man, some that. Last year the better minds decided that this was all nonsense and that it would be a good idea if everybody went to Philadelphia agreed on one man. Then, if *he* didn't go over on the first couple of ballots, the state chairman would be in a position to handle his delegation as a solid block in further negotiations. What happened, it seems, was that the dummy candidate decided to run in earnest, on a fine, expansive scale worthy of William Jennings Bryan. "We drafted this monkey," says one humble worker in the vineyard, "and, by Jesus, he took it serious."

This would not be a particularly alarming situation for the New York strategists if the primaries in other states hadn't made it clear that a good many romantic citizens were also inclined to take Dewey serious—so many, in fact, that at the moment it is quite possible that he will go to Philadelphia so firmly established as the People's Candidate that the boys in the back room, who would almost prefer to run Mr. Beebe, will have to climb on the band wagon. Incidentally, they will not be able to tempt him with the lesser rôle of the Vice-Presidency. Dewey says emphatically that he is not interested in anything but the White House, explaining to one interviewer that it would be impossible for him to live suitably in Washington on $15,000 a year. "I can't afford it," he said. "It costs money to be a Vice-President."

What Dewey would be like in the White House can only be deduced rather arbitrarily from his history up to now. His early life in Owosso, as previously noted, was suitable but dull, and so were his years in college, where he won singing and debating contests, got an adequate B grade in his studies, but was on the whole practically indistinguishable from his contemporaries. Dewey's actual career, it might be said, dates from the summer of 1925, when, on a bicycle tour of France, he decided to grow a mustache. It turned out to be a dream—bushy, dramatic, an italicized swearword in a dull sentence. From then on, things began to happen. Later that year, he went to work prosaically for a law firm in New York, but he rose rapidly and by 1931, when he was twenty-nine, he was earning $8,000 a year. Furthermore, according to Rupert Hughes, whose biography of Dewey compares very favorably with some of Albert Payson Terhune's hymns to the collie, he "was handling most of the litigation in his office." This statement is rather crossly denied by fellow-employees of the period, but there may be prejudice here, and anyway he was doing all right.

The big break, however, came when he served on a case with George Z. Medalie and impressed him so vehemently that when Medalie took the post of United States Attorney for the Southern District of New York, he offered Dewey a job at a salary around $3,500 as one of the sixty assistants on his staff. Dewey, whose indifference to money is such that he can remember offhand how much he was making at any given day in his life, even for singing in choirs, politely declined that, as well as a subsequent bid of $6,000. He finally accepted only when Medalie had raised the ante to $7,500 and the position to that of chief assistant.

In the two years and nine months that followed, the United States Attorney's office successfully prosecuted such middle-sized kings of the underworld as Legs Diamond and Waxey Gordon, and a lot of minor nobility, including James Quinlivan, a vice cop whose moral fervor had netted him $80,000 in three years, and James J. (Cupid) McCormick, the clerk in charge of the Marriage License Bureau, where, it seems, the pickings were also very nice.

In 1933, Medalie resigned and for five weeks, until Martin Conboy succeeded him, Dewey was in charge of the office. During this period the newspapers casually referred to him as the Acting United States Attorney, a title to which Dewey objected vigorously. In a letter to the editors, he advised them that they'd better omit the word "Acting," and they did, so, when he went into private practice a month later, he was able to call himself a former United States Attorney. Once again, Dewey had made something look good on the record.

Dewey says he was immensely successful in private prac-

tice, estimating the take at between $50,000 and $75,000
a year, a figure which even his best friends consider im-
aginative. Except for this financial item, nothing much
developed in the eighteen months he worked for himself,
although they marked his first encounter with Lepke, a
genuine crowned head, and his satanic prime minister,
Gurrah. In this case the victory seems to have lain with the
forces of evil, since the baking company which had employed Dewey to straighten out its labor difficulties was
still paying tribute to Lepke and Gurrah when he retired.
Talking of this now, the candidate pops his eyes and says,
"Isn't it awful? They were so scared, they were even afraid
to tell *me*."

The next step up the ladder, and a big one, was his appointment as Special Prosecutor, which came about in
July, 1935, after the grand jury had finally broken with District Attorney William C. Dodge and asked Governor Lehman to appoint somebody to investigate racketeering and
vice in New York. At the instigation of Medalie, who by
this time regarded his protégé as one of the fanciest blood-
hounds in the business, the Governor chose Dewey, though
not before four other prospects had refused the job. His
salary, which he set himself, was $16,695, the same as the
District Attorney's. The expenses of his office, during the
years 1935, 1936, and 1937, were $793,502.92, of which
$117,994.63 came under the useful heading of "contin-
gencies."

Dewey established his first offices in the Woolworth
Building, where he set up elaborate defences against the
hosts of darkness, including a twenty-four-hour police
guard inside the building, secret entrances, and a special
untappable cable connected directly with the main office
of the Telephone Company. After examining some four
thousand applicants, he picked four chief assistants, sixteen

assistants, ten accountants, and nine investigators. Then, with the Governor and the Mayor, he called on the public to come forward with information on racketeering, assuring witnesses of protection. The first, and rather discouraging, fish to fall into this net was a nineteen-year-old boy whom Dewey's agents caught breaking windows, but soon the big ones began to come along.

The biggest unquestionably was Lucky Luciano, who, in the eyes of casual newspaper readers, soon came to bear the same relation to organized prostitution that the late John D. Rockefeller once bore to petroleum. Luciano's tentacles were everywhere, his income was fabulous, there wasn't a sporting lady in New York who didn't shiver in her chemise at the mention of his name. Rupert Hughes, giving a little shudder himself, called him "the deadliest and most evil genius in the whole country."

There are those, even among his enemies, who claim that Luciano never got a dollar from prostitution in his life, and it is known that he was doing nothing more deadly than making book at Saratoga when he was surprised to learn that Dewey had crowned him King of Vice. Nevertheless, sex being what it is, the trial was a tremendous artistic success. In addition to revealing the gay and provocative names which most of the girls had thought up for themselves, the testimony was gratifyingly explicit and gave the public a good working picture of the technical structure of a pretty complicated business. A lot of the entertainment also lay in the relations between Mr. Dewey and his staff and the witnesses who eventually won the case for the prosecution. From the beginning, the young women were treated with exceptional tenderness and chivalry, even though one of the investigators persisted in wearing gloves throughout the trial and several of them were rather ungallantly mystified when their clients insisted they were vir-

gins. As the girls began to come through with the right kind
of testimony, they were shown even more consideration.
They were set up in apartments and hotels around town,
given spending money, taken to the movies, on shopping
trips, out to cocktails, and even to night clubs. This last
practice, however, fell into disrepute when one of them, in
the company of an assistant prosecutor, was observed by
the opposition having a fine, though somewhat incoherent,
time at Leon & Eddie's on Fifty-second Street. This incident
went on the record, where it did not look good at all.

It was after the trial, though, that the prosecutor really
showed that his heart was in the right place. In order to
protect them from the vengeance of any possible surviving
vice kings, two of the girls were given a trip abroad, spending four months in England and France with all expenses
paid. Two others took a studio in New Rochelle and got
$50 a week each for ten weeks while a writer from *Liberty*
interviewed them. They also got $500 bonuses. With this
money, the ladies bought a car and went to California,
where they opened a filling station, whimsically christening
it The Rooster. Contented letters came back to the prosecutor's office, reporting that business was fine. "We're selling more gas already than the other two stations near us,"
wrote one of the partners. "Regards to Mr. Dewey."

While the money kept coming in, everything was lovely
between these far-flung witnesses and Uncle Dee, which
was their pet name for the scourge of the underworld. When
it stopped, however, and the Dewey office was unable to
help *Liberty* sell their life stories to Warner Brothers for a
movie, the girls began to get rough. In the middle of
March, 1937, Luciano filed a motion for a new trial with
affidavits from Nancy Presser, Mildred Harris Balitzer, and
Cokey Flo Brown, in which they repudiated their previous
testimony. Miss Presser said that she had spent most of her

time in the prosecutor's office drinking liquor and listening
to people shouting that they "had to get Lucky." Miss
Brown went even further. Her testimony against Luciano
was all made up, she said. Why, she had never laid eyes on
the man in her life.

In spite of the fact that the motion for a new trial was
denied, this ingratitude was discouraging, and so was the
common report that most of the ladies had gone back to
their regular work as soon as the heat was off. Mr. Hughes,
it is true, wrote that one of them had "become a blooming
bride after a year of hard work and clean living," but less
roseate authorities were pessimistic. In fact, Samual Marcus, counsel for the Society for the Prevention of Crime,
was able to dig up Stone-Faced Peggy at an address on
West End Avenue, where, with six assistants, she was established in a penthouse from which she was sending out
cards to her old clients, announcing the arrival of "the
latest fall neckware." This enterprise, according to Mr.
Marcus, was partially financed with money Peggy earned
as a Dewey witness.

The rest of Dewey's term as Special Prosecutor never
rose to the dramatic level of the Luciano trial. Restaurant,
poultry, and baking empires were overthrown, but, generally speaking, it was dry stuff, with no sex appeal and not
much gunfire. It was not until December 31, 1937, when
Dewey took office as District Attorney, that the fun began
again. Richard Whitney, Jimmy Hines, Fritz Kuhn, and
Lepke were all men of substance in one way or another, and
lent themselves well to florid treatment both by Dewey
and the newspapers.

The Hines case—the only one, incidentally, which the
District Attorney prosecuted in person—was probably the
best, with its rumors of bodies done up in concrete and
sunk forever in the East River; its suggestion, always agree-

able to the public, that every member of Tammany Hall is on the payroll of the underworld; and its remarkable cast of characters, including the beautiful Hope Dare, who handled Dixie Davis's laundry, and the fantastic Abadaba, who could do quadratic equations in his head.

In this case, too, Dewey was conspicuously gentle with the witnesses for the People. Not only was Davis permitted to leave his cell and go visiting whenever he felt like it, but later, when the first effort ended in a mistrial, he and two other witnesses, George Weinberg and Harry Schoenhaus, were removed from the Tombs—they had been complaining about the heat—and shipped out to a country club on Long Island, where they learned to play badminton. When that got tiresome, the District Attorney fixed them up with a private house in White Plains. It was here that Weinberg ungratefully shot himself with a cop's gun, to the irritation of the owner of the property, who claimed it had a bad effect on real-estate values.

For everybody except Weinberg, who was dead, and Hines, who got from four to eight years, the case ended happily. Davis was given a year, but the sentence was shortened on the ground that he had theoretically served half of it while held as a witness; Schoenhaus got a suspended sentence; and the District Attorney's office, which apparently had a persistent enthusiasm for belles-lettres, encouraged Hope and Dixie to write their memoirs for *Collier's.* They got $6,300 apiece. The policy game, according to reliable reports from Harlem, is still running just about the way it always was.

The Whitney and Kuhn cases also had their points (Lepke was rather an anticlimax because of the annoying circumstance that the G-men got to him first), but defalcation and propaganda are never as interesting as vice and gambling, and relatively they attracted less attention.

Dewey's expenses as District Attorney from January 1, 1938, to the present have been $2,146,509.03, including $201,183.44 for "contingencies."

While all this was going on, Dewey heard the call to run as Republican candidate for Governor in the fall of 1938. He devoted over a month to the campaign, but was defeated by Lehman by a margin of approximately 67,000 votes. Undeterred by the fact that he had won only one elective office in his life, Dewey made formal announcement on December 1, 1939, that he was a candidate for the Republican nomination for President of the United States. Since then there hasn't been much of interest happening in the District Attorney's office, and during the past six months the boss has been absent some sixty-five days, though still, of course, on the payroll.

People who have watched Dewey perform in court sometimes wonder how the same technique would work in larger fields. His manner before the bench is as exasperating as it is in private. A distinguished attorney, who suffered from it painfully in the Hines trial, says that the District Attorney seems to feel that any lawyer who would stoop to defend a man indicted by the Dewey office must either be a crook himself or else corruptly allied with criminal interests. If a ruling is unfavorable to the People, Dewey will rise from his chair, slow and aghast, the blood mantling his neck, and cry, "Do you mean to say that the Court will not allow the District Attorney of New York County," etc., etc. During the first Hines trial, while the policy broker Spasm Ison was on the stand, Dewey sat slumped in his chair, pretending to read a Harlem dream book. Occasionally, without rising, he would drawl, "I think I'll object to that," and once, to Justice Pecora's indignation, he varied this formula. "I suppose it won't do any good," he said wearily, "but I think I'll object."

It is also part of his system to make the jurors feel that they are part of the prosecution, not a difficult feat with a blue-ribbon jury, which usually imagines that it has been divinely appointed to convict, anyway. When opposing counsel scores a point, Dewey turns to the jury and beats his breast to let them know that the People are being crucified. When an attorney for the defence says anything derogatory about him or any member of his staff, he objects thunderously to "this insult to the representatives of the People of New York," a classification, of course, including the jury. Sometimes, when things aren't going too well for his side, he is apt to stifle a yawn and saunter out of the courtroom for a smoke and a chat with the reporters.

Dewey's most annoying mannerism, however, is drinking water. He is one of the greatest water drinkers of our time, estimating himself that he gets away with more than three quarts a day, and he has learned that it is a wonderful way to harass the opposition. While Stryker was examining key witnesses against Hines, Dewey made many leisurely trips to the water-cooler near the jury box, filled himself a Lily cup, and ambled back to his table, looking bored to the edge of imbecility. This finally worked on Stryker to such an extent that the next time Dewey got up to get a drink, he waved him back to his chair, poured out a cup himself, and carried it politely over to the prosecutor's table. There can be no question that The Boy has mastered the art of getting on people's nerves.

After the second Hines trial, Dewey announced that he didn't propose to go into court again until after the election, but his technique is almost as effective in private life. His vanity is enormous, a fact of which he is aware and even rather proud (he once refused to appoint an otherwise capable man, saying seriously, "Why, he's as arrogant as I am"). When he was chosen to run for District Attorney on a ticket with LaGuardia, the Mayor suggested that it might be wise if he didn't have much to say to the papers until they had planned their campaign. "I can't do that," said Dewey. "My public will want to hear from me." Recently, when somebody asked him if he wasn't afraid that John T. Cahill's mounting reputation as a United States Attorney might come to eclipse his own, Dewey was reassuring. "No, I don't fear that," he replied earnestly. "After all, the public knows there was only one Lindbergh."

Last year, a former United States Attorney named Green was nominated by the Republicans to run against Mayor Kelly in Chicago. Green was the prosecutor who sent Capone to Alcatraz for income-tax evasion, and consequently he had a local reputation as a gangbuster almost equalling Dewey's. Since his campaign against the corrupt Kelly-Nash machine was based on the need for divorcing crime from politics, the same war whoop that Dewey had been finding so useful in the East, Green's backers thought it would be helpful if the New York prosecutor came to Chicago and made a speech endorsing their man. Dewey declined after some thought. "There's only one thing that would pull Green through," he said, "and that's if I went out there." "But if I did," he continued, "everybody would know what had happened. I think the people of Chicago would resent having me come out there and elect their Mayor."

Dewey reached his peak, though, in the reply that went back to Anthony Eden, who, on his trip here in December, 1938, said that he would like to meet New York's celebrated crusader. The man who tried to arrange the interview got a brief telephone call from Dewey's office. "I have your message to Mr. Dewey," a voice said. "He has asked me to tell you that he will be glad to meet Mr. Eden if he will call at the District Attorney's office on Centre Street."

The advent of the Deweys would certainly mean a new era of simplicity in official Washington society. Mrs. Dewey, who once sang in a road company of "George White's Scandals," is probably not temperamentally opposed to a little gaiety around the place, but lately she has grown increasingly conscious of her responsibilities as the candidate's wife. Political topics are taboo with her and she is fairly cautious on all others, so conversation is something of a strain.

Dewey himself is simply a man with no time for comedy or other irrelevancies. His life outside his work is a little like the interval between rounds in a prizefight—a period of rest, therapy, and reflection about what to do next. He gets up at the same time every day, eight-thirty, and eats the same breakfast. His lunch, which he usually has at his desk, never varies either, consisting of fruit salad, a chicken sandwich on white bread, milk and coffee, cheese and crackers. He lets himself go at dinner, but not recklessly. He limits himself strictly to one package of cigarettes a day and, since repeal, two highballs at a sitting. During prohibition he never drank or allowed alcohol in his house. If he was offered a drink at a party, he would smile tolerantly and say, "No, you go ahead and have a drink if you want one. That's your business. None for me." He plays penny-ante poker with a nickel limit, and usually wins. His chauffeur, who used to have a job driving an old lady around, is right at home with him, because Dewey hates speed and objects to anything over fifty miles an hour, even in the open country.

The candidate is a great man for getting his sleep and

always bundles Mrs. Dewey up at eleven-thirty and takes her home, no matter what's happening. He hasn't been inside a night club since his appointment as Special Prosecutor. To make up for this, the Deweys organized a private dancing group among their friends, hired an instructor and a small orchestra, and met regularly at one another's apartments for dancing parties. They did this for a season or two and then gave it up. It may have been too exclusive.

Dewey is terribly down on sculpture, but he says he likes all the other arts and is sorry he hasn't the time to get at them any more. He used to go to the opera quite a lot (he admires Wagner especially) and to the Sunday concerts at Town Hall almost every week. That's out now and so is the theatre. The only play he saw this season was "Ladies and Gentlemen," with Helen Hayes, whom he likes, though not as much as Ina Claire. When it comes to books, he reads history, biography, and mystery stories, volunteering that he's read just about all of Edgar Wallace. The only books currently visible in his office are *Who's Who in America* and "Debate Outlines on Public Questions." Dewey has even given up his own singing except for rare duets with his wife and a rich, baritone solo now and then in the bathtub, where he sings the Prologue to "Pagliacci," but he still gets to church. When interviewers ask his press secretaries how often he manages to get there, they say, "Not as often as he'd like to—about once every month or so." When they ask Dewey the same thing, he thinks it over for a while and answers, "Not as often as I'd like to—about once every month or so." Incidentally, while the candidate has only two official publicity men, at salaries of $6,500 and $5,000 a year, practically everyone in the office these days is coöperating with the Republican Party, including many of the Assistant District Attorneys. Considered on a man-hour basis, it is probable that the people of New York are spending $500 a week to send their prosecutor to the White House.

In winter the Deweys live in an eight-room apartment at Fifth Avenue and Ninety-sixth Street, which has nothing remarkable about it one way or another. Their elder son, Thomas, Jr., who is seven and a half, goes to a private school, although both his parents can hardly contain their admiration for the public-school system. John, four and a half, hasn't started yet. For the past three years, the family have been spending their summers on a 300-acre farm near Pawling, which Dewey bought last year. Before that they went to Tuxedo, until Dewey discovered that his neighbors led a "manicured existence." "Between you and me," he says, "that Tuxedo crowd is a bunch of snobs. I want my children to grow up with farm children." At Pawling, Dewey gets up early to go riding with Lowell Thomas, who more or less sets the social and intellectual pace for the colony. After that, he has the standard breakfast and then plays golf, shooting around a hundred, usually with Carl Hogan, a Madison Avenue furniture dealer and probably Dewey's closest friend; Kenneth C. Hogate, publisher of the *Wall Street Journal;* and Ralph Reinhold, publisher of an architectural magazine called *Pencil Points.* He plays earnestly, watching his opponents like a hawk so they won't try to chisel on their scores. Sometimes he plays softball with Thomas's Nine Old Men. He used to pitch, but he always tried to strike out the batter, and, as the game is played mostly for fun, they shifted him to second base. There is quite a lot of visiting around at Pawling, but no cocktail parties or other rough stuff. Altogether, it is a simple, earnest, and healthy way of life. How it would look to the British Ambassador or someone like Mrs. Longworth, there is no way of telling.

Dewey's speeches have been described as the best that money can buy, and they are delivered in a voice that even Mr. Stryker has been obliged to admit is "quite an organ," but up to now nobody seems exactly sure what he has been talking about. Generally speaking, he is apparently for everything that's good and against everything that's bad, which naturally includes most of the activities of the administration. In spite of this vagueness—Raymond Clapper has written in the *World-Telegram* that most of the Dewey policies are about as mysterious as love—his campaign has been an astonishing success. As a candidate, if you care to listen to his admirers, he is a cinch for the White House. They see him as America in microcosm—the small-town boy who demonstrated to the people not only that the cities were as wicked as they had dreamed but also that wickedness is helpless when confronted with rustic purity. He is the hope of the world, the Plumed Gang-Buster. Berton Braley, a poet who once accompanied the Ford Peace Ship to write odes to Mr. Ford, has summed the District Attorney up lyrically:

> Let Dewey do it! And Dewey did.
> Dewey's "magic" was simply that
> He did the job he was working at!
> But do we duly do honor to
> The work of Dewey? We do! We do!

To his critics, this picture seems a little too rapturous. Some have complained that a man who spends a good part of his first year in office running for Governor and even more of his second and third running for President can't exactly be described as doing the job he is working at. Robert Moses, a forthright man, said frigidly that it seemed to him Mr. Dewey had "no manifest experience or probable qualification for the job," and Mayor LaGuardia, returning thoughtfully from a visit to "Abe Lincoln in Illinois," dismissed all the current Republican aspirants with the word "phooey." The Arab in William Saroyan's play called "The Time of Your Life" probably came closest to getting at what a good many people have been trying to say about the Boy from Owosso in his reiterated refrain: "No foundation. . . . No foundation. . . . All the way down the line."

One with Nineveh

One recent Sunday afternoon, following a well-blazed trail, I went over to Weehawken, New Jersey, for cocktails with Lucius Beebe and Charles Clegg, whose private car was moored there on Track 1 in the New York Central yards. A strange excursion for a Sunday afternoon—strange for my wife and me, to whom Mr. Beebe and, to a lesser extent, Mr. Clegg are memoranda from the remote and jocular past; strange indeed for our sixteen-year-old daughter, who has seen few millionaires in the flesh, and none ever on a siding.

"Just who *is* this Mr. Beebe?" she asked as we sped in the taxi from Eighty-second Street to the foot of Forty-second, where the ferry Utica lay.

"A friend," I replied. "A fashion plate. A sport."

"You and your friends," she said with habitual derision, but pressed the point no further. My answer was a poor one, though, and I am trying now to amplify it in my mind.

It was, I find on reference to *Who's Who*, in 1929 that Mr. Beebe first swam hugely into the life of this metropolis. He was twenty-seven then, and his career already had certain legendary aspects. He had attended Yale but, proving too vivacious for the faculty, had moved on to Harvard, where he was graduated, though not without some official misgivings, as a Bachelor of Arts. His bent, in the under-

162

graduate years, was poetic, and he had issued feuilletons on Villon and Edwin Arlington Robinson. He also wrote verse of his own, and, for some inscrutable reason, a fragment that won the Richard Memorial Prize at Yale in 1923 is still in my possession. The first and final stanzas will suffice:

> I am weary of these times and their dull burden,
>> Sweating and laboring in the summer noontide,
> And the hot stench of inland forges
>> Sickens my nostrils.

> Soon there will be no more metals to plunder,
>> There will be no more forests to slash and dismember,
> Then, O chosen people, nation of fortune,
>> Where is thy glory?

This poem, I am in a position to add, was reviewed, in question-and-answer form, in the *Yale Daily News:*

Q. What is the theme?
A. Defeat, foreseen or expected, lying in wait for American materialism.
Q. What does the author indicate will remain after said defeat?
A. Nothing.

Other and less spiritual tidings preceded the youthful Beebe into town. At Yale, it was his merry custom, on returning from weekends in New York, to attend his first Monday-morning class in full evening dress, wearing a monocle and carrying a gold-headed cane, and the *News*, stunned by such gloss in a contemporary, reported that "two hemispheres knew him at nineteen." At Harvard, his room contained a roulette wheel and a bar equipped to

make any drink a guest could name. His departure from
New Haven was partly the result of his appearance in a
stage box at the Hyperion Theatre extravagantly bearded
and brandishing a bottle and shouting that he was Professor Henry Hallam Tweedy, of the Divinity School. His stay
at Harvard was enlivened by his circulation of a ballot to
determine how the college stood on trading President
Lowell and three full professors for a good running back-
field. These exploits and several like them, being so accurately part of the climate of a peculiar time, were widely
reported in the press, and Mr. Beebe showed up in this
parish trailing, if not clouds of glory, at least a certain
antique and fashionable radiance.

Reading over what I have written, I can see that it will
convey little to young and sober readers, who almost surely
have no idea how whimsically celebrity was come by in
the twenties. The New York chapter of the saga, I'm afraid,
will be hardly more illuminating. I remember I thought
about that as the Utica cleared her slip and, lurching and
clanking, set out for the western bank. The cabin of the
ferry was a good place to think about the past, since, except for the advertisements on the wall, it differed little
from those in the old sidewheelers that used to take me to
and from Palisades Park. The ladies in my party, assailed by
many searching aromas (less vehement, however, than those
diffused by the horses of my youth) and highly suspicious
of a craft with a propeller at each end, behaved rather
badly on the seven-minute passage, but my own mind was
calm and clear. I am soothed by anachronisms, being, I
suppose, so nearly one myself.

To the best of my recollection, I met Mr. Beebe first during the winter of 1931. It was in one of the speakeasies

that then contained so much of our social life, and I remember him, immense, pink, and menacingly groomed, standing at the bar and booming out a denunciation of the Newspaper Guild, which he appeared to regard as a branch of the Maffia. Additional jocosities had already collected around him. His salary as a reporter on the *Tribune* was, I think, only thirty-five dollars a week, but his private means were boundless and his wardrobe consisted of no fewer than forty suits, none, of course, duplicating another. It was rumored that he had once gone out to report a negligible fire in a morning coat, and a tedious dinner of the Landscape Gardening Society in top hat and tails. His jewelry, according to further material in my files, included three gold cigarette cases, valued at approximately seven hundred dollars each; a Kashmir sapphire cabochon ring, at twelve hundred dollars; a single emerald stud worth five hundred dollars; and a platinum evening watch that cost a thousand. His attitude, in general, was that a decent respect for the profession of journalism demanded all these accessories. "I wear formal clothes, morning or evening, whenever they are called for," he was quoted as saying at the time, "and regard them quite literally as the livery of my business. As a reporter for the *Tribune*, I would no more think of entering a restaurant in the evening out of dinner dress than I would in swimming shorts."

In spite of this almost sanctified approach, he was, I'm afraid, never much of a reporter. For one thing, the outrageous majesty of his appearance was often too much for the people he was dispatched to interview, many of whom suspected him of being an elaborate practical joke on the part of the *Tribune's* management and clammed up accordingly. For another, he had little interest in the small triumphs and disasters that constitute the bulk of each day's news, and he wrote about them with blank distaste and only a perfunctory attention to the spelling of the names.

The *Tribune* soon discovered that an error had been made, and the young man was transferred to the drama department, where he lingered long enough to describe Hollywood as "the outhouse of civilization" and the men and women of the theatre, with a few icily cultivated exceptions, as "preposterous bores and mountebanks." It was not a successful experiment. In June, 1934, however, he came at last to what must have seemed the goal of his dreams. This was his appointment to conduct a weekly department called "This New York." In essence, it was a gossip column, but it was different from any seen before or since. Unlike Winchell, Walker, Sullivan, or Lyons, Mr. Beebe was not concerned with the gritty amours of midtown Manhattan, the ineligible suburbs, or the unspeakable cities of the plain. He had no political convictions, except perhaps that all politics are vile, and he was not impressed with the usual objects of public veneration, having other and far more elevated standards of his own. The particular charm of his work lay in the rigid boundaries of its subject matter. "This New York" was concerned exclusively with the goings on of a group of people making up something known as Café Society, and Mr. Beebe's requirements for membership were stern. "A general definition of Café Society," he wrote, "might be: an unorganized but generally recognized group of persons who participate in the professional and social life of New York available to those possessed of a certain degree of affluence and manners." There were, he added, no more than five hundred men and women in all the world fit for the dizzy heights.

The crumbling files yield visions of this spacious life:

Doris Duke has nine Rolls-Royces . . . M. André Simon of the Wine and Food Society ordered a bowl of spring flowers removed because it infringed on the bouquet of the Château Latour '20 . . . Margaret Valdi Curtis, a relative of Lord Asquith, is around town singing Tahitian songs in a straw skirt . . . Mrs. Graham Fair Vanderbilt's butler is reported to have been dismissed for saying "O.K., Madam" . . . Prince Kyril Scherbatoff, A. K. Mills, and this department discovered the other day they were wearing identical suits. Tony Williams is a wretch to have duplicated them on us.

And:

Cecil Beaton, the languid photographer of folk who count, is back in town from London, and bravely carrying the torch for clothes that set Manhattan's lorgnons a'quiver. He showed up at the Colony for lunch last week in a little number Lanvin had run up for him in a pale shade of apple green, with a darker green waistcoat, double-breasted and buttoned with gold and emerald links. Everyone remarked how fine and brave he was.

I regret to say that I took almost no part in these festivities, partly because I lacked the appropriate suits and partly because my vitality has never been intense. For this reason, I encountered Mr. Beebe only in the lobbies of theatres and in saloons that catered to the working classes, especially newspapermen. His attitude in these establishments now seems to me to have been indulgent. My own is harder to define. I understood, that is, that Mr. Beebe was intended to represent a Charles Dana Gibson illustration for a book by Richard Harding Davis, and I was impressed both by the fidelity of the likeness and by the astounding amount of effort that had gone into producing it. The object of the whole charade, however, was almost completely inscrutable to me.

The riddle still persisted twenty-five years later as our ship put in at Weehawken and I led the ladies, twittering like birds, out into the terminal. The car was not hard to find. Red as blood and yellow as scrambled eggs, it lay some fifty yards due west. Its name, Virginia City, was painted on its side, but even without that it would have been unmistakable in that blasted landscape. A pretty toy, a jewel box, a dream on wheels. Mr. Beebe himself greeted us from the observation platform, and I was gratified to note that his culture was still intact. "Welcome to Walden Pond!" he cried.

It is one of the melancholy facts of human experience that memory is a sorry cheat. The mansions of our childhood, revisited, are only houses after all; the mountains, hills; the rivers, little trickling brooks. The great personalities are especially diminished by this unpleasant chemistry, and the arrogant giants we knew are too apt to turn into small and querulous men. My only excuse for introducing this tritest of all reflections is that it was so emphatically not true of Mr. Beebe. He was precisely as vast and stylish as he had ever been, and the years, if anything, had added something senatorial to his aspect. The fact that he had grown a trifle deaf only conferred a special awful distance on him. I shuddered to remember that it was sometimes our drunken custom, late at night, in the lost and dissolute past, to address this monument disrespectfully as Lou or Beeb. "It's nice to see you again, Lucius," I said, and entered never-never land.

The magic elegance of the interior of the Virginia City is beyond the descriptive powers of any journalist today, and Mr. Beebe, who has suffered too often from the kind of reporting that attempts to conceal ignorance with levity, has met this problem squarely. As I write, I have beside me a chaste pamphlet, presumably of his own composition, entitled "Vital Statistics of the Private Car 'Virginia City.'" The simple physical facts are easy to compress. The car is ninety-three feet long, weighs a hundred and eighty-five thousand pounds, and consists of a twenty-three-foot observation-drawing room, three master staterooms (each with its own toilet facilities), a small Turkish bath, a dining room seating eight, a galley with a fifty-bottle wine cellar, an extra seven-hundred-pound refrigerator on the forward platform, and crew quarters for two. Each room is wired for music, which comes from a mechanism that plays eight hours of uninterrupted tape recordings; there are three conventional telephones to the outside world, and a radio telephone for use when the proprietors are in motion. The car can be carried at the end of any passenger train in the United States at a cost per trip of eighteen first-class fares. When it is on a siding, the daily storage charge is forty cents a running foot. It is capable of generating its own electricity, heating its own water, and disposing of its own waste. Nothing is said about what Mr. Beebe and Mr. Clegg have spent on the Virginia City, but some estimates have set the original purchase cost at two hundred thousand dollars and the remodelling at a hundred and twenty-five thousand more.

These data, though impressive, suggest little of the real splendor of the carriage, and for this I am obliged to turn to the actual phrasing of the script:

The decor is Venetian Renaissance evolved by the Doges of Venice when that country became the richest cultural nation in the world, a decor which was copied in the following centuries by the leading crowned heads of Europe for their palaces, a fine example being the hall of mirrors in the Palace at Versailles.

Mr. [Robert] Hanley made a trip to Europe to secure authentic period furniture and fixtures for the car. The crystal chandeliers in the observation-drawing room were purchased in Venice as was the baroque gold cherub mirror over the fireplace. The dining saloon's gold vein diamond paned mirrors were manufactured especially for the car in Italy.

Throughout the car all mouldings and decorative reliefs are of 14K gold leaf, the gold plated lighting fixtures are from France, and the rugs were especially designed for each individual room in the car, hand woven and shot with gold thread.

The ceiling murals were copied from those in the Sistine Chapel in Rome and the paintings on the upper berths in the three master staterooms are scenes of the famed Virginia and Truckee Railway which once ran to Virginia City, Nevada, after which the car is named.

I can think of nothing to add to this except that the artificial logs in the fireplace, fed with propane gas, really burn, though decorously, and that the apparel of the proprietors is worthy of its surroundings. It is not Venetian, but it is the work of patient hands and also liberally shot with gold, Mr. Clegg's watch chain, composed of matching nuggets, being especially rich and strange. In addition to Mr. Beebe and Mr. Clegg, the premises are occupied by a chef, a steward, and an enormous St. Bernard, weighing a hundred and eighty-five pounds. The total weight of all the inmates (Mr. Beebe, two hundred and ten; Mr. Clegg, a hundred and eighty; their two employees, perhaps a hundred and seventy-five apiece; and the dog, as noted) is thus in the neighborhood of half a ton. Unaccustomed to such splendors, my daughter, still barely poised on the threshold of womanhood, could only murmur, "Wow!" My wife, however, though a registered Democrat, was nearly beside herself with rapture and stated that she'd like to live there all her life.

The talk that afternoon, I'm afraid, was hardly up to its

jewelled setting. Our hosts were on vacation from Nevada, where they conduct a weekly newspaper, and the conversation dwelt largely on that. This was entertaining in a way, because, just as he did so long ago in New York, Mr. Beebe is intent on imposing an older and more jovial system of manners on a community not always quite sure what is expected of it, and even occasionally hostile. In his fond imagination, everyone in that part of Nevada greets the rising sun with two ounces of bourbon and ends the day prostrate on a barroom floor, and gamblers, prostitutes, and quaint survivals of the roaring past disport themselves with terrible enthusiasm. The paper reports this gaiety conscientiously, and some measure of its success may be gathered from the fact that it has picked up the largest weekly circulation west of the Mississippi and about five hundred and eighty-five thousand dollars' worth of impending lawsuits of one kind and another.

My own tales of the society our hosts had abandoned were in a melancholy minor key. Many of our common acquaintances had died, some picturesquely but more just sorrowfully withering away, unwanted strangers in a new and vulgar world. Others were visibly ailing and could hardly hope to see another spring; still others, like me, had married and produced hostages and lived lives hard to contemplate without a kind of wry hilarity. One of the brightest spirits we had ever known was in jail, having written too many facetious checks.

Mr. Beebe listened sombrely to all this intelligence. "Change and decay," he said. "What are you drinking?"

"Ginger ale," I said with embarrassment, because I had hoped to conceal this humiliating circumstance.

"My God!" he said. "You sick?"

Breeding, however, overcame his horror, and in the end I got the ginger ale. Mr. Beebe himself was drinking Mar-

tinis. To my astonishment, they came out of a bottle—a
trade preparation, already mixed. "You like that stuff?"
I asked as he was poured another.

"Not particularly," he said. It developed that gin struck
him as faintly disgusting, however served, and he saw no
point in making a witches' brew of his own when industry
was prepared to do it for him. He was drinking it now, I
gathered, as a concession to barbaric Eastern tastes. My
wife is still innocently convinced that there are degrees of
merit in Martinis, and I could see that she was not favorably impressed with this ultimate sophistication.

Conversationally, as I've said, the gathering never really
got off the ground. Mr. Beebe and I were, I think, glad to
see each other again, but our paths had been too far
apart. I had a feeling that we were characters in two wildly
differing comic strips—his infinitely more colorful and ven-
turesome, mine perhaps a shade more closely related to
usual mortal experience. There could be little real communication between a man who clearly regarded his presence in a golden coach on a private siding as a lull between adventures and one who had undertaken a short ride
on a ferry only with the deepest misgivings.

We were diverted momentarily by the entrance of the
dog, whose name is T-Bone Towser. He is the biggest dog
I have ever seen, and, like everything else about the
Virginia City, he is somewhat top-heavy with publicity,
being, among other things, equipped with a special brandy
cask obtainable only at Abercrombie & Fitch. The ladies
professed themselves enchanted with him, and in a measure I was, too, though I was not entirely convinced by
Mr. Beebe's assurances that he was as gentle as a lamb. His
gaze, when it rested on me, was hooded and speculative,
and it occurred to me that he was simply biding his time. I

was vaguely relieved when Mr. Clegg took him out for a walk.

So our visit wore away. There was a strange peace about it. Enclosed in the golden box, warmed by propane and lulled by Ampex, surrounded by the treasures of older civilizations, we were wonderfully insulated from time and the nagging circumstances of daily life. Once, three proletarian noses were flattened against the window of the door leading out onto the observation platform, and Mr. Beebe rose and snapped down the shade. "They think we're with a circus," he observed genially. "The freaks, probably. It happens everywhere we go."

We left shortly after that. Aboard the Utica again, with the lights of Weehawken diminishing behind, I found that my thoughts were rather tedious and ornate, having to do with Mr. Beebe and his symbolic presence on a siding— and with the presence, by extension, of all my contemporaries on sidings of one kind and another. My companions, however, were troubled by no such immensities. They had had a wonderful time. They had been cheered by the vision of an almost incredibly jaunty past, and they had also, I could see, placed me firmly in the middle of it, a battered survivor of God knows what bygone revelries. Altogether, it had been a singularly rewarding trip and one they were unlikely to forget. They only regretted that nobody had had the presence of mind to swipe a 14K Renaissance ashtray.

Battle's Distant Sound

It was a hard week, of course, for all journalists, but probably nobody suffered as acutely as the daily sporting and night-life specialists. The winter had been widely advertised as the gayest since 1928. There was money in the night clubs, where the velvet rope was seldom down; money in the theatre, where one exhibit had already opened at an eight-eighty top; money at Madison Square Garden, where the Louis-Baer fight had been announced at thirty dollars ringside; there were drunken sailors, male and female, loose with money in the shops; money everywhere, money for everybody. When the dream blew up at Pearl Harbor, the reporters assigned to the Broadway front blew up with quite a bang themselves.

Monday was a dreadful day. Lieutenant Commander Walter Winchell of the *Mirror*, who had occasionally given the impression that he was going to be in personal charge of the war with the Axis, had nothing whatever to say about it when it came. The only remotely Oriental item in Dorothy Kilgallen's column in the *Journal-American* dealt with a girl from the mysterious East called Noel Toy, whose pet name for George Jean Nathan appeared to be "Mah Lao Doy," meaning her little pet monkey. Miss Kilgallen's other intelligence was equally singular, but timeless; "The chap who stole the Doris Duke Cromwell art wanted the money for a nose bob" was a typical example. The other gossip columnists were also substantially speechless.

On the society pages, things were almost as discouraging. In approximately fifteen hundred words of copy, Cholly Knickerbocker of the *Journal-American* was able to devote only a hundred and seventy to the crisis. Most of these concerned a rumor that Japanese bombs had exploded on the lawn of Doris Duke Cromwell's estate in Hawaii. "Truly this old world of ours has gone mad," exclaimed Mr. Knickerbocker with horror. Nancy Randolph of the *News* also touched on the Cromwell outrage, describing the exasperating day Mrs. Cromwell spent trying to get her caretaker on the telephone. Everybody else just ignored the whole distasteful business, with Elsa Maxwell of the *Journal-American* achieving perhaps the loveliest detachment. "There is something in the nature of food that brings out man's noblest qualities," she wrote dreamily. "I've always distrusted people who don't eat."

In the sports department, the boys were also taken by surprise. Joe Williams of the *World-Telegram* turned over most of his column to the war, but it was clear that his mind was still reeling. "It's a grim picture," he said, prophesying that a good many celebrated performers would soon be called to the colors, "one to nobody's liking, but it's War." This, in fact, was the general note. "All the club-owners are worried over the war situation," wrote Daniel, also in the *World-Telegram*, "and there is a feeling that 1942 will find a lot of big leaguers at army training camps." Stanley Frank of the *Post* was another man able to look the facts squarely in the face. "The drafting of Greenberg, then Feller, the biggest names in the game, is a stern warning that baseball can expect no favors during the period of national emergency," he observed bravely.

"This is as it should be. . . . Today it does not seem dreadfully important whether there are low-run or high-scoring games in baseball."

By Tuesday everyone had begun to catch his breath, although the coverage was by no means perfect. The Lieutenant-Commander was still mute, but Leonard Lyons of the *Post* had got around to Doris Duke Cromwell, George Ross of the *World-Telegram* noted briefly that the customers were rather upset at Sardi's, Miss Kilgallen, in a hasty roundup of her beat, reported that on the first night of hostilities nobody asked Joe DiMaggio or Franchot Tone for his autograph, and Danton Walker of the *News* broke his silence with a handsome generalization. "War, we will discover, is a grim business," he wrote. Nick Kenny, a radio commentator on the *Mirror*, came up with a timely poem beginning:

> The Samurai of old Japan was honest,
>   brave, and true—
> At stabbing neighbors in the back he
>   would have looked askew.

The society writers were getting warmed up, too. Cholly Knickerbocker gave a hushed description of a luncheon at Tony's Trouville. "It was a poignant moment," he breathed, "pregnant with solemnity, as the fashionable group in both bar and restaurant stood at attention while our National Anthem was played." Mr. Knickerbocker also took about four hundred words to discuss whether, in view of the emergency, Mrs. Frederick Payne might not be well advised to abandon her nickname of "Tokio." No decision was reached. Patricia Coffin of the *World-Telegram* appeared for the first time with a few grace notes on sacrifice in high places, quoting in particular Mrs. Vincent Astor. "The sight of ermine and chinchilla makes my stomach turn," Mrs. Astor seems to have said. "I am making a point of wearing the simplest clothes for the duration." Miss Maxwell still clung to her splendid isolation, this time analyzing the qualities that make Clark Gable, Gary Cooper, and Charles Boyer especially appetizing to females. She was joined by Malcolm Johnson of the *Sun,* who began his notice of some ceremonies at a night club with what sounded like a paraphrase of "The Shooting of Dan McGrew": "It was opening night at the Café Lamaze and there was a million dollars' worth of talent in the band."

The sportswriters were still more or less groping their way in the dark. "The President of the United States had just asked the joint session of Congress for a declaration of war, and now making small talk with the young giant seemed terribly futile, even facetious, in this moment of grave crisis," wrote Stanley Frank in an only partially successful attempt to explain how he happened to be interviewing Buddy Baer. Joe Williams agreed with Cholly Knickerbocker that it was a mad world. The erudite John Kieran of the *Times* and "Information Please" found himself involved in a rather untidy analogy between the United States and a college with two first-string football teams. Jimmy Powers of the *News* and Richard Vidmer of the *Herald Tribune* conceded that sports might not be so awfully important but remarked wistfully that they might have some value as escape mechanisms. Only Daniel seemed to have shaken off the general depression. "Major league magnates and managers today began to emerge from the anæsthetic administered by the first shock of war news, and show some life in negotiations for players," he wrote briskly. Obviously he felt that it was about time.

Wednesday came and went with no word from Winchell, and for the most part his colleagues were transferring their vagrant attention to something else. Danton Walker noted that the patrons at the Versailles got quite a nasty little scare when a defective fuse blew out the lights; Ted Friend of the *Mirror* scooped the field with a schedule of cover charges for New Year's Eve, adding a warning that "grave affairs will make hilarity difficult"; "Heartening has been the Broadway reaction," observed Ed Sullivan of the *News*, applying timestyle to Armageddon. But on the whole the tempo was slackening.

Society was calmer, too. "C'est la guerre," wrote Nancy Randolph philosophically, describing a visit to a night club which contained little except Mrs. Byron Foy, looking wonderful in a strapless black grown. Patricia Coffin began a story "Mrs. Henry J. Topping, Jr., clutched the telephone, her eyes widening," but nothing much came of it. Even the great Knickerbocker appeared to be running down. Miss Maxwell, however, maintained her spectacular composure with a funny story about how she had been mistaken for a ski champion. This was notable chiefly for an interesting translation from the French of François Villon—"Well, much snows have melted since yesteryear."

Sports continued in about the same key. Two writers happened to hit on a very similar device. "The Little Brown Men have turned out to be yellow," wrote Dan Parker in the *Mirror*. "The little brown brothers, eh?" said Joe Williams indignantly. "The little brown b——s!" It was impossible to say whether Mr. Williams or the *World-Telegram* copy desk decided to keep this remark so demure.

On Thursday, Winchell published a rather elementary biography of General George Armstrong Custer, who died in 1876, and things were moderately quiet on all other fronts. Mr. Knickerbocker, Miss Coffin, and Miss Randolph all noted that the war was seriously interfering with the matrimonial designs of various young ladies of distinguished position, but they let it go at that. The imperturbable Miss Maxwell told of a talk she once had with Diamond Jim Brady. They discussed his ice. Sports were almost back to normal.

On Friday the great silence was broken at last. The Commander's column contained three items about the war, including a pun on the Hawaiian word "poi" which was old. The only other contributions of any interest were a parody of "The Night Before Christmas" by Nick Kenny, who, like Mr. Knickerbocker and Mr. Williams, was of the opinion that the world was going mad, and Miss Maxwell's majestic progress on her untroubled way. This time she wrote about the Marx Brothers.

On Saturday there was only one great question still left to be answered. "What on earth is Lucius Beebe going to say about all this?" the members of Café Society asked themselves anxiously as they rang for black coffee and the *Herald Tribune*. The reply was reassuring, though perhaps not entirely unexpected. The war was out of luck. Mr. Beebe had cut it dead.

Robert Benchley: In Memoriam

One afternoon about two years ago, Bob Benchley dropped in at my home for a drink. It was at a time when my life had got more or less turned around backward, something apt to happen to a drama critic, and as usual I was still in my pajamas, though it was about six o'clock in the evening. The idea of not dressing till nightfall seemed rational enough to me, since I had nowhere in particular to go in the daytime, but it was a matter of some concern to my son, who was just eight, and attending a school where, it seemed, the other boys' fathers performed respectably, and suitably clothed, in their offices from nine to five. Apparently, the jocular explanation among my son's classmates who came to call on him from time to time was that I was a burglar by profession, and it caused him intense embarrassment. When Benchley finally got up to go, and I went to the door with him, it was more than the child could peaceably bear.

"Gee, Dad, you're not going to start going out in the street that way, are you?" he cried in dismay.

"No," I said. "I'll try to spare you that final humiliation."

It was hardly a notable remark, but it seemed to amuse my guest, who chose to regard it as somehow typical of my domestic life, and he laughed very gratifyingly thereafter whenever he happened to think of it. This anecdote, dim and aimless in itself, is illuminating only in that it shows how politely anxious, how delighted he really was to promote his friends, and I certainly wasn't an especially old one, to the pleasant company of fellow-humorists.

When you were with him, in the wonderful junk shop he operated at the Royalton in "21," or in less fashionable saloons which had the simple merit of staying open all night, you had a very warm and encouraging feeling that you were a funnier man than you'd previously suspected, the things you said sounded quite a lot better than they really were and, such was the miracle of his sympathy and courteous hope, they often actually *were* pretty good. He wanted his guests to feel that they were succeeding socially and he did his best to make it easy for them. The truth, of course, was that Benchley himself maneuvered these conversations, tactfully providing most of the openings for wit, but the effect was that people were mysteriously improved in his company, surprisingly at home on a level of easy charm of which nobody would have dreamed they were capable. This willingness to play straight man to amateur but hopeful comedians is rather rare in the world he inhabited, where it is not customary to give very much away, but he did it instinctively.

I have used the word "courteous" before, but it seems inevitable. He was one of the most courteous men I ever knew, in the sense that whenever he was aware of a feeling of insecurity or inadequacy in anyone he met, he was automatically their genial, admiring ally against the world. It committed him to a great many bores and some men and women who used him rather shamelessly, and he knew it all right, but he was helpless. Perhaps it was a price he had agreed with himself to pay for the luxury of knowing that he had failed very few people in kindness.

Most of the available anecdotes about Benchley have re-

cently been put through the giant mangle operated by the
gossip columnists, coming out in the form of an extremely
depressing hash, and I have no intention of adding to them
here. Anyway, his humor didn't fall very easily into formal
patterns. He was enchanted once when a young woman employed to grapple with his wildly tangled affairs remarked
quite unexpectedly, "Sniff. Sniff. Somebody in this room
has brown eyes" (I have probably butchered that one as
cruelly as the genius on *The Post*), and most of the things
he said or wrote himself that reflected his personality most
accurately had the same quality of almost-logic, the same
chilly, fascinating little skid off the hard road and right
to the edge of the swamp, where the mind goes down and
doesn't come up.

Though a great many earnest students have tried, the
nature of humor has never been very satisfactorily defined
—there are too many tastes and nothing is terribly funny
to everybody—and it is a reckless thing to try to put any
writer into a neat and permanent compartment. It is
especially hard for me with Benchley, because the extra fact
of known personality inevitability gets into it, too. Rereading his pieces, that is, my judgment is influenced by a clear
picture of how he would have looked telling the same story,
punctuating it with the abandoned laughter that used to
be so famous at opening nights, and assisting himself with
gestures of quiet desperation.

It is also conditioned by another absurdity not apparent
in the text. For the most part, he wrote about his own
polite New England bafflement in the face of strange but
negligible crises; the actual fact was that he led one of the
most insanely complicated private lives of our day and did
it, on the whole, with extraordinary composure. It is possible that this secondary information makes his stories seem
funnier to me than they really are, so that my estimate of

his talent may be a little high. I can't honestly say that he made me laugh more than any other humorist writing in his time—some of Thurber's maniacal experiences in Columbus, Ohio, still seem to me incomparable as examples of comic genius operating on what must have been an extremely favorable environment—but I think he was, by far, the most brilliant and consistent of the school, originating with Leacock, who performed such dizzy miracles with parody, *non sequitur,* garbled reference, and all the other materials of off-center wit.

He avoided with a very acute instinct the monotony that can come from a reiterated comic device and the disaster that comes from crossing the strict line which divides high comedy from awful foolishness. He was sure, wonderfully resourceful, and his style, really based on a lifelong respect for good writing, would have been admirable applied to anything. It was no secret, I guess, that his later appearances in the movies and on the radio bored and depressed him, though he was enormously successful at it, for he was dedicated to writing, and he suffered bitterly when, mistakenly or not, he decided that he couldn't do it any more, and never did.

In commenting on him as a critic, an editorial note in *The New Yorker* said:

His reviews had a quality now largely missing in criticism in that they reflected a complete personality, genial, sensitive, informed, too mature and tolerant to care about the easy, rather discreditable reputation for wit that can come from hasty and intemperate ridicule. It was a weapon he didn't need anyway; his disapproval was all the more effective because it always seemed clear that his kind heart was far more anxious to admire and praise.

That was true of all his work and, in a sense, of all his life. His death was a sad loss to thousands of people who never knew him; to his friends it still seems almost incredible. He took up so much room in so many lives.

SO-SO STORIES

Outwitting the Lightning

There was an article somewhere a while ago about how to keep from getting hit by lightning. I don't remember much that it said, because our cook was reading a serial in the same issue about a girl who fell in love with a jai-alai player, and took the magazine up to bed with her every night, so that I didn't get very far with the lightning article except to learn that you mustn't stand around under trees, and I knew that already.

It reminded me, though, of the times my aunt and I used to have with thunderstorms when I was a child. My aunt's major obsession is cats, which she thinks climb up on people's beds at night and smother them, but lightning comes next. I have heard that the fear of lightning is congenital, but I doubt it, because I can't remember that it ever bothered me until I went to stay with her on Long Island.

On the South Shore, storms come up very quickly. The clouds mount, purple on black, in the west. There is a stiff, hot wind that turns up the under sides of the leaves, giving everything a strange, end-of-the-world effect, and the next thing you know you're in the middle of it. Sometimes, of course, the storms go rumbling and flashing out to sea, but not often, and when they do, they're as likely as not to come back treacherously from the east, where you least expect them. These storms are hardest of all for my aunt to bear. They put her in a sort of double jeopardy and her nerves go all to pieces, so that she usually ends up sitting on a raincoat in the cellar.

I was about eight when I had my first experience with Long Island lightning. I was sitting on the floor cutting out the wings for a cardboard airplane with a pair of scissors when my aunt came in the room. She was wearing a pair of my uncle's rubbers and her head was wrapped in a towel, because thunderstorms always made it ache. She looked unusual and mildly deranged, like the White Queen. When she saw me, she gave a negligible squeal.

"Put down those scissors!" she said.

"They haven't any points," I said hastily. My mother was almost as theatrical about scissors as my aunt was about cats, her theory being that an enormous number of people committed involuntary hara-kiri every year by falling on the points.

"It isn't the points," said my aunt. "They're *steel*. Put them down before—oh, *dear!*"

There had been a violent crash just then, apparently directly outside the window. My aunt leaned against the door, shuddering.

"My, but that was close!" she gasped. "It must have hit one of the maples."

I got up and ran to the window, but there wasn't much to see. The rain was coming down straight and blinding, and everything looked very queer in the yellow glare. The trees seemed all right, though.

"I don't see—" I began, but she caught me by the shoulder.

"Come away from that window," she whispered fiercely. "Do you want to get killed? Never, *never* stand near a window when there's a thunderstorm."

It was a bad storm and it lasted all afternoon. By the

time it had gone muttering off to sea, I knew everything that you mustn't do during a thunderstorm.

In the first place, you mustn't use the telephone. If it rings, don't answer it. In spite of uninformed persons who imagine telephone receivers are rubber, they are made of steel. Touch one, and up you go. My aunt's explanation of that is quite simple: anything steel (and all the metal in the house automatically becomes steel with the first gathering thunderheads) attracts electricity. When it attracts enough, it blows up, along with anyone imprudent enough to be attached to it. My aunt's horror of the telephone extends to everything else that works by electricity. No matter how dark it gets, she never turns on the lights; she uses candles. If she happens to be in her car when a storm breaks, she turns off the switch and sits there, to the confusion of traffic, until it is over. This is purest agony, because the car is steel too, and liable to go wham with her at any moment.

Next to steel, water is the most dangerous thing in a thunderstorm. It conducts electricity. This is a somewhat vague term in her mind. She doesn't mean that water conveys electricity from one place to another. She means, in a large way, that any body of water becomes impregnated with electricity at the outset of a storm and stays that way until it is over. Anyone foolish enough to get in it is briskly and competently electrocuted. This theory applies equally to our bathtub and to the Great South Bay, except that the bay, being larger, holds its electricity longer. She considers it very unwise to go swimming for at least an hour after a storm is over.

Draughts are another thing. In spite of the shattering violence of which it is capable, lightning strays like smoke along the faintest current of air. When a storm begins, she shuts and locks every door and window in the house. That makes everyone pretty hot and uncomfortable, but it doesn't do much good. There are always strange breezes around her ankles, any one of which may easily carry a bolt which will demolish the house. The fireplace is the most perilous source of draughts. It is an open, almost suicidal invitation to destruction, and she avoids it carefully. As a matter of fact, a fireplace had very nearly been the end of my grandfather, who had been sitting in front of one when a ball of fire rolled down the chimney and out on the hearth, where it oscillated for some time, looking at him, before it rolled thoughtfully away and disappeared in the cellar.

That is another of the perils of lightning: its ability to assume practically any form you can think of. It can be a bolt, or a ball, or even a thin mist, luminous but deadly. You can take all the negative precautions you want—avoiding metal and draughts and water—but it will get you anyway if it's in the mood. There is only one positive cure for lightning, and that is rubber. My aunt has the utmost faith in rubber, which she thinks confers a sort of magic immunity. If you wear rubber, lightning can't get at you, not even if it strikes in the same room. Like all her precautions, however, even that has one miserable flaw. You have to be *all* rubber. If there is a single chink, however small, the lightning gets in, and you're done for. When a storm gets really bad, my aunt always spreads one raincoat on the floor and sits on it. Then she puts another one over her head, like a tent. She sits that way until the storm is over, when she reappears tentatively, a little at a time. It always seems to astonish her mildly to find the rest of us alive and unsinged, but I think she puts it down mostly to luck, and is convinced that in the end we'll pay for our mad and unprecedented recklessness. It is a tribute to her training that even now, with the first far-away roll of thunder, I think so too.

Ring Out, Wild Bells

When I finally got around to seeing Max Reinhardt's cinema version of "A Midsummer-Night's Dream," and saw a child called Mickey Rooney playing Puck, I remembered suddenly that long ago I had taken the same part.

Our production was given on the open-air stage at the Riverdale Country School, shortly before the war. The scenery was only the natural scenery of that suburban dell, and the cast was exclusively male, ranging in age from eleven to perhaps seventeen. While we had thus preserved the pure, Elizabethan note of the original, it must be admitted that our version had its drawbacks. The costumes were probably the worst things we had to bear, and even Penrod, tragically arrayed as Launcelot in his sister's stockings and his father's drawers, might have been embarrassed for us. Like Penrod, we were costumed by our parents, and like the Schofields, they seemed on the whole a little weak historically. Half of the ladies were inclined to favor the Elizabethan, and they had constructed rather bunchy ruffs and farthingales for their offspring; others, who had read as far as the stage directions and learned that the action took place in an Athenian wood, had produced something vaguely Athenian, usually beginning with a sheet. Only the fairies had a certain uniformity. For some reason their parents had all decided on cheesecloth, with here and there a little ill-advised trimming with tinsel.

191

My own costume was mysterious, but spectacular. As nearly as I have ever been able to figure things out, my mother found her inspiration for it in a Maxfield Parrish picture of a court jester. Beginning at the top, there was a cap with three stuffed horns; then, for the main part, a pair of tights that covered me to my wrists and ankles; and finally slippers with stuffed toes that curled up at the ends. The whole thing was made out of silk in alternate green and red stripes, and (unquestionably my poor mother's most demented stroke) it was covered from head to foot with a thousand tiny bells. Because all our costumes were obviously perishable, we never wore them in rehearsal, and naturally nobody knew that I was invested with these peculiar sound effects until I made my entrance at the beginning of the second act.

Our director was a man who had strong opinions about how Shakespeare should be played, and Puck was one of his favorite characters. It was his theory that Puck, being "the incarnation of mischief," never ought to be still a minute, so I had been coached to bound onto the stage, and once there to dance up and down, cocking my head and waving my arms.

"I want you to be a little whirlwind," this man said.

Even as I prepared to bound onto the stage, I had my own misgivings about those dangerously abundant gestures, and their probable effect on my bells. It was too late, however, to invent another technique for playing Puck, even if there had been room for anything but horror in my mind. I bounded onto the stage.

The effect, in its way, must have been superb. With every leap I rang like a thousand children's sleighs, my melodies foretelling God knows what worlds of merriment to the enchanted spectators. It was even worse when I came to the middle of the stage and went into my gestures. The other ringing had been loud but sporadic. This was persistent, varying only slightly in volume and pitch with the vehemence of my gestures. To a blind man, it must have sounded as though I had recklessly decided to accompany myself on a xylophone. A maturer actor would probably have made up his mind that an emergency existed, and abandoned his gestures as impracticable under the circumstances. I was thirteen, and incapable of innovations. I had been told by responsible authorities that gestures went with this part, and I continued to make them. I also continued to ring—a silvery music, festive and horrible.

If the bells were hard on my nerves, they were even worse for the rest of the cast, who were totally unprepared for my new interpretation. Puck's first remark is addressed to one of the fairies, and it is mercifully brief.

I said, "How now, spirit! Whither wander you?"

This unhappy child, already embarrassed by a public appearance in cheesecloth and tinsel, was also burdened with an opening speech of sixteen lines in verse. He began bravely:

> "Over hill, over dale,
>   Through brush, through brier,
> Over park, over pale,
>   Through flood, through fire . . ."

At the word "fire," my instructions were to bring my hands up from the ground in a long, wavery sweep, intended to represent fire. The bells pealed. To my startled ears, it sounded more as if they exploded. The fairy stopped in his lines and looked at me sharply. The jingling, however, had diminished; it was no more than as if a faint wind stirred my bells, and he went on:

"I do wander everywhere,
Swifter than the moone's sphere . . ."

Here again I had another cue, for a sort of swoop and
dip indicating the swiftness of the moone's sphere. Again
the bells rang out, and again the performance stopped in
its tracks. The fairy was clearly troubled by these interrup-
tions. He had, however, a child's strange acceptance of
the inscrutable, and was even able to regard my bells as
a last-minute adult addition to the program, nerve-racking
but not to be questioned. I'm sure it was only this that got
him through that first speech.

My turn, when it came, was even worse. By this time
the audience had succumbed to a helpless gaiety. Every
time my bells rang, laughter swept the spectators, and this
mounted and mingled with the bells until everything else
was practically inaudible. I began my speech, another long
one, and full of incomprehensible references to Titania's
changeling.

"Louder!" said somebody in the wings. "You'll have to
talk louder."

It was the director, and he seemed to be in a dangerous state.

"And for heaven's sake, stop that jingling!" he said.

I talked louder, and I tried to stop the jingling, but it
was no use. By the time I got to the end of my speech, I
was shouting and so was the audience. It appeared that I
had very little control over the bells, which continued to
jingle in spite of my passionate efforts to keep them
quiet.

All this had a very bad effect on the fairy, who by this
time had many symptoms of a complete nervous collapse.
However, he began his next speech:

"Either I mistake your shape and making quite,
Or else you are that shrewd and knavish sprite
Called Robin Goodfellow: are you not he
That . . ."

At this point I forgot that the rules had been changed and I was supposed to leave out the gestures. There was a furious jingling, and the fairy gulped.

"Are you not he that, that . . ."

He looked miserably at the wings, and the director supplied the next line, but the tumult was too much for him. The unhappy child simply shook his head.

"Say anything!" shouted the director desperately. "Anything at all!"

The fairy only shut his eyes and shuddered.

"All right!" shouted the director. "All right, Puck. *You* begin *your* next speech."

By some miracle, I actually did remember my next lines, and had opened my mouth to begin on them when suddenly the fairy spoke. His voice was a high, thin monotone, and there seemed to be madness in it, but it was perfectly clear.

"Fourscore and seven years ago," he began, "our fathers brought forth on this continent a new nation, conceived . . ."

He said it right through to the end, and it was certainly the most successful speech ever made on that stage, and probably one of the most successful speeches ever made on any stage. I don't remember, if I ever knew, how the rest of us ever picked up the dull, normal thread of the play after that extraordinary performance, but we must have, because I know it went on. I only remember that in the next intermission the director cut off my bells with his penknife, and after that things quieted down and got dull.

The Secret Life of Myself

(*With a Peck on the Cheek for James Thurber, Who Wrote* The Secret Life of Walter Mitty)

The rehearsal was going very badly. For at least the fifth time, the leading lady had come to the line which was supposed to read, "From now on, darling, you'll have to be strong for us both," and simply shaken her head in pretty despair.

"It's no use, Max," she said at last to the director. "I simply don't *feel* this scene. It sounds so damn silly. I know it's supposed to be sophisticated comedy. 'One of Charles L. Bedrock's urbane and searching studies of a woman's heart.'" She laughed unpleasantly. "But nobody can tell me that any woman in her right mind is going to leave her husband for the *Wagner* Act. Especially to take up with a man who keeps on telling her what a terrible time she's going to have. 'I'm afraid I can't promise you anything for a long time but all my love and the clean satisfaction of a good fight.' For God's sake, what is that supposed to be? Churchill? I'm sure Bedrock is a great writer, but somebody ought to tell him he isn't Lillian Hellman."

They all looked at her helplessly, because it was obvious that the scene couldn't be played as Bedrock had written it. It was disastrously naïve in the way that often happens

196

when a poetic and essentially cloistered talent attempts to deal with the affairs of the changing world.

"Perhaps you have some constructive suggestions, Miss Rembody?" said the director sardonically.

"No," she replied. "All I know is it stinks."

"God," he said. "I wish Wolcott Gibbs were here. He's only a drama critic, but I understand he's been called in a couple of times—secretly, of course—to advise Behrman and Robert E. Sherwood and a couple of others. I bet he'd know what to do."

"Perhaps I would, Max." The quiet, rather tired voice came from the back of the darkened theatre and it was a moment or two before the others could identify the speaker in the gloom. It was indeed Wolcott Gibbs, however, and as he spoke he came slowly down the aisle, furling his umbrella.

"I just dropped in for a moment to get out of the damn rain," he said, "but now that I'm here, of course, you're quite welcome to any assistance I can give. Would you mind trying that line just once more, Miss Rembody?"

"'From now on, my darling, you'll have to be strong for both of us,'" she began, responding automatically to his easy charm, as so many women had.

"I see," he said. "The idea, as I get it, is that you're prepared to give up your old life at the Stork Club and '21' to help your lover gather material for his book on the evils of the vertical hookover system in the automotive industry."

"Whatever that may be," she said.

"But you're a little afraid not only of giving up financial security but also of the ridicule of all your old friends?"

"That's it," she said. "Isn't it silly?"

"Precisely," he said. "It's a basically preposterous situation. Even a Theatre Guild audience would laugh it off the stage. Let me see." For a moment he was lost in thought while they watched him anxiously. At last he snapped his fingers and turned to the director.

"You got your secretary here, Max?" he asked. "I can't guarantee that these are exactly the final lines, but at least it's something for Bedrock to work on. All right, Miss . . . ?"

"Grismund, Mr. Gibbs," she said rather breathlessly, for it was the first time she had met a critic in the flesh. "Yes, I'm ready. If you don't go too fast."

"Here we go, then," he said. "Instead of having Miss Rembody looking out of the window and saying that last line, she goes over to a little bar in the corner—you'll have to put that in, of course—and makes herself a cocktail. Very slowly and carefully, because she's trying to make an important decision. We see only her back for a minute, but when she turns around she has a glass in her hand and there's a curiously ironic little smile on her face. 'Marsden,' she says, or whatever the guy's name is, 'Marsden, did it ever occur to you that I'm a beautiful woman?'"

"Well, that's more like it," said Miss Rembody.

"Naturally, you're a little startled by that, Mr.—ah—van Drum, isn't it?—but you recover in a second. 'Of course, everyone knows you're the loveliest thing in New York, Bedelia,' you say, giving a little bow."

"As I understand this character," said Mr. van Drum, "he is one of those crusading journalists, like Quentin Reynolds or Ralph Ingersoll—you know, a sort of slouchy, Lincoln type. It seems to me that a sophisticated note like that is a little out of key. More for somebody like Coward, I'd say. Anyway, I don't see how I'm going to learn damn near a whole new part with the show opening this Saturday night."

There was dismay on every face, for not only was Forrest van Drum a notoriously slow study but it was also clear that this new conception of the part was fatally at variance with his rough-hewn appearance and his pleasant but unmistakably Middle Western accent. At last Darius Portaman, the old producer, who was an almost legendary figure in the theatre, sighed and shook his head.

"I'm afraid it's no go, as you youngsters put it," he said. "I think Mr. Gibbs is on the right track, but nobody else could possibly learn the part in time, unless"—his eyes lighted for a moment, but then he gave a rueful smile— "but, of course, that's out of the question."

"What?" said Miss Rembody.

"I was going to say unless Mr. Gibbs would consider taking it on himself, but I'm afraid that was just a dream. I'm sure his profession has taught him practically all there is to know about acting, but naturally he isn't an actor himself.

To everyone's surprise, Miss Rembody gave a delighted little laugh.

"Perhaps he isn't now," she said, "but he certainly was once."

"What do you mean by that, Miss Rembody?" asked Mr. Portaman. "I don't think this is exactly the time for levity."

"I'm not joking," she said. "It was a long time ago, when I was a very little girl. I had a brother up at the Riverdale Country School and one spring my mother took me up there for their spring play. It was *A Midsummer Night's Dream* and Mr. Gibbs was Puck. I'm sure you'll laugh, but it was one of the most astonishing performances I ever saw in my life. He was only a boy, of course, but it was really brilliant—confident and gay and absolutely professional. I'm sure exactly what Shakespeare meant Puck to be."

"Is that so?" said Mr. Portaman. "Well, this is certainly a great stroke of luck. Think you could see your way to

giving us a little hand around here, Mr. Gibbs? I'd certainly appreciate it."

"I don't know, sir," said the critic rather doubtfully. "I'm afraid a man's apt to get a little rusty after thirty years."

"Nonsense, my boy," said Mr. Portaman. "Acting is something in one's blood. Either you're born with it or you aren't. I've got a pretty big investment represented in this show—about four hundred and sixty-five thousand dollars, I think—and if I'm willing to take a chance on it, I don't see why you shouldn't be. After all, what have you got to lose?"

"Well," said Gibbs, with his melancholy but rather charming smile, "you can never tell about those sons of bitches in the Drama Critics Circle, but . . ." He gave a quick shrug, obviously having come to a decision. "Ah, the hell with them. The worst they can do is take away my membership, and I don't think they'd dare go as far as that. After all, I know where a good many bodies are buried. It's a deal, Mr. Portaman! I'd be delighted to play Marsden Barlock for you!"

"Thank God!" breathed the old man. "You've saved the day. Miss Grismund, take a note to arrange for Mr. Gibbs' Equity membership on your way home this afternoon. After all," he said with the ghost of a chuckle, "we might as well do these things according to Hoyle."

"That's right, sir," said Gibbs, taking off his overcoat and assuming the position on the stage rather irritably vacated by Forrest van Drum. "Now, where were we? Oh, yes, I've just said, 'Of course, everyone knows you're the loveliest thing in New York, Bedelia,' and now, Miss Rembody, you say—let me see—yes, you'd better say, 'Thank you, kind sir. And that's precisely why I can't go on with this. I don't wish to seem cynical, Marsden, but I can't

help feeling that there is a certain absurdity in the spectacle of a beautiful woman, clearly designed for love, carrying one of those little signs in a picket line.' "

"By God, I think he's got it!" whispered the director, as the clear, unhesitating voice . . .

"For heaven's sake," whispered Mrs. Gibbs, tugging at her husband's sleeve. "*Now* what's the matter with you?"

"Eh?"

"I don't know," she said. "You were muttering and tossing around as if you were having a nightmare. You weren't really asleep, were you?"

"Certainly not," he replied. "May have just shut my eyes for a minute, that's all."

"Well, you'd better try to keep them open," she said. "After all, that's what you're supposed to be paid for, isn't it?"

"Oh, God, I guess so," he said, and focussed grimly on the stage, where Marsden Barlock was just clasping Miss Rembody in his arms and from the context it appeared that they had decided to take the midnight for Detroit. I still think it made more sense the way I had it, he thought, and if that van Drum can act, I'm Ty Cobb.

Song at Twilight

He was getting along beautifully until he shot that pickerel," said Mrs. Crane.

"He did *what?*" said Mrs. Anderson. They have been
discussing a man called Ed Herlicher, whom they had both
known several years before—one of those rather mysterious
young men who for a little while turn up everywhere in
New York, spending a good deal of money and acquiring
a certain reputation either as comedians or beaux, and
then vanish back into the social underbrush from which
they came.

"He shot a pickerel," said Mrs. Crane. "With a double-
barrelled shotgun. It was one of those absurd stories, like
the things that happen in Evelyn Waugh."

The seven people on the porch of the Cranes' ocean-
front cottage looked at her hopefully, but she seemed to be
overcome by the murmuring sea and the gentle evening
air and leaned back with her eyes closed.

"Wake up, dear," said Mrs. Anderson. "Tell us the rest
of it."

"That was all," said Mrs. Crane in an exhausted voice.
"He shot this fish and that was the end of him."

"No, it wasn't," said her husband. "Not the way you told
it to me before."

"Well, it was terribly silly," she said, reluctantly return-

ing to the mortal world. "This Ed Herlicher got around a
lot, you know, and one week-end Jimmy Betts asked him up
to his place in the Adirondacks. He had a hunting lodge
on a lake, and a lot of them used to go up there to fish
and shoot and—oh, whatever people like Jimmy Betts do
when they aren't annoying girls or going to football games.
Give me a drink, George."

She held out her glass and George Crane filled it from
the shaker.

"Where was I?" she asked. "Oh, yes. Jimmy's lodge.
Well, they had a lot of childish ideas up there, but I guess
the worst was about this fish. It was supposed to be the
biggest fish of its kind in that part of the world and they
kept seeing it all the time right off the end of Jimmy's dock
or somewhere, but it was too smart for them and nobody
had been able to catch it. It got to be a legend. You know,
the way people go on about that kind of stuff in the *Saturday Evening Post*."

She seemed about to fade away again but her husband
caught her eye and shook his head.

"All *right*," she said, "but that's really about all there
was. Ed listened to them practically all one night and then
early the next morning when he must have been still drunk
he went down to the dock and when the fish came up, he
shot it with one of Jimmy's guns. They couldn't even tell
how big it had been because he blew it right in half. As
I said, it was the end of him socially. They hardly talked
to him for the rest of the week-end, and when he got back
to town, it must have got around '21' and places that he
wasn't, well, quite a gentleman because pretty soon he
just disappeared. He may have shot *himself* for all I know."
She yawned and settled back in her chair. "I told you it
was a pretty dull story," she said.

In the silence, George Crane looked around at the cocktail party, which had been going on now for about an hour.
It was apparently one of his failures. His wife was clearly
in a mood when any social effort seemed to tax her unbearably, and his friends, Mark and Virginia Anderson, who
could generally be relied on to keep a conversation in motion also had a rather limp and unpromising air. The other
three were comparative strangers—a Mr. and Mrs. Derleth,
whom he had known slightly in town and who had just
taken a house a little way down the beach, and a man
named Freddy Basker, a Princeton classmate of Mark Anderson's, who was out for the week-end. The Derleths
weren't particulary hard to classify. They had usually gone
to Black Point in the summer, but this year they had
switched to Fire Island in the hope that the sea might do
something for her asthma. Mr. Derleth had complained several times that he missed his golf, and Mrs. Derleth found
herself unable to get used to the fact that no considerable
trees grew on the island. There was a noble elm on her
lawn at Black Point, much admired by artists, that had
once cast its shadow on the soldiers of a king. Nothing,
however, was precisely clear about Mr. Basker, a hoarse,
reddish man of about thirty-five, except that he was quite
drunk and obviously willing to get a good deal drunker.
From time to time, he had filled his glass, without urging
from his host, but, except for a low, tuneless humming, that
had been the extent of his activity. Mr. Crane was about
to give them all up—he had had a good many drinks
himself and the role of conscientious host had begun to
bore him—when help came from an unexpected source.

"You know Mrs. Crane's pickerel reminds me of our rac-
coon, Amy," said Mr. Derleth, chuckling and addressing
his wife.

"Oh, yes, tell them about that, Sam," she said. "It was

awfully sweet. There was this little brook behind our house
in Black Point and almost every morning . . . no, but you
go ahead, dear."

"As my wife has told you," said Mr. Derleth, looking at
her with faint disgust, "there's a little brook behind our
place—empties into the Sound finally, I guess—and . . ."

Mr. Basker was sitting beside Mr. Crane, who suddenly
found he could detect a sort of lyric in his guest's humming. "Empties into the *Sound*," hummed Mr. Basker. "You
don't say. Into the Sound. Well, my God and my Jesus."
Mr. Crane looked at him sharply but there was no particular expression on his face.

"And one winter morning," Mr. Derleth was saying
when his host caught up with him again, "on my way
out back to get the car, I saw this coon sitting on the
bank, hell of a cute little specimen . . ."

"What sex?" hummed Mr. Basker, but this time he was
audible to them all.

"I beg pardon?" said Mr. Derleth politely.

"Unimportant point," said Mr. Basker, waving his hand.
"Let it go." He began to hum again.

"Anyway," said Mr. Derleth, "he was sitting there, and
what do you suppose he was doing?"

"Well—" began Mr. Basker.

Mr. Crane cleared his throat. "What *was* he doing?" he
asked hastily.

"He'd broken the ice with his little paws," said Mr.
Derleth, "and he was sitting there washing his face. Looked
just like my own Timmie. That's our little boy."

"How *cunning*," murmured Mrs. Crane, giving him a
bright smile, and Mrs. Anderson also made sounds of sweet
approval.

"Yes, sir," said Mr. Derleth, "and after that I'd see him
practically every day. I guess he got used to me because

after a while he didn't pay any attention to me at all.
He'd just come down and break the ice with his little
paw—"

"How thick?" Mr. Basker asked. He was leaning forward
and his eyes had a bright, peculiar fixity.

"What?" said Mr. Derleth.

"I said how thick was this ice," repeated Mr. Basker.
"Approximately? Couple of inches? A foot? What did he
do? Take a rock to it?"

"No," said Mr. Derleth. "It was very thin, of course.
He just had to tap it with his paw."

"How cunning," said Mrs. Crane, rather desperately.
"How terribly, terribly cunning. But everyone says they're
awfully intelligent."

Mr. Basker gave her a tolerant smile. "You keep out of
this," he said. "You're just supposed to be the pickerel expert." He turned back to Mr. Derleth. "Then what did he
do? After he got finished with washing his face?"

"How do you mean?" asked Mr. Derleth, whose geniality
was beginning to show signs of strain. "That was all he did.
Just washed his face."

"Oh," said Mr. Basker. "Well, it's a damn good story,
anyway. You'll never have any occasion to regret *that* story,
old man."

"*Well*," said Mrs. Derleth, but apparently he didn't hear
her.

"Damn good story," he repeated and got up and poured
himself another drink. He sat down again and for a little
while stared out to sea first with concentration, then suddenly with a look of deep, inward pleasure on his face.

"Reminds me of a somewhat similar experience *I* once
had with a couple of rats," he said at length. "You want to
hear about the experience I once had with a wonderful
couple of rats?"

"Sure," said Mr. Crane. "What about these rats?"

"It was when I had an apartment down on Tenth Street," said Mr. Basker. "I wasn't married at the time, though God knows how that happened because I've been married off and on to various women since I was nineteen. It's a hell of a thing, you start marrying dames and the first thing you know, you begin marrying them *all*. It's like—like collecting almost any kind of stuff." He stopped and looked doubtfully at Mr. Crane. "Say, listen," he said, "what the hell was I talking about?"

"Rats."

"Rats?" said Mr. Basker and he frowned with brief perplexity. "Oh, sure. *Rats*. That's right. It was down on Tenth Street. I had this apartment down there and for a long time I kept missing—ah—tennis balls. Many as two or three a week sometimes." His rather coppery eye fell on Mrs. Derleth and he winked at her genially. "I used to ask girls up there now and then," he said, "and for a while I thought *they* might be taking them. But then I thought now what the hell would *they* want with tennis balls. Whatever about these girls, they weren't much for playing tennis. I remember an Agnes used to come up there—*you* remember Agnes, Mark . . ."

"I've *heard* about Agnes, Freddie," said Mr. Anderson. "You better get back to the rats."

"O.K.," said Mr. Basker. "The rats. Let me see. Well, after I decided it wasn't the girls, or even Virgin Birth—"

"Virgin Birth?" said Mrs. Crane.

"Some name like that. One of Father Divine's Angels. Anyway, my cook. She was always taking stuff up to Harlem with her after she got through, but only out of the icebox. Not sporting goods. Well, I was ready to give up until one night I was lying in bed reading when I suddenly heard this noise—kind of a squeak and some scratching

—in the corner. I looked around and there, by God, was one of the damnedest rats you ever saw. I figured he came out of the closet, which naturally emptied into the bedroom."

Mr. Derleth, looking slightly harassed, went over to the table and mixed himself another drink. Mr. Basker waited politely until he had finished.

"So I just lay there and watched," he said, "and what do you suppose the little son of a bitch did?"

"Listen, Freddie," began Mr. Anderson.

Mr. Basker ignored him. "I forgot to tell you there were a couple of tennis balls lying right there on the rug," he said rapidly. "Well, this rat went right up to one of them and gave it a little shove with his nose. Cutest thing you ever saw."

"How about another drink?" said Mr. Crane.

"Sure," said Mr. Basker and held out his glass. It was clear, however, that he had no intention of being diverted. "All right, I thought, this is the bastard that's been stealing my balls, but *how?* That's what I asked myself. *How* is he going to get it out of here? He can't take it in his mouth because it's too damn big and he can't carry it because his little arms are too short and I can't see him getting to work and eating it right there on the rug. *How the hell is that damn rat going to get that ball out of the room?* I asked myself. That was my problem. *How—*"

"He pushed it along with his nose, Freddie," said Mrs. Anderson. "That's easy."

Mr. Basker looked at her blankly for a moment and Mr. Crane had a momentary impression that the well had run dry. He was mistaken, for Mr. Basker's face suddenly cleared and he beamed at her delightedly.

"Mmmm," he said. "Well, I suppose he *could* have done that, but the point is, he didn't. I'll tell you what he *did*

do, because I think it's terribly cute. And I'm sure Mr. and
Mrs. Deluxe will back me up."

"Derleth," said Mr. Derleth.

"Derleth. All right, here's what he did, and stop me if
you don't think it's terribly cute. He lay down on his side
next to one of the balls and he reached out his little paws
and took it right in his arms. Then he rolled over until he
was lying on his back. Just like a kid with a damn doll. Just
like—"

"Drink?" said Mr. Crane. "You better let me get you a
fresh drink."

"No," said Mr. Basker. "You wait. Damn good story.
Where—oh, yes, there he was on his back with the ball in
his little arms." He bent forward and tapped Mr. Derleth on
the knee. "*Then* what did he do?" he asked more hoarsely
than ever. "Give you any number of guesses. It's hopeless."

"All right. I give up," said Mr. Derleth, who was nothing
if not a good sport.

"You'd better," said Mr. Basker, "because he didn't do
a damn thing. Not personally. He just lay there on his back
and the first thing I knew, *another* rat came sniffing out
of the closet. The female, of course. The little girl rat."

"Oh?" said Mrs. Crane.

"Certainly," said Mr. Basker firmly, "and pretty as a picture, too." He closed his eyes as if reviewing the scene and
it was clearly hard on his composure because he choked
and had to wipe his eyes. "And what did *she* do?" he said
when he had recovered. "Well, sir, she went right up to this
boy rat, the husband, and she grabbed the end of his tail
in her teeth and, by God, she pulled him right across the
rug, ball and all, and right into the closet." He looked
around at the members of his audience and his expression
was bland and courteous, that of a man only anxious to instruct and entertain. "In a couple of minutes," he said,

"they came out after the other ball. Same thing all over again—he rolled over with the ball in his arms and she pulled him the hell out of the room. Damn if it wasn't the cutest thing you ever saw."

"Well," said Mrs. Derleth, after a considerable pause, "I guess we'd better get started if we're going to get any dinner. Come on, Sam."

She got up and produced suitable farewells.

"Good night," she said to the Cranes. "It's been so nice. Good night, Mrs. Anderson, Mr. Anderson. I'm so glad to have met you."

Her little nod to Mr. Basker was admirable—containing just the correct mixture of ladylike tolerance and amusement. It was wasted on him, though, because by that time he was clearly lost in another of his foolish and disreputable dreams, humming to himself and tapping on the arm of his chair.

Crusoe's Footprint

It wasn't a very promising day—a strange, level wall of copper-colored clouds was building up in the west and the wind from the ocean was driving the waves higher and higher up the beach. Since the previous afternoon, the radio had been reporting a hurricane on its way up from the Florida Keys, with storm warnings already flying as far up the coast as Hatteras, but the inhabitants of Fire Island, who had twice seen the sea come smashing over their dunes, had developed an irritable fatalism about the weather and paid little attention to these alarms that always sprang up in September. A few nervous people still moved back to town with the first breath of danger from the South, but most of them, confident that the storm would either whirl harmlessly out to sea or else that the Coast Guard would give them ample warning of its approach, stayed where they were, feeling reasonably safe and agreeably heroic.

It was a Sunday afternoon, and in spite of the radio and the threatening sky, the beach was crowded. The sun, seeming to shine with an extra and rather unearthly brilliance over the low barrier of clouds, heightened the gay colors of the ranked umbrellas and the blue sea, and in its light the tanned bathers also seemed to have a more than mortal glow. It was all as pretty and vulgar as a postcard, thought George Crane, who was lying on the sand in front of his summer cottage. He had just been rereading Henry James and felt in a rather supercilious and Continental mood.

"Let's take a walk," he said to his wife, who was spread out beside him on a blanket, inert but not quite dead. "Too damn many people."

"All right," she said amiably. "Where to?"

"I don't know," he said. "The lighthouse, I guess. We haven't been there for quite a while."

"It's a long way. Five miles."

"Three," he said. "And the sand is good and hard. It won't kill you."

They stood up and started down toward the edge of the water.

"Look at that tide," she said. "Do you think we'll be able to get back all right?"

"Sure. We can walk on the dunes if we have to."

They set out west along the beach. It was a walk they had taken many times that summer, almost precisely as often, in fact, as they had gone the other way, to the eastward communities of Point o' Woods and Cherry Grove, and Mr. Crane, familiar with the scenery, found his mind free to wander back over the summer so nearly gone. He'd had a good time, he decided. His closest friends, Mark and Ginny Anderson, were pleasant people, generally tranquil in disposition, and articulate without feeling obliged to prove it by holding too many interesting literary and social opinions. I am a very tolerant man, he thought, but God I get tired of these ambitious conversations. Their other acquaintances on the beach and the guests who'd come down for week-ends had also been entertaining on the whole, though there had been a few too gifted raconteurs among them and one or two who were clearly not adapted to the innocent monotony of life on a beach. There had been the trouble about Miss Deedy Barton's cat, and he remembered a man called Francis Bidwell who had come to visit the Andersons, trailing an impressive reputation for persuading ladies against their better judgment. Mr. Bidwell had been responsible for a rather difficult night at Sweeney's when he had attached himself much too purposefully to a girl who was generally conceded to be the property of one of the lifeguards. The guards had closed in quietly, moving as one man, and it had required the combined fascination of Mrs. Anderson and Mrs. Crane . . . He looked at his wife, who was wandering along the water's edge, still intent on finding the perfect shell that had been eluding her all summer.

"I must say I find you extremely companionable, Emily," he said, parodying the fashionably constricted accents of Noel Coward in *Private Lives*. "There isn't a part of you I don't know, remember, and love."

"My," she said. And then as a wave swept over her ankles and ran high up on the beach, "Look at that. I told you were were going to get caught in this damn tide."

"What do you care? You haven't anything on to get wet."

She ignored that and began to whistle "Can't We Be Friends?" for she had a sweet, melancholy taste in music. His thoughts went back to the summer just behind them and presently he began to laugh.

"Remember Mark and that damn woman?" he asked.

"Mrs. Wilmot?" she said, referring to a rather troublesome experience Mr. Anderson had had with a lady who had made up her mind that, as a writer, he was cramped by his family ties and had offered him her own house to work in. It was hard to say whether or not another promise

had been contained in this suggestion, but anyway, between them, Mrs. Anderson and Mrs. Crane had fixed Mrs.
Wilmot.

"No," he said. "The other one. That time at Sweeney's."

"Oh, yes," she said. "About the hair. That was funny."

It had been funny, too. There had been about eight of
them sitting there at a table by the dance floor one Saturday
night. They had been watching the dancers—there was a
never-ending fascination for Mr. Crane in the wild abandon
of the steps they did and the certainly questionable postures they assumed and its contrast with the cold, inscrutable expressions that they chose to wear—when they gradually became aware that Mr. Anderson was involved with a
red-haired girl at the next table. She was very drunk,
though no drunker than the three delicate young men she
was with, and her passion for Mr. Anderson was open and
explicit. Mr. Crane found that most of the conversation
was still fresh in his memory.

"Listen," she had said, addressing them all, "I *love* this
man." She had hitched her chair away from her own table
and so was in a position to put her arm around her victim's neck. "You got such wonderful beautiful hair," she had
said fondly. "What's your name, honey?"

"Anthony Comstock."

"O.K. if I call you Tony?" He had said it was and she
had proceeded even more directly. "Whyn't we go out
to the bar, Tony?"

"Sure," he'd said, "but what about your friends?"

"Oh, *them!*" It had amused her to be frank about her
friends, and they had looked down at their bracelets in
embarrassment and delight. Just then, one of the lifeguards
had come to claim her for a dance, and she had gone, though
smiling back at him with unmistakable promise. During
the dance, though Mrs. Anderson had urged him warmly

to enjoy himself, he had changed places with Eddie Willard, who had been sitting across the table.

"Tell her you're John S. Sumner," he'd said. "Just tell
her you're crazy about sex."

The lady had come back but such had been her exer-
tions on the floor that she walked in a daze and sat down
without looking behind her. In a moment, however, her
hand had gone out, found Eddie Willard's shoulder, worked
its way lovingly up his neck, and come to rest at last on
his head, which was as bald as an egg. For a moment, her
fingers had tapped doubtfully, then incredulously, and
then she had swung around and finding only a naked skull
where she had expected wonderful, beautiful hair, her
mouth had dropped open in dismay and she had given a
small, ladylike scream.

"My God," she had cried with horror, "what's *happened*
to you, Tony?"

The summer had been full of experiences like that—
small, neat absurdities, in most of which, he reflected, his
friends' behavior had been a credit to him. They were not
humorists, thank God; they just seemed to show a certain
presence of mind in unlikely situations. It occurred to him
briefly that financial security sometimes has a good deal
to do with charm; that the native Fire Islanders, that is,
who were in the business of renting houses and selling
food, might naturally be inclined to make humor easy
for transients, and even that the soft, mysterious young
men, who made up such a large part of the summer population and had practically no money at all, might also find
it intelligent to tolerate the whims of the solvent.

He remembered another evening at the bar, when Horace Giddings, an actor who had been visiting him, had
raised some doubt in his mind about the real quality of
what might be called privileged wit. There had been a

crowd nearly three deep at the bar and getting drinks to
bring back to their table had been a tiresome problem.
Mr. Giddings had solved it briskly. Throughout the room
there were a good many tables whose occupants were all
male though their gaiety held a note of birds, and Mr.
Giddings soon adopted the practice of waiting until a
round of drinks had been secured for one of these and
then approaching it courteously.

"I'm sure you won't mind, old man," he'd say, putting
down a dollar and picking up one of the glasses. "For a
lady, you know."

The owner had usually confined his protest to a rather
breathless "Well," and the whole idea had seemed funny
enough at the time, but now Mr. Crane remembered it
with faint embarrassment. It would have been fine if one
of them had taken a poke at Mr. Giddings, he thought, but,
of course, he'd known damn well they wouldn't. However,
Horace was a special case, an actor's actor; generally his
friends had been admirable. He had a brief, self-conscious
vision of himself as a rather distinguished figure in the community; the senior member, you might say, of a pleasantly
worldly group, augmented from time to time by urban
celebrities, that still understood the value of the simple
life and had adapted themselves to it gracefully, without
perceptible condescension.

Mr. Crane was brought out of these agreeable thoughts
by the thunder of a wave and then a rush of water across
his knees. "That was a hell of a big one," he said, bracing
himself against the backwash.

"I told you the tide was coming in," said his wife. "Want
to turn around?"

"No," he said. "Let's go a little further anyway."

The wall of clouds had begun to cut across the bottom
of the sun, which now shone level and blinding in their

eyes. The wind had increased and the waves, which had been breaking on a bar about a hundred yards offshore, rolled across it, mounted as the still water piled up under them, hung suspended for an instant, and then broke tremendously, making the beach tremble under their feet. There had been more spectacular surfs that summer, but somehow none quite as ominous. These waves were not so much breakers as slow, enormous swellings of the sea. I don't know about any hurricane, he thought, but there's a hell of a storm out there somewhere. Mrs. Crane had been walking on a higher part of the beach, where it was still dry, and suddenly she stopped and looked down at something at her feet.

"Hey," she called. "Somebody's shoes."

He joined her and found a pair of moccasins lying neatly side by side on the sand. They were quite new and obviously feminine.

"That's funny," he said. "Where do you suppose . . ." He picked one up and as he tilted it in his hand looking for a label, a woman's wristwatch slid down out of the toe. "Saks," he said. "E.M.K. on the back."

There were a pair of sun-glasses in the other shoe and they, too, were impressive in design. From where they stood, they could look along the beach almost to the end of the island. There was no one in sight.

"We didn't pass anybody coming up either," Mrs. Crane said. "I guess she must be lying up there behind the dunes."

"Not around here," he said. "Not unless she flew. Look."

The only footprints in the sand came from the east, from the direction of the lighthouse, and whoever made them had been wearing shoes. Obviously the woman had sat down where they were standing and taken them off. Beyond these clear marks, there were only two or three bare prints in the sand, leading toward the ocean. As they watched, a wave came hissing up and washed a print away.

"I'd better go and take a look anyway," said Mr. Crane uneasily. He walked across the narrowing strip of beach and clambered up one of the dunes. From the top of it, he could see the few houses that made up a settlement called Lonelyville scattered along the margin of the bay about a quarter of a mile away. No one was visible on the barren stretch of sand and marsh grass that lay between, but the land was hummocked with smaller dunes and it was possible that the woman was lying behind one of them. It was really absurd to think so, though, not only because of the absence of footprints up from the beach but also because the grass would have been wickedly sharp for anyone walking in bare feet, and even on the height where he stood the air was thick with gnats. He rejoined Mrs. Crane at the edge of the water.

"No," he said. He looked again up the beach toward the lighthouse. There was always a chance that the woman had walked off in that direction barefoot and that the waves had washed away her prints, but there were a good many things against it—the moccasins and the watch left so near the water with the tide coming in so fast, the threatening storm (the sun by now was almost buried in the clouds), the beach clearly empty for at least three miles.

"Well," he said. He handed her his own watch and his cigarettes and matches.

"She wouldn't still be out there, George," said Mrs. Crane.

"I'll just go out to where they're breaking," he said.

He started wading through the shallow, fast-running water. The footing was bad. There was a strong pull to the east, and the current was scooping out deep holes in the bottom. The ocean sucked at his knees, and shells, sliding along the bottom, pulled roughly across his ankles. As he got nearer to them, the waves began to seem enormous—tons of water lifting appallingly over his head, hanging in instant, incredible suspension, curling and crashing down in great smothered explosions. He struggled out to within four or five yards of where they were breaking, keeping his feet with difficulty and half-blinded by the spray as the wind tore it from the crests of the waves. The hell with it, he thought. Emily was right, there would be no chance of finding anything out here. He took another doubtful step and the bottom fell away under his feet, dropping him to his armpits in the water. As he turned to fight his way back, the current caught him and pulled him off balance, twisting him around so that again he was facing out to sea.

He saw the big wave coming and realized with horror that it was going to break almost exactly where he stood. For a moment he stood idiotic with panic and then he threw himself forward and began to swim desperately toward it. He knew at the last second he was too late—the water around him was running swiftly uphill, sucked upward into the base of the wave—and he threw his arms around his head and tried to go under it. He saw the wave coming down and then it hit him, shook him with fierce, wrenching blows, ground him down to the bottom and dragged him furiously along it, flung him up in a boil of white water, threw him somehow to his feet, only to pull him down and roll him along the bottom again, in a nightmare of shells and sand and strangling water. He got up in the shallow water at last and stumbled up onto the beach. He heard Mrs. Crane's voice, but the roar in his ears and the floating white lights were too much for him and he put his head down between his knees.

"Son of a bitch," he gasped finally. "That one *got* me."

"Yes," she said. "You all right now?"

"I guess so." He turned his arm over and found a long scratch from wrist to elbow. "God, look at that. You got the cigarettes?"

"They're up the beach," she said. "You stay here. I'll get them for you."

He smoked for a while in silence and then reached over and picked up the moccasins. "I guess the only thing to do is tell them at the Coast Guard," he said.

"I suppose so," she said. "Do you want me to go? It's up back of the lighthouse, isn't it?"

"That's right," he said. "No, we'll both go. Wait'll I finish this."

Presently Mr. Crane threw the cigarette away and got up, and he and his wife started off for the lighthouse, still about three-quarters of a mile down the beach. The sun had disappeared behind the clouds, which now formed a black band halfway up the sky, and the wind was blowing much more strongly off the sea. Mrs. Crane estimated the width of the remaining beach.

"We'll have to walk back on the dunes," she said.

"Yeah, I guess so."

He couldn't tell precisely what was in his mind. It seemed to him almost certain now that the woman was drowned and, in conjunction with his own experience in the water, the idea made him feel sick at his stomach. He was also disgusted with the emotions—an almost pleasurable excitement, a sense of self-importance, though he had certainly had no heroic intentions—that he had felt when he waded out into the surf. He found he was shaking as he transferred the moccasins from one hand to the other.

They had walked about a hundred yards when Mrs. Crane touched his arm.

"Isn't that a jeep coming?" she asked.

"Yes," he said. "Probably *that's* the Coast Guard now."

The car was bouncing along by the water's edge, occasionally throwing out sheets of spray. Mrs. Crane began to wave and it slowed and soon pulled up beside them. The driver was very young, a self-possessed boy, with flanking ears and a sharp nose. His blue shirt was open at his mahogany throat and he wore his uniform cap jauntily, on the back of his head. There was a girl in a brief, black bathing suit on the seat beside him, and she, too, was young and quite handsome, though her face wore a sullen and arrogant expression, clearly habitual.

"Something the matter, Jack?" asked the driver.

Before Mr. Crane could answer, the girl leaned forward and stared at him with surprise.

"Look," she said. "That man has my shoes."

"Oh," he said, holding them out. "Are these yours? We found them on the beach. I was taking them to the Coast Guard Station."

She held out her hand silently and Mr. Crane gave her the moccasins.

"I had some glasses and a watch," she said with no particular expression.

He had fogotten them but they were in his other hand and he extended them to her.

"Yes," he said, "we found them, too."

She inspected them carefully and there was a silence.

"Well, thank you," she said at last. "I'm sorry I haven't got my purse, but if . . ."

"For God's sake," he said with exasperation, "we thought you were drowned. We were on our way to get the Coast Guard."

She looked surprised. "Oh," she said. "I'm sorry. But, of course, that was absurd. I was just walking down toward the Point and this man picked me up—because of the storm."

"Naturally," he said, but she clearly suspected no irony.

"Well," she said. "It was very kind of you anyway."

The driver had been listening to them impatiently and now he addressed Mr. Crane. "How'd you come to cut yourself, Jack?" he asked.

"That? I got caught by a wave."

"You mean you been in?" His tone was incredulous. "You oughta have sense not to go in a day like this." He looked at them curiously. "Say, where do you folks live?"

"Ocean Beach," said Mr. Crane. "It's a couple of miles down the beach."

"I know where Ocean Beach is at, Jack. Listen, you ain't going to get there walking, the way this ocean is."

"Oh, we'll get there all right," said Mr. Crane, hoping he sounded airy. "We can walk on the dunes."

"Don't you folks ever listen to the radio?" said the driver. "There's supposa be a hurricane coming up. You'd be in fine shape caught on this beach in a hurricane. Come on, you better get in here. I'll run you down."

Mr. Crane protested, but without much conviction. The sky was definitely alarming now and the sea might easily be gathering itself for a really dangerous effort. He climbed in, followed by his wife, and they sat humbly together on the narrow seat in the back, hemmed in by tarry coils of rope and many cans of paint. As the car jounced along, throwing them from side to side and drenching them with spray, he felt as foolish as he ever had in his life. Gradually, however, his embarrassment and indignation were succeeded by an overpowering weariness, and when the jeep pulled up in front of his house, his head was on Mrs. Crane's shoulder and he was sound asleep.

The Courtship of Milton Barker

Milton Barker, the car checker, stood at the window, looking out at the freight yard. It was mid-April. A thin rain was blowing in from New York Harbor in little gusts and showers, filling the usual melancholy of the yard with further desolation. The dirt and cinders between the ties had turned to gray mud, and the smoke from a switching engine, idle in one of the leads, was flattened down by the rain and trailed off along the ground. The intricate steel towers that held the machinery for handling the car floats stood up dimly against the sky. Ben Rederson, the old switchman, went by with a lighted lantern, although it was only three o'clock in the afternoon.

"God," said Milton Barker, and rubbed the pane where his breath had clouded it.

The yardmaster looked up from the waybills he was checking.

"Some day, ain't it?" he said.

"For ducks," said Milton, who was no man to slight a ritual.

"Yeah."

"You got no kick coming, sitting there on your fanetta," said Milton bitterly. "Take *me*, now."

"I been out in plenty rain worse than this in my time," said the yardmaster. "Say, when I was braking on the Santa Fe . . ."

Milton yawned.

"O.K., Pop," he said. "You already told me."

There was a potbellied stove in the middle of the office and a battered kettle on top of it. Milton took the kettle down and looked inside.

"You want coffee?"

"It's a pity one of you guys couldn't wash that pot once in a while," said the yardmaster. "It's got a cake inside of it, like in a pipe."

"You drunk worse things, Pop," said Milton.

He found a tin cup and a paper bag full of sugar in one of the lockers along the wall and took them to the stove. The coffee poured black and thick. Milton carried his cup over to the window and sat down.

"How you like to be in Pom Beach, Pop?" he said, and when the yardmaster didn't answer, he found peace in the *Daily Mirror*.

After a little while a telephone bell rang.

"Get that, will you, Milty?" said the yardmaster.

"Get it yourself," said Milton, who was reading with some dismay that a famous moving-picture star, weary of tinsel, had decided to immolate herself in a convent.

"Listen, you," said the yardmaster.

"All right, all right," said Milton, and reached over and picked up the telephone, though without removing his eyes from a photograph of the actress, taken in an earlier and more secular mood. "Harbor Yard."

The telephone chattered and Milton, abandoning the paper, wrote as he listened.

"Circus train . . . Layton & Crowley . . . Five P.M. from Greenville . . . To lay over until nine A.M. . . . Yes, sir. . . . Yeah, I got it."

He hung up the receiver and looked at the yardmaster.

"Well, can you tie that?" he said.

"Circus train?" asked the yardmaster.

"Yeah. Layton & Crowley. That ain't one of the big ones, is it?"

"Nah. A mud show. Plays like Lowell and Attleboro, them places."

"Well anyway."

"Five o'clock from Greenville? That means the float ought to get here around seven. Tell the yard crew it goes up in number three on the Hill."

"O.K."

"And listen, Milty . . ."

"Yeah?"

"It ain't like the *Follies*, see? I wouldn't be figuring on nothing if I was you."

"You ain't talking to me, Pop," said Milton, and he went out to find the yard conductor.

The circus train arrived on the float at half past six and by seven the yard engines had pulled it up on the Hill, where it was to lie until the following morning. Milton Barker, who had observed the cars sharply as they were pulled off the float, was able to report that nine of them were boxcars which presumably contained animals and stage properties, and that the tenth was a passenger coach which had its curtains drawn but must nevertheless contain the ladies and gentlemen of the cast.

"It cert'n'y *smells* like a hell of a cheap circus," he now told the yardmaster, staring up toward the Hill, where the circus train lay between two lines of empty boxcars.

"It's them elephants," said the yardmaster. "No matter what you do."

Milton nodded. The commonplace aspect of the boxcars and their outrageous fragrance had left him feeling cheated and slightly empty. He took a pair of shears out of a table

drawer and began to cut the picture of the actress out of
the *Mirror*. Suddenly there was a knock at the yard-office
door.

"C'min!" he shouted.

The door opened, letting in a gust of rain from the yard,
and he looked up with annoyance.

"Say, how's for . . ."

He got no further because there were strangers in the
doorway—two women and a man—and it was clear that
they were not native to his world or even anything he
could hope to classify from his previous experience.

The man, who was carrying two empty buckets, was
sheathed in a purple suit. It was an opium-eater's dream
of a suit, with lapels that rose vivaciously into two points
that menaced its wearer's ears; the openings of the pockets
ran up and down instead of crosswise and they were
trimmed with braid; the trousers, which constricted him
too lovingly, terminated in a pair of long, narrow suède
shoes, turning up at the ends like little skis. Beneath the
upper part of these antic vestments he wore a checked vest
of horrible design. His face was pale and, in relation to the
rest of his body, much too large. The expression it wore
was arrogant but harassed—Monseigneur taunted by the
rabble. Like his two companions, he was damp from head
to foot, and in the sudden warmth of the yard office he had
begun to give off a frail steam.

The two ladies each carried a bucket. They wore dresses
which remained defiantly frilly in spite of the rain, and
spoke somehow of the indolent South. Their faces, above
this girlish finery and beneath two hats that were identical
garlands of drenched flowers, were somewhat surprising.
There was a prettiness about them, but it had a furious
quality, a sort of triumphant ferocity. The ladies indeed

looked as if they had just dispatched an enemy in a manner that had given them some dark pleasure and as if presently they hoped to do so again. They were almost exactly alike and it seemed reasonable to Milton to suppose that they were twins or at least sisters.

"Was there something I could do for you?" he asked cautiously.

The three came forward and surrounded the stove.

"You the yodmaster?" asked the man in a hoarse whisper.

"No," said Milton. "Him."

"Oh," said the man. "One of the shacks told us we could get some drinking water."

The yardmaster pointed to the washroom door.

"Hep yourself," he said. "You folks with the circus?"

"Yeah," said the man. He paused, clearly trying to think of something to say about the circus.

"Go on, halfwit," said one of the ladies. "Get the water."

"All right, Mildred," said the man sadly. "You don't have to holler."

She looked at him somberly, and he picked up the four buckets and disappeared into the washroom.

There was a silence in the yard office while the ladies steamed and brooded in front of the stove. Suddenly the air was filled with the smell of singeing cloth.

"*Now* what the hell?" said one of them, sniffing sharply.

"It's your skirt, Babe," said the one called Mildred. "It's on the stove."

"Well, for God's sake," said Babe, though without any special emotion. With one accord, the ladies drew back from the stove and sat down on the edge of the table by the window. Their sultry eyes swung around the yard office and rested at last on Milton.

"You," said Mildred. "What do you do here? What's your job?"

"He's just the clerk," said Babe wearily. "Forget it."

"Well," said Mildred, "he's better than the other one. That other one is dead, if you ast me."

"Say," the yardmaster began, but he was chilled by their bleak and impersonal stare, and subsided.

"Listen," said Mildred to Milton. "You know where's a drink around here?"

"I told you it's just the clerk," said Babe. "He wouldn't know. Strictly a dummy."

"Gin or whiskey," said Mildred. "I wouldn't care."

"Well," said Milton slowly, "there's no bars around here. You could ast at the lunch wagon. If they knew you.

"They know *you?*"

"Sure."

"What do they carry?" asked Babe.

"Only grappa. It's some kind of a Greek drink."

"Oh, my God," said Mildred. "Well, all right. Get two of them. Two bottles."

"Well . . ."

"It's all right. We'll give you the dough."

"It ain't that," said Milton. "It's only I oughtn't to leave the yard."

"We'll take care of the yard," said Babe. "You get the what's-this."

"You don't have to worry," said Mildred. "I'll handle any trains."

They watched him as he shrugged into a raincoat and went out the door. "Hurry back, dear," said Mildred.

Babe looked at the washroom door.

"I think that bum is drowned," she said. "Your husband. I think he fell in."

"Well, that would be O.K.," said Mildred.

When Milton came back with the grappa, Mildred and Babe were still sitting on the table, and the man was standing by the stove. The four buckets, full of water, were on the floor outside the washroom. The yardmaster was finishing a story. "So when she found out I didn't have no dough, she threw my shoes out of the window, right in the hobber." He looked at them, shaking with laughter. "Right in New York Hobber. I liked to died."

"You ought to be ashamed of yourself," said Babe coldly. "And old dope like you."

"Hello, dear," said Mildred to Milton. "Did you get it?"

"Yes," he said. He took the two bottles out of the paper bag and put them on the table. The man picked one of them up and held it against the light.

"What is it?" he asked. "Mule?"

"Grappa," said Milton.

"What's this grappa?"

"You ought to know," said Mildred. "You're part Greek or something, ain't you?"

"Ah, don't be like that, Millie," said the man. "I only ast him a question."

He took the cork out and held the bottle up to his nose. "It don't smell much."

"Well," said Milton, "a bomb don't smell either."

"Listen, you can't drink that stuff in here," said the yardmaster.

"Why not?" said Mildred.

"The superintendent is liable to show up any time," he said. "He's regularly down here every time we get a circus train."

"Ah, tell him—"

"No," said the man. "Wade a minute. Wade a minute. What would he do?"

"Plenty," said the yardmaster. "Drinking on railroad property."

"He can't do nothing to me," said Babe.

"You want to try and tell that to the railway cops?"

"Oh," said Babe. "Well, O.K."

She looked at the four buckets.

"Say, who's going to carry them things?"

"Milty," said Mildred promptly. She put her arm through his. "Ain't you, Milty? Babe and I can each take one of the bottles and you and Stupid can carry the pails. We'll have a little drink up at the train."

"Say, I'd like to," said Milton, "but I better not leave the office, had I, Pop?"

"I don't care what you do," said the yardmaster. "I don't even care if they cut your throat."

"See," said Mildred. "He says it's O.K. Come on, Milty."

"Better leave me hold your watch," said the yardmaster.

It was raining even harder as they started across the yard toward the Hill, where the circus train lay. The flood-lights on the float were enough to throw a pale gleam along the rails, but the ties were invisible, half drowned in the muddy water. Milton picked his way along them expertly, but he could hear Babe and the man with the other two pails stumbling and cursing up ahead in the darkness. Mildred came last and she too seemed to be having trouble and spoke sullenly about it.

"You need to be a duck or something," she said.

"Walk where I do," Milton told her. "Keep on the ties. I should of brung a flashlight."

"That's right," she said bitterly. "Now is when to think about it."

They were halfway up the Hill when she pulled at his sleeve.

"Let them go on ahead," she said.

"Why, what's the matter?"

"I ain't taking drinks to all that mob," she said. "There's fifty of them in that car. We wouldn't get no more than a smell. We better drink it right here."

"Listen," he said, with a daring that rather astonished him. "All them boxcars alongside your train. They're empty. How about if we go and sit in one of them for a while?"

"We-ell . . ."

"We could have a little talk," he said carelessly. "Just the two of us."

"Why, Milty," she said, and laughed unreasonably in the darkness. "All right. Whatever you say."

"Come on," he said. "Let's get going."

They reached the top of the Hill and started down the black aisle between the circus train and the empties.

"We better get far enough away from the passenger car," he said. "Some one of your friends might be coming out."

"My!" she said.

They had to walk single file between the cars. Mildred went ahead and Milton followed her with the buckets. It was very dark and the strangling smell of the animals was heavy in the air. Suddenly the night was split by hideous laughter; it was inhuman; the laughter of the demented or the damned.

"Hey," said Milton. "What's that?"

"It's only Orson Welles," she said.

"What?"

"The hyena. We call him Orson Welles."

"Oh."

At last he stopped before one of the boxcars. The door was open and he peered inside.

"This one looks all right," he said. "It's got some hay in it."

"You think we come far enough, dear?" she said with a giggle.

"I guess so."

"O.K. Hep me up."

He boosted her in the car and then swung in himself, leaving the buckets outside on the ground. The car had apparently contained bricks, because the floor was covered with broken fragments and little piles of straw. Mildred kicked a pile of straw together against the wall facing the open door and sat down on it with a sigh.

"My God," she said, "am I ever pooped."

He sat down beside her on the straw.

"Say, this is all right, ain't it?" he said.

"Well, it's prolly better than the rain." She picked up the bottle and pulled out the cork with her teeth.

"This had better be good," she said.

She drank in the darkness and gave a little shiver.

"You sure that Greek didn't make no mistake, Milty?" she said. "Like giving you kerosene or something?"

"Let me see it," he said, and drank cautiously. "No, that's the grappa all right. It don't taste very hot, but it's got a wallop."

"It better," she said. "Give us a cigarette, huh?"

The match lit up the interior of the boxcar and even threw a brief yellow light on the car across the way. Milton noticed that the door of that was open, and there were bars across the opening. The car seemed to contain some kind of cage. In the flare of the match Milton thought he saw vague shadows, stirring enormously.

"What's in there?"

"Some one of the animals," she said indifferently. "I wouldn't know."

"Oh."

Mildred drank again, deeply and this time without apparent displeasure.

"Maybe you was right about this stuff," she said. "I begin to feel like I might live."

"You better take it a little easy," he said. "It's stronger than you think if you ain't used to it."

"Listen, Milty," she said. "You know what happened the last guy told me that? They had to scrape him off the floor."

"I'm only telling you," he said.

She drank again.

"No, that ain't bad stuff at all," she said gratefully. "I got to remember to get some more of that stuff sometime. What did you say its name was?"

"Grappa."

"Grappa. I like it. Hey," she said with a sharp note of inquiry in her voice. "What seems to be eating *you?*"

Milton, who had put his arm cautiously around her shoulder, withdrew it.

"Nothing," he said uneasily. "I only thought you might find it more comfortable."

"Well, for the love of God," she said. "Milty the Raper."

She laughed coarsely at this exhibition of poor taste and in the darkness Milton blushed.

"All right," she said, relenting. "Go on, put it back, Milty. I ain't sore. It's only you surprised me."

They sat for a little while in silence, in tentative embrace. Mildred's face, lighted intermittently when she drew on her cigarette, seemed relaxed and peaceful, almost amiable. Milton, his eyes more accustomed to the darkness, could see the cage in the other car quite clearly now. There really was an animal in it, a big animal, pacing soft and deadly behind the bars. He could hear the sound of its heavy breath and the creaking of the cage when it threw its weight against the bars. The cage seemed to Milton a frail and ridiculous barrier for an animal that had really made up its mind to get out.

"Say, what *is* that over there, anyway?" he asked nervously.

Mildred glanced at the cage.

"It looks like the lion," she said. "Yeah, that's what it is. Say, is he ever a crazy bastard."

"How do you mean 'crazy'?" asked Milton with anxiety.

"He gets in these crazy spells," she said. "You dassent get near him. Like the time he chewed up this fellow's arm."

"He did?"

"Like hamburger," said Mildred with satisfaction.

"He didn't ever get loose, did he?"

"Not yet. But he can give those bars hell when he gets in one of these crazy spells."

The lion had apparently noticed their voices, because he had stopped walking up and down in the cage and was standing facing the door. Milton could see his wild and luminous eyes searching the darkness. A growl, low and distant like the roll of a train on a faraway bridge, began to stir in his throat. He was rapidly developing all the symptoms of a crazy spell.

"He ain't going to bother us," said Mildred, noticing that Milton seemed tense. "He's practically a tame lion compared to some of them."

She drank again and then laid her head on Milton's shoulder.

"Listen, Milty," she said, and now unexpectedly there was pathos in her voice. "I guess you think I'm just a tramp, don't you? I guess you don't think much of a girl that would drink this grappa, laying around with a fellow in a boxcar. I guess that's what you been thinking about me, ain't it, Milty?"

"I ain't given the topic so much as a thought," said Milton gallantly, though with a wary eye on the lion.

"Shut up before I spit in your eye," said Mildred, addressing the lion, which had begun to growl in earnest. "Listen, Milty, you try being a living statue off and on for ten years, and see how you like it. When I think the number of times I been Fame leading that God-damn horse. Maybe I ain't always been a plaster saint, but what the hell kind of a life is that for a girl, I ast you?"

She drank, moodily.

"Nobody is calling me no tramp," she said furiously. "That louse in Wilmington. I guess he ain't passing no more remarks about people being tramps."

"Who?" said Milton.

She must have been a volatile girl, because now she laughed merrily.

"This fellow in Wilmington," she said. "Say, that was comical! This fellow was in the act, too. He was the General—you know, sitting on the horse—when I was Fame. Well, one night we all get stiff in a bar and this fellow called Babe and me a tramp. We didn't say nothing at the time, but the next night when he's the General and I'm Fame and Babe is some kind of an angel or nimp or something laying on the ground behind the horse, she takes this big pin and sticks the horse in his backside. Well, I'm hardly out of the way before he's down off the stand and like a bat out of hell for the exit. The General can't hardly keep on a horse staying still, so he gets tossed off in one of the boxes. He busted four ribs.

"Well," she said, with another of her dark and inexplicable changes of mood, "I ain't a tramp, and I don't want to have to tell you again, Milty, that's all."

"But I didn't—"

"Let it pass," she said magnanimously.

The rumble in the lion's throat had been growing steadily stronger and now it deepened into a passable roar. He flicked his paw tentatively at the bars, which rattled ominously.

"Pipe down, you," said Mildred.

"Say, maybe we better—"

"You, too, Milty," said Mildred, speaking with some difficulty because the neck of the bottle was in her mouth. "Both of you. Pipe down."

There could be no mistake this time about the lion's roar, and he lunged heavily against the bars.

"Well, for God's sake," said Mildred disgustedly. She had been smoking a cigarette, and when the lion roared again she threw it irritably toward the cage.

"Lay down, screwball," she said.

As Milton watched with dismay, the cigarette curved through the air, between the bars, and hit the lion sharply on the nose. A little shower of sparks enveloped his head, glowed, and went out.

For a moment nothing happened, and then the lion exploded. They could see him only dimly, a black and monstrous shape, tearing at the bars, but his intentions were clear and awful. The roaring had given way to a strangled, deadly snarl, and sometimes he spit like a cat. Beneath these louder sounds Milton could hear the even more paralyzing groan and creak of the tortured bars. Mildred added her own frail voice to bedlam.

"Shut up, shut up, shut up!" she shouted. "Shut up, *shut up*, SHUT UP!"

"My God," whispered Milton, "he's breaking the damn thing down!"

She didn't hear him or, hearing, paid no attention.

"I'll fix the crazy bastard!" she cried passionately, and while he watched in agony she scrambled down out of the car and picked up one of the buckets of water.

Milton waited for no more. He vaulted down out of the car and fled desperately into the darkness. For a little while, as he ran, he could hear Mildred arguing with the lion, but presently all sound died away. It occurred to him that this might mean that the lion had got Mildred and was eating her. He thought of this gruesome possibility with horror, but there were other emotions, too.

When Milton Barker got back to the yard office, haggard, panting, mysteriously encrusted with mud and straw, the yardmaster looked at him curiously.

"Well, you cert'n'y ain't wasting no time, Milty," he said admiringly. "How'd you make out? Them babies treat you all right?"

Milton gave him a secret smile, implying many fascinating things.

"What do *you* think, Pop?" he said darkly.

Somewhere down in the yard Orson Welles laughed his mad, derisive laughter.

Feud

"What a dame!" said the callboy, finishing his apple and throwing the core over his shoulder. "No sooner we figure Baldy's checked in at the yard—I'd stopped in at his place to call him for the six-o'clock Fresh Pond—than I'm laying there on his sofa and she's pouring me out a hooker of rum."

The yardmaster yawned.

"Some night one of them shacks is going to get home early and kick your teeth in," he said.

"Nuts to them," said the callboy.

"All right," said the yardmaster, "I'm only telling you."

It was eight o'clock. All the regular car floats had come in and the Brooklyn interchange yard was quiet except for the occasional cough and scuffle of a switch engine on the hill. Nothing was scheduled now until the midnight freight from New Haven got in with a train of refrigerator cars to be loaded on the floats and towed across New York Harbor to Greenville, where they'd be turned over to the Pennsylvania.

"Stick on the phones, Al," said the yardmaster. "I'm going to lay down a while."

He took off his coat, balled it up into a pillow, and put it on the table. He had scarcely laid his head on it before he seemed to be asleep. The callboy sat down at the yardmaster's desk and put his feet on the edge. He picked up the outside telephone and presently was connected with a lady called Myrtle, to whom he was able to speak frankly.

"Why don't you lay off them tramps?" said the yard-master without opening his eyes.

"You're a fine guy to be talking about tramps," said the callboy. "How about that big Swede I seen you with at the Coliseum? How about that dizzy—"

"All right. All right," said the yardmaster. "Skip it."

He turned over and this time actually slept. The callboy took a folded copy of the *Journal* out of his pocket and turned to "Popeye the Sailor."

At nine o'clock there was a ring on the direct wire from Greenville.

"Bay Ridge," said the callboy. "O.K., Greenville, let's have it."

"Penn floats five-o-three and five-o-six, tug twenty, leaving Greenville at—make it nine-o-five. Thirty-eight cars, one livestock for Manhasset," said the receiver hollowly.

"What the hell kind of time is this to be sending out floats?" said the callboy indignantly. "Don't you guys ever give nobody a break?"

"What's the matter, dear?" said Greenville solicitously. "Was you asleep?"

"All right, wise guy," said the callboy, and hung up the receiver. It would take the floats about three-quarters of an hour to cross the harbor. When they got in, he would have to sort out the waybills, print destination cards from them, and then go out on the floats and tack the cards on their corresponding cars. In the dark this was a disagreeable and even a dangerous job. It was slippery on the icy floats, and the cars were lined up in three rows with barely enough space for a thin and active boy to move between. A checker carried his flashlight in one hand and a railroad spike and the stack of cards in the other. He kept the tacks in his mouth. Expert checkers were usually able to finish the floats before the switch engines came and began to pull the cars off, but sometimes the engines didn't allow enough time and the checker had to flatten himself against one row of cars while projections on the moving row scraped across his back. Livestock cars were worse because they were moved at once, and you could be sure the engines would be coupled on and pulling almost as soon as the floats were fast in the slips.

"Lousy bastards," said the callboy, referring to the Pennsylvania Railroad.

At nine-thirty he went over and shook the yardmaster.

"Come out of it, Jake," she said. "Floats on the way. They got cows."

When the tugboat captain came in the office with the waybills, they found that the livestock car was far back in one of the middle rows, which, for a technical reason, is the most inaccessible position possible.

"That's perfect," said the yardmaster bitterly.

"Don't tell me about it," said the tugboat captain. "I don't load floats."

As the callboy went down the yard toward the bridges, he could see that the two floats were already fast. The switch engines, then, were probably on their way down from the upper yard. He had arranged his cards in order, meaning to tag the cars in rotation, but now he decided to tag the livestock first. They'd switch that right out and take it away. He could get the others in the yard later if he had to. Float 503, which had the cattle car, was in the right-hand slip and he climbed up on it, lighting his flashlight. The passageway between the cars was even worse than usual because there was a thin sheen of ice on the deck of the float.

"Oh, sure," he said bitterly, starting to worm his way back to the livestock car. Its number was PRR 637601, and presently he picked it out with his flashlight. As he started to hammer on his card, there was a stirring and grunting in the dark interior, and a piebald face peered at him through the wooden bars. The callboy looked at it nervously.

"Go on, beat it," he said, "before I spit in your eye."

He waved at the cow with his spike and it disappeared, snorting. The callboy put his flashlight up to the bars, illuminating the interior of the car. Eighteen or nineteen cows were standing together at the far end, their heads lowered, their eyes incandescent in the beam from the flashlight. He swung the flashlight around until it came to the floor of the car directly in front of him. Another cow was lying there, pressed against the side of the car. The callboy poked it gingerly with his spike.

"All right, on your feet, sister," he said.

The cow was motionless, however, and he poked it harder. Nothing happened, and he thrust his light through the bars and studied the cow more closely. It had, he saw now, a curiously flat and rigid appearance, and its eyes were closed. He focussed the flashlight on its ribs, and saw that there was no motion. The cow was dead, and there were indications that it had been dead for some time.

"Ain't *that* something," said the callboy. He took a last look at the cow, and then squirmed back through the alley between the cars. The switch engine was just rumbling up on the lead to the bridge when he came out, the conductor waving it on with his lantern. The callboy went up to him.

"Better hold it up, Eddie," he said. "One of them cows is stiff. I'm going in now to tell Jake."

"Yeah?" said the conductor. "Well, we ain't got all night."

"You got all night if Jake says so," said the callboy, and went away, whistling.

"Find it all right?" asked the yardmaster when the callboy came in.

"I found it," said the callboy, "but it ain't all right. One of 'em's dead."

The yardmaster swore.

"Did you look at it good?" he asked.

"I smelled of it," said the callboy simply.

"O.K. Go out and tell them shacks to pull five-o-three, switch out the cow car, and shove it back on the float. They can drag the rest of the cars up the yard. I'll talk to them dummies at Greenville."

The callboy went out, and the yardmaster spun the crank on the direct wire to Greenville.

"Hello, Maloney? Harvey. Listen, lug, I ain't running no tannery."

"Tannery?" said Greenville, and laughed with a light assumption of bewilderment. "What do you mean you ain't running a tannery, Mr. Harvey?"

"You know god-damn well what I mean," replied the yardmaster. "I mean I ain't got no use for any dead cows."

"Dead cows?" said Greenville, still seeming bemused. "What dead cows?"

"Nuts to you," said Harvey. "One of them cows is dead, and the tug is taking it back as fast as I can switch it out."

"Oh, *them* cows," said Greenville. "Well, I'm afraid there's some mistake, Mr. Harvey. Them cows were in number A-1 shape when they left here. Prolly them gorillas of yours broke their necks switching them."

"This cow has been dead a week," said Harvey. "It stinks."

"They were fresh as daisies when they left here," said Greenville. "I seen them myself."

"Never mind about that," Harvey said. "I'm only telling you the car is on its way back."

Greenville became official.

"You know we can't accept any dead cows, Mr. Harvey," he said. "You know we can't be liable just because you take some poor damn cow and bust its neck switching it."

It was clear to the yardmaster that he was up against a more active mind, and he abandoned the unequal struggle.

"I'm only telling you," he said, and hung up.

PRR 637601 made four trips back and forth across the harbor that night. Harvey persistently refused to accept it at Bay Ridge; Greenville politely insisted that the cow was in perfect condition when it left him, that Harvey had broken its neck, and that he was now transparently trying to foist the damages on the Pennsylvania Railroad. The car came over with every consignment from Greenville, and each time it was switched out and sent back with the returning load. The yard crew, which had at first been inclined to regard all this as a humorous variation of their routine, grew bored at length and complained that the cow was deteriorating rapidly and had indeed begun to affect their digestions. The surviving cows also appeared to suffer from their morbid ferrying, and lay trembling and panting on the floor of the car.

At six o'clock the Long Island dispatcher at Jamaica called Harvey.

"What in God's name are you monkeys doing down there?" he demanded.

"Doing, sir?" repeated Harvey, who by this time had the sense that his mind was ticking like a bomb.

"Yeah. I got eight interchange reports here, and the same damn car on every one of them. Penn 637601. It don't seem possible that you've got the same car from the Penn four times, and sent it back four times. I mean, it don't make sense that you've been shipping the same car back and forth across the harbor all night, but I'm damned if I know what *else* to make out of it."

"No, that's right," said Harvey.

"Well, for God's sake, *why?*" said the dispatcher. "You ain't doing it just for the fun, are you?"

"No," said Harvey wearily. "It's on account one of them damn cows is dead."

"What?"

Harvey explained at length and bitterly about the dead cow, and the evidence that it had died while under the jurisdiction of the Pennsylvania Railroad, if not a long time before. The dispatcher listened, but not sympathetically. At the end, he said, "Well, I guess you finally gone screwy, Harvey, but that ain't the point. Who's got the car now?"

"It's here," said Harvey hopelessly. "It just came in again on the five-thirty."

"All right, get out there and dump that damn cow in the harbor. Then pick up the car and put it on the first freight you got out of there."

"But—"

"Never mind 'but.' God almighty, you want *twenty* dead cows on your hands? You think it's good for them other cows to be riding around the bay all night with a stiff?"

"Yeah, but the Penn's got no right—"

"We'll take care of the Penn. You get after them cows."

"Yes, sir."

He called a brakeman and they went down to the float and found the car. Harvey broke the seals and pulled open the door, and, while the rest of the cows shuffled nervously, they rolled the dead cow out onto the float and then pushed it off into the water. It sank for a few seconds and then came up again, ten yards away, bobbing and twisting in the dirty current. Harvey watched it till it was out of sight, then he turned and looked gloomily across the harbor to Greenville, where the Pennsylvania humorist was probably already aware of his victory, and prepared to make the deadly most of it.

The Curious Incident of the Dogs
in the Night-Time

"This is a nice place, Freddy," said Harrington, looking around the noisy, crowded room. "You come here often?"

"I used to," said Goetz. "A few years ago, before I got married. Not any more. Ellen claimed it made her head hurt."

"Oh," said Harrington. "That's quite a thing, you getting married," he said after a pause. "That's certainly one nobody ever figured on. What's she like?"

"Ellen?" said Goetz. "She's a wonderful girl, Tom. I want you to meet her."

"Swell," said Harrington. "We'll have to get together sometime. I'll get Jane."

"Who?" said Goetz.

"Jane Inman," said Harrington. "But on second thought I guess not. She's no girl if your head happens to hurt."

The two men had been standing at the bar for about half an hour. When they came in, at seven-thirty, there had been no tables vacant, and the captain had suggested they have a drink while they were waiting.

"Why don't you gentlemen just stand right up here to the bar," he had said. "I'll let you know the first moment there is anything free."

They were on their fourth Martini now, and in the silence following Harrington's last remark they were both suddenly conscious of the passage of time.

"Listen," said Goetz. "We ought to be sitting down pretty soon. Where the hell is that waiter?"

"Over there," said Harrington. "Leaning up against some damn thing. Hey, captain."

The captain moved slowly toward them. He had a pale, impassive face and an air of having formed a rather low opinion of his surroundings.

"Gentlemen?"

"How about that table?" said Goetz.

"Yeah," said Harrington. "How about us sitting down one of these days?"

The captain looked around the room, tapping his fingers on the menu card in his hand.

"I'm sorry, gentlemen," he said. "I still got nothing free. I'll let you know."

"You said that before," said Harrington.

"You gentlemen get the first table that's free."

"All right, see that we do," said Harrington.

"Yes, sir," said the captain contemptuously, and moved away.

"Now you got him sore," said Goetz.

"Good," said Harrington. "I'm sore, too. How about another drink?" He tapped on the bar. "Hey, a couple more Martinis here."

"This is the one I don't need," said Goetz when the drink came.

"What do you mean you don't need?"

"The one that gets me drunk," said Goetz.

"What's the matter with that? What are you saving yourself for, Freddy? You planning a career or something?"

"Career, hell. I got to get up in the morning. I *work*."

"No. You're saving yourself. I know you married bastards. You plan ahead."

"That's right, Tom," said Goetz pacifically. "I'm planning a career. I want to be a waiter."

"You're too old," said Harrington. "You got to start young in that business. You got to be born in a linen closet or some damn place. All the really great waiters have been born in linen closets. It's like those trunks in vaudeville."

He was interrupted by the return of the captain, who gave them what he conceivably regarded as a smile.

"I got that table now, gentlemen," he said.

"Thank you," said Goetz, finishing his drink. "All right, Tom, let's go."

"Just a minute," said Harrington. "I wonder if I could put a question."

"Yes, sir?"

"This gentleman and I were having a little argument. I wonder if you'd mind telling us if you happened to be born in a closet."

"Sir?" said the captain, looking at him sharply.

"Never mind, captain," said Goetz. "You just show us that table."

"All right, you drunken half-wits," said the captain's expression quite plainly, but aloud he only said, "This way, gentlemen," and led them to the table, which was off in one corner of the room. At his signal, a waiter came up and handed them each a menu.

"We better have another drink first," said Harrington. "Bring us a couple of Martinis. No, you better make that double Martinis. Two *double* Martinis."

"Two double Martinis," said the waiter, and left them.

"That's a good man," said Harrington. "Knows how to take an order."

"Listen, Tom, how about taking it easy? You're getting pretty soused."

"You don't know what soused *is*," said Harrington. He concentrated on the menu, shutting one eye. "Say, what *is* all this stuff? What nationality?"

"Italian," said Goetz.

"Well, it's a terrible language," said Harrington. "You know what I want? Just some eggs. Some scrambled eggs."

"I'm going to have the *cacciatore*. They do that pretty well here."

"They do, do they?" said Harrington. "You know something about you, Freddy? You talk like a God-damn tourist."

The drinks came and they gave their order.

"Some pretty interesting people used to come here, Tom," said Goetz. "The Baker Street Irregulars."

"Who?" asked Harrington.

"The Baker Street Irregulars. The Sherlock Holmes experts. *You* know."

"Oh," said Harrington. "Yeah, I guess I read about them. Woollcott or somebody. This where they met, eh?"

"They did when I used to come here. Here or someplace very much *like* here. Maybe they still do. Woollcott, Morley, Tunney, Elmer Davis, some guy called Starrett—oh, a lot of 'em."

"That's a lovely bunch of boys," said Harrington. "What did they do? All I remember is they wore funny hats."

"They used to ask each other questions," said Goetz. "You know, about the stories. Like the name of the dog in 'The Sign of the Four.'"

"Toby," said Harrington promptly. "A lurcher, whatever the hell that is. And it's 'The Sign of Four.' No second 'the.'"

"The hell it is," said Goetz.

"All right," said Harrington. "Look it up. 'The Sign of Four.' I got five bucks says no second 'the.'"

"I'll take your word for it."

"You better. All right, ask me another. Ask me anything. Any of the stories. No, I'll ask *you*. What's a Penang lawyer?"

"Cane," said Goetz. "Dr. Mortimer carried it in 'The Hound of the Baskervilles.' Dr. James Mortimer, M.R.C.S."

"All right," said Harrington. "How many orange pips? How many Napoleons?"

"Five and six," said Goetz. "In that order. For God's sake, is that the best you can do? How about three stories with 'three' in the title?"

"Well, there's one with a funny word in it," said Harrington. "'Garribeds'? No, 'Garridebs.' 'The Adventure of the Three Garridebs.'"

"That's one."

There was a long silence while Harrington stared at the tablecloth.

"O.K., Freddy," he said finally. "You win on that one. I give up."

"'The Three Students' and 'The Three Gables,'" said Goetz. "You're a hell of an expert if you don't know that."

The two friends went on like that for some time. Goetz horrified Harrington by not remembering that the villain of "The Speckled Band" was called Dr. *Grimesby* Roylott, and somehow or other Harrington missed on the last name of Jefferson Hope's fiancée, which, of course, was Ferrier, but on the whole they did remarkably well. Time passed, and though the eggs and the *cacciatore* remained substantially untouched on their plates, the double Martinis continued to arrive and vanish.

"Listen," said Goetz suddenly at ten o'clock, "maybe they *still* come here."

"Who?" said Harrington.

"The Baker Street Irregulars," said Goetz, managing so many consonants very successfully, all things considered. "Maybe they're here right now."

"Those sons of bitches," said Harrington. "A lot they know about it."

"Sure they do," said Goetz. "They write articles."

"Not Tunney," said Harrington. "He's no writer. He just *reads*. Mostly Shakespeare."

"Well, all the rest, then."

They considered this briefly, and Harrington snapped his fingers. "Test 'em," he said.

"What?"

"We go up and test 'em."

"Find out they here first," said Goetz.

"Sure," said Harrington. "Find out. Ask *him*. Hey, waiter."

The waiter came over reluctantly, for he had been instructed to serve no more double Martinis and he saw trouble ahead.

"Sir?"

"You got a meeting here tonight, waiter?" said Goetz.

"Meeting?"

For a moment, the name of the Holmes admirers escaped Harrington. "Bunch of boys with funny hats," he said. "Ask each other questions."

"There's some fellas upstairs," said the waiter. "Some society. I don't know about the rest of it."

"Called Baker Street Irregulars," said Goetz. By this time, however, the Martinis had got in their work and his speech was somewhat blurred.

"Some name like that," agreed the waiter. "Some so-ciety."

"Whereabouts?" said Harrington. "What floor?"

"Right up at the head of the stairs," said the waiter, and then, belatedly grasping their intention, "It's a private party though, sir."

"It's all right," said Harrington, getting to his feet. "We're friends."

"Old friends," said Goetz, also rising. "Fellow-members."

"Well . . ." said the waiter doubtfully.

"Old, *old* friends. Don't give it a second thought," said Harrington. "Dismiss it from your mind. Here, let's have the check."

The waiter produced the check from somewhere inside his coat and added it rapidly. The total came to twenty-three dollars and twenty cents, and Harrington gave him three tens.

"O.K.," he said. "You keep that."

"Thank you, sir," said the waiter. There was still a doubtful expression on his face as his customers started across the room but he made no effort to detain them or to communicate with the captain, who would certainly have been opposed to the project they had in mind.

Goetz and Harrington turned to the right when they left the dining room and started up the stairs.

"Listen," said Goetz when they were halfway up. "Who you going to be?"

"Be?"

"Yes. I just remembered they all pretend to be somebody. Some character in the stories."

"All right," said Harrington. "I'm Holmes. You're Watson."

"Too obvious," said Goetz. "Anyway, they must *have* a

Holmes and Watson. Probably the president and vice-president."

"All right," said Harrington. "*Mrs.* Watson. Mrs. Watson and Mrs. Hudson."

"No," said Goetz. "It isn't that kind of kidding. You got to stick to the right sex."

"Mycroft and Pycroft," said Harrington. "Addison and Steele. Gallagher and Shean." He laughed immoderately, holding onto the railing along the wall, but Goetz was not amused.

"No, the hell with that kind of stuff, Tom," he said. "Listen, how about Gregson and Lestrade?"

"Those dumb bastards," said Harrington. "No. I tell you —Moriarty and Moran. First and second most dangerous men in London."

"Good," said Goetz. "Which one you want? First or second most dangerous?"

"Moriarty," said Harrington. "First most dangerous. Naturally."

Since one of the two doors at the top of the stairs was labelled "Men," they turned to the other.

"After you, Professor," said Goetz.

"Thank you, Colonel," said Harrington, and flung open the door.

There were perhaps twenty men in the small room. They were sitting at a long table and they appeared to be engaged in some general and earnest discussion. They wore no hats. Except for the table and the chairs, there was nothing in the room but a small piano, off in one corner.

"Gentlemen," said Harrington. "The chase is on!"

A silence fell on the room, and then a small, red-faced man got up from the table and approached Goetz and Harrington. He had on a rather jocular suit, but his manner was formal. "Some mistake, fellows, I think," he said.

"Not at all," said Harrington. He waved his hand at Goetz. "Like you to meet Colonel Sebastian Moran, late of the 1st Bangalore Pioneers. I'm Professor Moriarty."

"Of Reichenbach Falls," said Goetz. "Who are you supposed to be?"

The red-faced man cleared his throat. "Well, I'm Ed Tracy, of Denver," he said, "but—"

Goetz looked inquiringly at Harrington. "How about it?" he said. "You know that one?"

Harrington shook his head. "Might be 'A Study in Scarlet,'" he said doubtfully. "One of the Mormons. I don't remember him, though."

"I told you these boys made it tough," said Goetz. "All right," he said to the red-faced man, who had begun to wear a hunted look. "We give up. What story?"

"I don't know what you fellows are talking about," said the man helplessly. "This is a private party."

"I know," said Goetz. "We just thought we'd drop in. Great admirers."

"Disciples," said Harrington. He spoke thickly, and Goetz was surprised to see that his face was pale and beaded with perspiration.

"You O.K., Professor?" he asked.

"No," said Harrington simply "Better sit down a minute. Better *lie* down."

He swayed visibly as he spoke, and Goetz caught his arm.

"You going to be *sick?*" he demanded.

Harrington shook his head and then rose to a kind of heroism in his extremity.

"No," he muttered. "Just a touch of enteric. Old trouble of mine. Ever since Ladysmith."

His appearance actually was alarming, and between them Goetz and the red-faced man got him to a chair at the table. The other guests looked at him with a mixture of apprehension and respect.

"What's the matter with him?" said one of them. "What'd he say he got?"

"Enteric," said Goetz. "The curse of our Indian possessions."

"Yeah? What does he do for it?"

"Whiskey," said Harrington in a much stronger voice. "Only known cure for enteric. The Fuzzies live on it."

A bottle and a glass stood on the table near him, and without waiting for an invitation he poured himself a rather staggering drink. After a moment's hesitation, Goetz did likewise. Then, suddenly and simultaneously inspired, they raised their glasses in the air.

"To the Woman," said Harrington solemnly.

"To the Woman," repeated Goetz. "To Irene Adler."

The two emptied their glasses and, still in unison, they sent them both crashing to the floor.

"Listen, fellows," said the red-faced man. "*Please.*"

Afterward, Goetz had no very clear memory of the rest of the evening. Sometimes, in the tormented and fragmentary glimpses he got, he seemed to be shouting at a table of men who retreated from him, gradually and indignantly, until he was left alone at one end with Harrington, who sometimes shouted, too, and sometimes just slept. Sometimes he must have realized that these were not Sherlock Holmes experts, as the waiter and his own romantic heart had somehow led him to believe, but instead simply the innocent conclave of roofing experts from the West that their appearance and conversation indicated that they were. If he did occasionally recognize this for the discouraging truth, however, he never did so for long, and there were considerable periods when, noisily abetted by Harrington, he tried to force them into the shape of the Baker Street Irregulars, harassing them with unanswerable questions about the second Mrs. Watson and the Diogenes Club and whether Holmes went to Oxford or Cambridge. Once, he recalled, a waiter had been summoned and there had been some talk about putting them out, but that mysteriously had passed and there had been an interlude of great good will, when scrawled cards and promises of future gaiety were exchanged.

Goetz's only exact picture, as a matter of fact, was of the end of the evening. Harrington, somehow miraculously resuscitated, was seated at the piano and they were both singing, and it was his impression that they had been doing so for some time. He had looked up suddenly—this vision was as sharp as a photograph—and seen, to his perplexity, a line of figures, led by the red-faced man, tiptoeing from the room. After that, there was only the empty room and Harrington shouting and banging on the piano. Roofers or Baker Street Irregulars, the guests had gone, and they were all alone. His memory stopped there.

The Crusaders

On Thursday, Ralph Breck insulted Ellen Major for perhaps the fifteenth time that month. She would never have mentioned it to anybody herself, because she was that rather anachronistic and touching thing, a lady, and she wished to enjoy no special immunity on account of her sex. However, the walls of Breck's office were thin, and his secretary, who was subsequently replaced, was of a confiding disposition, and it wasn't long before the story got around. It seemed that Ellen had gone in with the proof of an advertisement for her employer's approval. The earlier part of the conversation had been amiable, or at least inaudible, but Breck's voice had risen toward the end. It had been rough and hectoring, and punctuated with jarring laughter.

"He sounded even more horrible than usual," the secretary testified.

Anyway, his final remark had been quite clear, and the secretary was able to report it verbatim.

"What the hell do you think this joint is?" Breck had shouted. "A God-damn kindergarten?"

Ellen had left the office rather pink and with tears of vexation in her lovely eyes.

Inevitably, this disagreeable episode soon came to the ears of three of Ellen's fellow copy writers, all of whom regarded her with respect, admiration, and hope untinged with vulgarity. This trio was composed of Alfred Mitchell, who might easily have been a poet in a sunnier climate and a more tranquil age; Henry Abbott, who was perhaps the most promising of all the younger men; and Elliott Fox, who had been very recently graduated by the Harvard Business School. Each of the three had suffered in his time from Breck's intractable disposition, which was, indeed, often indistinguishable from lunacy, but, being male, they were not disturbed by the steady, unaccented flow of blasphemy, and occasional obscenity, that passed with their employer for conversation. They pitied him for his poverty of expression, but since they also had the highest regard for his judgment, they were able to condone it, and even to find some entertainment in it.

With Ellen, however, things were, of course, quite different. The three men had come of age in a time of ever relaxing social standards, when a good many pedestals had been almost chipped away, but it still affected them unpleasantly to realize that Breck was in the habit of speaking to Ellen almost precisely as he spoke to them. They accepted this circumstance without comment for some time, hoping that Ellen's obvious gentility, her valiantly if unsuccessfully concealed discomfort when certain words were employed in her presence, would cause Breck to mend his ways. Their hope was vain. It may have been that Breck, aware of Ellen's embarrassment, honestly tried to restrain himself with her but that, being a man of drastically limited vocabulary, he was able to find no other words for those he was in the habit of using. Or it may have been that, quite aware of causing pain, he took a certain adolescent pleasure in continuing to do so. In any case, instead of improving, his behavior toward Ellen deteriorated rapidly. Mitchell, Abbott, and Fox watched with dismay as

Breck forgot himself with growing frequency and abandon, and as Ellen came to look more and more apprehensive and wistful. She had even, they couldn't help noticing, begun to lose confidence in those little mannerisms that had so endeared her to them all. For a long time, they hesitated to act, but Thursday's episode, coming, as it did, as the climax of a month of ever more aggressive assaults on her modesty, proved to be too much.

"I guess we're going to have to do something," Abbott said as the three gathered that night in a neighboring bar. "He can't go on treating her like this."

"I know," said Mitchell. "It isn't as if she was *any* damn woman. She *feels* that kind of stuff."

"You can count me in on this, fellows," said young Fox.

It was as a result of this conversation that the friends found themselves in the elevator on their way up to Breck's apartment on Saturday night. They had had dinner together and discussed the line they planned to take in insisting that their employer conduct himself in a more decorous manner.

"We'll have to be firm," said Mitchell as the car creaked upward.

"Yes," said Abbott. "Did he seem surprised when you telephoned him? Do you suppose he knows what we're coming about?"

"I don't think so," said Mitchell. "I didn't tell him, of course. I just said we wanted to talk to him."

"Good," said Abbott. "It may be helpful if he's surprised."

"Does Ellen know anything about this?" asked Fox.

"I mentioned it to her," said Mitchell.

"Oh," said the younger man, looking at him with faint dislike.

The door of the automatic elevator opened, and so, presently, did that of Breck's apartment.

"Hello, boys," he said. "Come in. Throw your stuff any damn place. Sit down."

They did so, and looked around the room, which was, indeed, a rather accurate reflection of their employer's bizarre personality. He had taken the apartment furnished, they knew, but the expensive reticence of the sofas, chairs, tables, and lamps had long since been overlaid with manifestations of a less coherent taste. The walls were covered with pictures—photographs of Breck's friends, usually in dissolute postures and facetiously inscribed; paintings and engravings that ranged erratically from kittens at play and young women enjoying the sun to tortured El Grecos and smoldering Gauguins; a color proof of an advertisement that an unfortunate slip of the engraver's tool had turned into a classic of impropriety. Books, also wildly various in subject matter, were piled everywhere, and there was a snowdrift of papers down from the chairs and tables across the floor. The proprietor himself was rather perplexingly arrayed. He had on the bottoms of a pair of pajamas, slippers, and the remnant of a panama hat. It occurred to his guests that he looked annoyingly frivolous, considering the nature of their errand.

Drinks were distributed, and for a time they sipped them in silence.

At last Mitchell cleared his throat and addressed Breck. "I'm afraid we've got a little problem, Ralph," he said.

"Well, who the hell hasn't?" said Breck, looking at him impassively.

"It's a little hard—" Mitchell began again, but before he could get any further he was interrupted by a strange and violent commotion in the wall behind his head—a thin whine of gears and the clanking of heavy chains.

"Problems," said Breck when this had died away. "You think *you* got problems. You hear that God-damn thing?" He gestured at the wall. "The lousy elevator. It does that all night. Right beside my bed. The little white Jesus knows the last time I got in a night's sleep."

"It's quite a noise," said Mitchell.

"Son of a bitch if it isn't," said Breck. "It's driving me nuts, Al."

"Well," said Abbott after a decent interval, "we wanted to talk to you about the office. That is—"

"The office?" said Breck. "You don't have to tell *me* about that office. I've worked there for fifteen godforsaken years. I've turned into a sick and beaten old man in that office. I used to have an appetite, Hank. I used to eat like other men. What do I live on now? Soup. No stomach, no teeth. I lost them in that office."

"Maybe you need a vacation, Ralph," said Abbott.

"Sure," said Breck. "And who's going to run the stinking joint? Except for you boys, what have I got? Women and children. God on a velocipede, *women!*"

"Maybe it's a little tough on women, too, Mr. Breck," said Fox.

Breck gave him a brief, sardonic smile. "*Everything* is tough on women, my boy," he said. "They make a career of having things tough. You know what Mark Twain said about women?"

"I'm afraid I don't," said Fox.

"He said they were beautiful creatures with pains in their backs," said Breck. "He had it right."

"Still," said Mitchell. "Well, in the case we wanted to talk to you about—"

"I don't know what the hell case you're talking about," said Breck. "There are all kinds of cases. You take my God-damn sister Muriel."

"We wanted to ask—"

"She keeps getting herself locked up," said Breck. "As a matter of fact, she's locked up right now. I don't suppose you knew that?"

"No, I hadn't heard," said Abbott, "but—"

"Well, she is," said Breck. "Some place up around Bridgeport. There's nothing the matter with her. Just every so often she feels she has to put herself away in one of these joints. She gets feeling picturesque or some God-damn thing and she slopes off to one of these joints. I wouldn't give a damn—it's her dough—except she keeps telling them *I'm* crazy. Maybe I am. You don't eat or sleep long enough, *anybody* is apt to go nuts."

While he stared at them defiantly, the elevator went up and down again in the wall, clanking and groaning, sending a small, unpleasant vibration through the apartment.

"What we came up about, Ralph—" said Mitchell uncertainly when the sound had ceased.

"Excuse me, Al," said Breck. He picked up a little bottle from a table beside him and shook a pill out onto his palm. "Supposed to quiet me," he said when he had swallowed it.

"You ought to be careful with those things, Ralph," said Abbott. "You can get dependent on that kind of stuff."

"Yeah, I know it," said Breck. "But what the hell. Drinking is no good. I've tried that. I don't get drunk. I just get depressed."

"Well, you ought to watch it, anyway," said Mitchell.

"A man has to relax," said Breck. "One way or another. You know that, Al."

"I know," said Mitchell.

"It's tough, Ralph," said Abbott.

"It sure is," said Fox.

"I'm thirty-seven years old," said Breck. "Supposed to be

the prime of a man's life. That's a laugh. Look at me. I live on soup and sleeping pills. For all I know, I ought to change places with Muriel."

"You do look kind of tired, Ralph," said Abbott.

"Tired?" said Breck. "God!"

"You ought to try and get some sleep, kid," said Mitchell.

"I don't know," said Breck. "Maybe I can. I feel as if maybe I might tonight." He yawned and closed his eyes, but opened them again almost instantly.

"But hell," he said, "you boys wanted to see me about something. What's on your mind, Al?"

"Ah, let it go, boy," said Mitchell. "We can take it up some other time."

"Sure, Ralph," said Abbott. "You just get your sleep."

"It wasn't important, sir," said Fox. "You get some sleep."

"Thanks," said Breck. "Perhaps I will. Well, good night, boys. Thanks for dropping around."

He yawned again as he showed them to the door.

It was some time before a cab came, and as they waited for it on the curb, they avoided one another's eyes.

"Poor guy," said Fox, tentatively, at last. "I hope he gets some sleep."

"Sure," said Abbott. He paused and slowly shook his head. "He seems to eat all right, though," he said. "At least whenever I'm with him."

"You're damn right he does," said Mitchell. Then he, too, stopped and stared off down the street. "I wonder . . ." he began again.

"So do I," said Abbott.

"You wonder what?" asked Fox.

"If the son of a bitch has really *got* a sister," said Abbott. "So do I."

WOUNDS AND DECORATIONS

The Country of the Blind

From early December, 1944, until September, 1945, I
was employed to review moving pictures for a magazine of
modest but genteel circulation. It was a makeshift arrangement, brought about by the war, and long before the ten
months were over, both the editors and I were aware that
a mistake had been made. Nothing was actually said, but
there was an air of constraint and embarrassment, rather
as if we had both made up our minds to ignore the fact
that I had suddenly developed a slight impediment in my
speech, and when in a moody moment I resigned, everybody was visibly relieved. Since the subscribers gave no
indication of either agreeing or disagreeing with anything
I wrote, it seemed permissible to deduce that they hadn't
bothered to read it. The only comment from the profession appeared in a screen writers' trade-paper on the Coast.
It compared me sardonically with Marcel Proust, the idea
being that I gave the impression of operating from an insulated cell, in a very fancy atmosphere of anemia and
corruption. Since one of my colleagues was described as
writing as if his upper plate had worked loose, however, it
was possible to regard this as a compliment.

The purpose of this essay is to explain, as clearly as I
can and while certain memories are still green, why it
seems to me that the cinema resists rational criticism al-

most as firmly as a six-day bicycle race, or perhaps love.
I am conscious of the danger of generalizing too freely
from a very brief experience and also of stating some things
that are both obvious and highly prejudiced. However, it's
a chance I'll have to take, and it is my indignant opinion
that ninety percent of the moving pictures exhibited in
America are so vulgar, witless, and dull that it is preposterous to write about them in any publication not intended to
be read while chewing gum. The exceptions to this indictment are the documentaries, which have of course, only
very limited opportunities to distort life; frank melodramas,
which have nothing to do with life and are therefore ex-
empt from criticism; and the occasional pictures, one or
two a year at most, which defiantly photograph some rec-
ognizable fragment of our common experience and generally lose a good deal of money. They are so few that
obviously no one could hope to find regular employment
writing about them, and consequently they can be ignored
here.

The explanation of the ninety percent is so elementary
and it has been offered so many times that it needn't detain us long. The cinema is a medium of entertainment
economically feasible only if it can be sold to an audience
of probably a hundred million in this country and God
knows how many more in the rest of the hemisphere and
across the sea. It must, of course, be intelligible to a vast
majority of these people. The common level of intelligence
in the world is presumably that of the normal adolescent,
who has no need or ability to relate the parts to the whole,
or the present to the total stretch of time. To him, that is, a
baby is a baby, cute and permanent; it has no future and
there are no conclusions to be drawn from it. (The persistent survival of Jackie Coogan as a middle-aged man,
with a divorce and thinning hair, incidentally, often has

an unnerving effect on lady cinema patrons, though they
are only vaguely aware of him as a symbol of their own
continuity.) The level of formal education, of course, is
even lower, so that any system of civilized reference is
obviously out of the question. To get in a picture, Homer
and Emerson must first be suitably defined, in words of not
too many syllables.

The third factor that has to be considered in this univer-
sal audience is the manner of life to which it is accustomed; its incredible extremes of wealth and poverty, its
varying social concepts, and its differences in language,
technical progress, and even climate and clothes. To
some extent, Hollywood has succeeded in imposing its own
vision of life on the world, so that a cocktail party on Park
Avenue need no longer be entirely mysterious to an Es-
kimo. However, while the cocktail party has gone far beyond life in gaiety and magnificence since people can be
taught to accept almost anything visually, it has been
necessary to scale it down almost to imbecility in behavior
since nobody can be expected to recognize a system of
conduct or conversation that has its roots in a more elaborate background than his own. The result of all this is that
very little seen or heard on the screen is precisely a picture
of anything.

As if these handicaps were not enough, a series of strict,
external codes, governing their political and moral content, have been imposed on the films either by organized
pressure groups or else by unorganized but highly vocal
minorities with a taste for out-size fig leaves. This makes it
impracticable to name political philosophies or explain
what they stand for, to discuss religion in any terms conceivably startling to the inmates of a parochial school or a
Baptist seminary, to speak disparagingly of any specific
business, except perhaps dope-running or the white-slave

trade, or to deal with sex in any way that might indicate that minor irregularities are not necessarily punishable by a lifetime of social ostracism and a lonely and untended grave. Hollywood, of course, did not frame these rules, but its own earlier excesses of vulgarity (not frankness or daring) were responsible for their existence in the first place, and it has not been noticeably heroic in combating them up to now.

Given all these restrictions, whether imposed by financial considerations or the Hays (now Johnston) Office, it is inevitable that the moving pictures should be just what they are—an astounding parody of life devoted to a society in which anything is physically and materially possible, including perfect happiness, to a race of people who operate intellectually on the level of the New York *Daily News,* morally on that of Dayton, Tennessee, and politically and economically in a total vacuum. I know, of course, that there are a great many pictures, usually "sophisticated" comedies or glum dramas of the soil, that *seem* to exceed this definition. It is only an illusion, however, though often an extremely clever one. Close attention will inevitably prove that no rules have been broken, that no sinister worldling ever says anything that would be essentially surprising from your grandmother, that no doomed sharecropper ever really criticizes anything more specific than the climate.

How the conscientious reviewer writes about the so-called A pictures (those that cost more than a million dollars to produce) is a small but fascinating literary comedy. Aware that he is dealing with names that are household words from Newark to Bangkok, with minds that command up to five thousand dollars a week for their power and agility, and with budgets that rival the national debt, he gets an uneasy feeling that such massive vulgarity somehow requires massive treatment, though those are not perhaps quite the words he'd use. Pictures are good or bad to him, for he has his standards, but their quality, whatever it is, is on the grand scale, and his discussion of it takes on a very peculiar accent, enormous, educated, and fuzzy. He writes, you might say, rather the way Henry Wadsworth Longfellow used to look.

Generally speaking, however, he has space for only five or six hundred words and very little time to put them down. The result is that he has developed a very special vocabulary in which words come to transcend their exact and customary meanings—in which, in a sense, they are detached from the language and inflated like little balloons, and presently sent spinning, lovely, iridescent, and meaningless, into the wild, blue heaven of critical prose. "Luminous" is such a word. Coming from the typewriter of a skilful operator, it means that the performance given by a young woman who has probably gone through each scene from ten to twenty times with her director and still has only the vaguest idea what it is all about is strong, beautiful, humorous, tragic, and lit with something of the same strange, devouring flame that once burned bright in Duse and Bernhardt. It means, that is, everything and nothing; it is both the non-word and the all-word. "Taut" is another and says, in reference to an actor's work, that he is somewhat greater than Booth or Salvini, and, in reference to a story, that it is high time for *Hamlet* to move over. There are a great many of these wonderful words —"haunting," "lyric," "brave," "tender," "compassionate," and, above all, "poignant" occur to me in passing—and they are invaluable in imparting such a cosmic air to a conversation that it is never quite apparent just what precisely is being discussed. The only trouble with all this, in fact, is that, habitually so used, these words can no longer be employed in their original and limited sense, and this is too bad because some of them were rather nice words in the beginning.

The reviewer is also remarkably talented in summarizing the complicated but fundamentally non-existent plots that come his way. These, too, he inflates to several times their natural size, colors with vague but impressive suggestions of other meanings than those that appear on the surface, and also sets adrift in space. In speaking, for instance, of a tornado that has apparently only a simple, melodramatic intent, he is apt to write, "There is, it seems to me, a profound and urgent ["urgent," by the way, is another favorite all-word] symbolism in the storm that carries away Miller's house and drowns his bed-ridden aunt." The symbolism is very seldom explained, but it is apt to delude everybody, including the writer, into believing that a subtle analogy has been offered, unerringly detected, and stylishly exposed.

In addition to complimenting the players and magnifying the plot, it is, of course, the reviewer's duty to go into the difficult matters of direction and photography. The first of these, since the mass mating of minds in any Hollywood picture makes it practically impossible for the layman to tell who did what, is usually conveniently dismissed by the use of a few all-words, or of phrases like "Mr. Desmond displayed great resource in his handling of nuclear mass," or "Mr. Drear's use of causal overtones is provocative, to say the least," both of which I presume mean something or other, though not to me.

Photography, on the other hand, is something actually visible on the screen and it is a good deal harder to brush off since the writer is confronted with an insanely complicated, endlessly refined, and wickedly deceptive technical process about which it is reasonable to assume that he knows about as much as he does about the inner workings of a seismograph. He has picked up a few useful terms like "lap dissolve" and "pan take," but for the most part he is obliged to rely on his personal artistic judgment, which, logically enough, since he is not an art critic, is apt to be unformed. He is a great one for "correct" or "striking" compositions, those, that is, that most closely resemble the paintings on sale in department stores, and he is a perennial sucker for the studiously telling details—a dead and falling leaf, a face in a crowd, a hand slowly relaxed —that are all part of a sort of primitive emotional shorthand used by the films to trap the unwary. Since photography is the one thing that Hollywood handles with invariable competence, and often with considerable taste and ingenuity, it seems too bad that the reviewers are neither mechanically nor esthetically equipped to deal with it adequately.

All that I have written, of course, has probably passed through the mind of anyone who has given any appreciable thought to the cinema. It took me ten months of notable physical discomfort and mental confusion, however, before I really saw, in the terms set down here, the whole absurdity of what I was trying to do—to write, that is, for the information of my friends about something that was plainly designed for the entertainment of their cooks—and before I realized that I had no intention of ever doing it again. I once knew an educated and almost excessively cultivated man who really enjoyed reviewing the movies. He was, however, a special case, in that he was unfailingly amused in his wintry way by sex in what he was pleased to call its "contactual aspects," and the idea of an art form fundamentally based on the slow, relentless approach and final passionate collision of two enormous faces struck him as convulsing. He wrote about it all with a wonderful, maidenly distaste, and to the total bewilderment of the motion-picture industry, but he really had the time of his life. He was also a very valuable critic since, free from the terrible spell of Love, he saw a good deal that escaped his earnest colleagues.

O.K., Zanuck, Take It Away

The career of Miss Gertrude Lawrence, up to now, has been a good deal like a superior moving picture—profuse in love, nicely arranged in a scale of mounting grandeur, and offering altogether very handsome opportunities for an all-star cast, bathed in Technicolor. The heroine has even furnished her own shooting script—a 238-page book about herself called *A Star Danced*, a title, of course, that would look lovely in lights. The strictly stylistic qualities of this document need very little discussion. It seems obvious that Miss Lawrence wrote it herself, composing, if a sample on the jacket can be trusted, in a round, maidenly hand on taupe paper with white ink. Apparently she was also somewhat pushed for time, since the useful dash is the backbone of her punctuation and the curly ampersand serves her faithfully as a connective. Nor is she an author whose ear is outraged by clichés—the waters of the world are the Seven Seas to Miss Lawrence and Timbuktu is her favorite symbol for all that's far away—or one to be daunted by the persistent recurrence of a word or sound. As early as her second page she writes, "And I might see Richard. That thought brought me out of bed and under the shower in one swift leap. From then on the next two days were one mad rush, winding up with the final leap to the airport," and her prose is full of girlish echoes to the end. This contempt for elegant variation, for the patient, hopeless struggle for felicity, is actually one of Miss Lawrence's most endearing young charms. She is a handsome woman, with a fine, arrogant spirit; a slavish attention to syntax would become her as oddly as a sunbonnet.

While the style of *A Star Danced* often suggests a young lady writing her parents from a camp in the Adirondacks, the content is rich and worldly and the point of view a winsome blend of Edward VII and Noel Coward, with brisk, practical overtones of Anita Loos. Miss Lawrence was born in Clapham, a section of London where it doesn't pay to be too nosy about other people's business, and she was christened Gertrude Alexandra Dagmar Klasen, for her father was Danish and these were royal names. Her early days were useful chiefly to establish her beyond any question as a character in a moving picture. There was Father, who sang huskily at smokers and in music halls, and drank, and presently abandoned his family for the less confining society of a minstrel show, where he took up with an amiable girl called Rose. Father was an artist, with all that implies in domestic confusion. Mother was also of the profession, though only dimly, since all her daughter seems to recall is that she was obliged to pad her thighs to land a job in the chorus. She was, in fact, mainly notable for her erratic selection of mates; after the Danish Thrush came Dad, a gambler of quite spectacular incompetence, who kept his family nervously alert for the sheriff. Of them all, the most vivid in her memory is Grandma, an imposing matriarch, who bred in her descendant that deep pleasure in royalty which was eventually to make Miss Lawrence regard the second World War primarily as a crusade to restore Edwardian securities. "The day will inevitably come," she writes at the height of the blitz, "when the established, comfortable, peaceful life, which every

British person considers no more than his due, will return."
And again, on a note of wonder, "The war has altered
some aspects of British life unbelievably. Daisy's door was
opened by her husband, Lionel. Butlers have become ex-
tinct, even in Eaton Square." Once, by some hideous mistake and in the presence of the commander of the Fleet,
she drank the King's health in *water*. "I felt like some
miserable figure in a Bateman drawing!" she confesses.

Miss Lawrence herself was distinctly a cinema personality. A plain, thin child (they stuffed her hopefully with
Scott's Emulsion and Parrish's Chemical Food, but she remained defiantly flat), she compensated for these deficien-
cies by following the traditional Hollywood patterns for
the early behavior of a star with incredible fidelity. "Suddenly," she writes in fond remembrance, "as against a
black-velvet backdrop, the past came back to me, and I
saw myself as a little girl, dancing on a sidewalk in Clapham . . . holding out my brief skirts." The music, suitably
enough, was provided by a wandering organ grinder, dis-
cordant but picturesque. She made her first sovereign
singing to a Bank Holiday crowd on the sands at Brighton.
" 'It ain't all honey, and it ain't all jam,' I carolled lightly,
twirling on my toes with my skimpy pink frock held out as
far as it would stretch." Sometimes the manager of a theatre gave her a pass to the gallery, where she sat transfixed,
dreaming the customary dreams. She went to a school for
professional children, where she met Noel Coward, "a thin,
unusually shy boy, with a slight lisp," and where the
clangor of Bow Bells was summarily erased from her accent. She appeared in Christmas pantomimes and in one of
Max Reinhardt's earlier scuffles with *The Miracle;* she went
on tour in the provinces, and once, when her employer
vanished with the receipts, she put in a week as a barmaid

to pay her board; in the end, the talent scouts caught up with her and, in almost less time than it takes to tell (seventy-seven pages), she was understudying Beatrice Lillie in one of André Charlot's revues.

It is all there, as tidy and satisfactory as the works in a little watch. It might even be said that it is *more* than all there, for Miss Lawrence is no girl to be content with the usual complexities of life or the accepted clichés of any rise to triumph in the theatre. When Miss Lillie obligingly fell off a horse and her understudy's great chance came, she was notably pregnant (she had married a dim, elderly character named Frank Howley in what appears to have been no more than a fit of abstraction) and only by reminding herself of the brave tradition of the theatre was she able to get herself out on the stage, tightly laced but still indomitably bouncy. Needless to say, she was magnificent. The child, whose sense of timing was also admirable, contrived to be born during one of the worst Zeppelin raids of the war, and Mr. Howley, having performed his whole function somewhat after the manner of the male spider, disappeared without a trace. It is almost permissible to suspect that Miss Lawrence ate him.

Before her marriage, she had been engaged to a young barrage balloonist identified only as Peter. "Whenever I would look up and see the big balloons bobbing lazily above the roofs and spires, like bubbles rising in an enormous glass of champagne, I had a cozy feeling of protection," she writes on page ninety-three. "My boy was up there looking out for me and for our city." Peter, a correct young man, took her to meet his parents and gave her a diamond-and-sapphire ring (subsequently hocked by Howley), but he had one fatal defect—the theatre bored him silly. In spite of the sense of security engendered by having a fiancé in a balloon, Miss Lawrence was quite un-

able to imagine herself as a suburban housewife. "The
more I thought about Peter and the life he pictured to me
. . . the more certain I became that it was not the life for
me. So I broke our engagement. Peter took it hard, but
gallantly." Like the spectral Howley, Peter was a mistake,
and Miss Lawrence was to make others. From now on,
however, they were to be on the grand scale, and so was
her life.

Since the book, like its author on her way to her shower,
leaps madly back and forth in time, it isn't easy to keep
Miss Lawrence's adventures in any rational sequence.
Here she is flying the Atlantic on her way to entertain the
troops in France. "How strange," she thinks idly, "was the
knowledge that far below was the stretch of tossing gray
ocean I had crossed so many times." Here she is standing
with Douglas Fairbanks, Jr., to whom a foolish rumor has
her engaged, in a crowd outside Buckingham Palace, waiting for news of George V. When a bulletin announces
that the King is dead, she is gratified to see a tall young
man sweep off his hat as tears run down his cheeks. "His
voice," she notes, "told me he was an American." He was
only a colonial, but he wept. In fact, her thoughts at this
period turned often to the United States. "I found a
tremendous interest in America—a genuine curiosity about
what Americans thought, what they were doing and how
they felt about the British. Everything sent from the U.S.A.
had become extraordinarily valuable and desirable. I don't
suppose that at any time since the reign of James I, when
the first British colonies were established in America, has
the world beyond the Atlantic held out such riches as it
does today. The British are rediscovering America."
Once Miss Lawrence came into her dressing room at
a London theatre to find the Duke of Kent trying on a

foolish blond wig before her mirror while the Prince of
Wales was democratically annoying her maid. "P.W., as
his intimates referred to him, had fulfilled all the promise
I had found in those early photographs of him which I
used to pin up beside my mirror. He was debonair, amusing, charming," she writes, adding, more or less cryptically,
"At that time, during the early twenties, no one in London
had even heard of Mrs. Wallis Warfield Simpson." It was
about this time that she met Captain Philip Astley, who
was "everything a knight in armor should be. He was born
at Chequers, which is now the official country home of all
British Prime Ministers. He was christened in the robes of
Oliver Cromwell, and educated at Eton and the Royal
Military College, added to which he was desperately good-
looking and had unparalleled charm. We had to fall in
love with each other. It was as natural and instinctive to us
both as it was for us to breathe." Captain Astley was more
durable than his predecessors, lasting for almost sixty
pages, but then she found to her horror that he, too, was
only feebly stirred by the theatre. There were other considerations, of course. "His career was as important as
mine, and it would have been wrecked had he married a
divorced woman. Though I was his wife, he could not
have brought me to Court, since etiquette forbade this.
He could not have entered the Royal Enclosure at Ascot—
something which is extremely important to English people
of Philip's position. . . . [His] income was not sufficient
to pay the heavy expenses of his clubs, his uniforms, and
all the obligations connected with his career in Court circles and to support me and a growing daughter." Also, he
called Miss Lawrence Dormouse, but she does not list this
specifically as a grievance. Anyway, Philip was out of the
question.

Fortunately, it was precisely at this vacant moment that Bert Taylor, a young man who she enthusiastically but incorrectly thinks was the son of the president of the New York Stock Exchange, came into her life. "This tall, dark-haired, stunning-looking American was like someone one only reads about," Miss Lawrence notes happily. "With a snap of his fingers, a glance, a quiet word, he had the power to bring about miracles. A banker in Bert's position could, and not infrequently did, make a profit of fifty thousand dollars in a day's trading on the Stock Exchange; and, exhilarated by this achievement, on his way uptown to his club he would drop in at Cartier's and spend a part of the day's bag on a gorgeous bauble to please the lady of his heart. Is it any wonder that Bert Taylor, who moved habitually in this fantastically luxurious world, should have swept me off my feet?" The dark, repetitive fates, however, were still dogging Miss Lawrence, and it was only a little while before she found herself involved in a familiar and disgusting conversation. "When I come home in the afternoon, I'm tired," said Mr. Taylor, obviously not in the tone of a man accustomed to pass fifty-thousand-dollar miracles. "I want to relax, have dinner, play a little bridge or something, and then get to bed at a decent hour. I don't want to sit around alone all evening until your show is over to take you out to supper, and then sit up half the night." Like Captain Astley, he also had a pet name for her. It was Peaches. When the circumstance that he seemed to be engaged to someone else (Captain Astley, too, had had a tiresome way of making alternate arrangements the minute her back was turned) made it clear that Bert would never do, Miss Lawrence was somewhat discouraged. "Would I always be too late for happiness?" she asked herself wearily.

For a while then, she had only more or less dispassionate admirers—William Rhinelander Stewart, who was also capable of quiet miracles and once sent a florist with orders to plant a garden in her back yard; Jules Glaenzer, the head of Cartier's New York branch and "one of those wonderful people, rare in any country and any society, who—though not artists themselves—are creative in their ability to encourage and develop artists of every sort"; Alexander Woollcott, a big, untidy man, with a lap like a lawn, known to her with fond derision as Uncle Aleck; Ernest Hemingway, who made her think tolerantly of "a rather mischievous small boy whose pockets are full of bits of string, old rusty nails, chewing gum, and maybe a pet toad or two"; George Gershwin, whose only interest in life unfortunately was his own music; and the young Prince of Hyderabad, or Baby, who, with the rather disconcerting humor of the mysterious East, gave her a miniature cannon, which fired lighted cigars, and a gold kidskin bag containing betel nuts.

In this emotional vacuum, the theatre was always a great consolation to Miss Lawrence. In John van Druten's *Behold We Live,* she felt that she had reached a milestone in her career. "I, who had begun in light musical comedy and revues, was now starring as a dramatic actress in a serious rôle with *other* truly great actors," she writes, though without the italics. "If there is another actress on the English stage who could give the performance you did on Monday night in Edinburgh, I don't know her," Charles B. Cochran told her after a tryout of Noel Coward's *Private Lives,* and Mr. Coward himself sent her a specially bound set of all his plays, bearing the inscription "For Gertie, with my undying gratitude for her exquisite, polished, and sensitive performance of Amanda."

Ill in a hospital in Toronto and deluged with flowers from all over the world (Florenz Ziegfeld sent his daily, on ice), she realized for the first time that "there was something wonderful in being somebody." The most impressive tribute ever paid her had been the one at the final New York performance of the 1924 *Charlot's Revue*. "The whole house stood up and cheered us. They pelted us with flowers. When the audience was finally pushed out of the theatre, several hundred of them merely adjourned to the stage door, where they formed such an imposing mob scene that traffic was clogged in Forty-second Street. When Bea and I came out, laden with flowers, to get into our waiting taxi, we found the roof of the vehicle packed with the more ardent revellers, who escorted us through the streets of New York singing our own songs to us."

Eventually the script was finished, except for a suitable fadeout, and soon that was provided, too. Happiness came to Miss Lawrence when she was trying out *Skylark* at a summer theatre on Cape Cod. Her producer was Richard Aldrich, a tall young American (all Miss Lawrence's beaux, of course, were tall and young) whom she had met casually in London several years before. "Richard and I took our time," she writes with a rather settled and matronly air. "We both wanted to be very, very sure. I had made one mistake in marriage. I did not want to make another. It was curious about Richard—it was as though he combined in one person the different things I had found and admired in Philip Astley and Bert Taylor. He was Boston and Harvard, and had been a banker, but above all he loved the theatre. He was the first man in my life who understood what my career in the theatre meant to me—the first man who really understood me. And so we were married." It was perfect. The only note, in fact, that might conceivably distress the Hays Office came in the form of a rather questionable telegram from that perennial bachelor who had always followed her career with passionate, if slightly sardonic, attention:

> Dear Mrs. A.,
> Hooray, hooray,
> At last you are deflowered.
> On this as every other day
> I love you—Noel Coward.

The Big Boffola

The Hucksters, by Frederic Wakeman, has not only been taken by the Book-of-the-Month Club as its selection for June, it has also been bought by MGM for $200,000, a pre-publication deal indicating, of course, high hopes on the Coast. In spite of these impressive votes of confidence, I'm afraid that it is a remarkably silly book. Mr. Wakeman's purpose, as I get it, was to write a sort of moral satire about the radio advertising business in which he himself was once successfully engaged. There is a hero, Victor Norman, who is able to view the absurdities of the profession with a detached, sardonic eye. Unfortunately, however, he is not sufficiently gifted to write a book about them, and instead we find him employed in an agency as an account executive in charge of radio programs for a soap company. For the benefit of those who have never grasped the technical mysteries behind the demented voices on the air, this means that it is his job to assemble a half hour of comedy, music, and commercial announcements, convince the president of the soap company that this entertainment will sell his product, and then arrange for its delivery over a radio network—or at least that's what I *think* it means. Anyway, he has accepted this position at an annual salary of $35,-000, plus stock, bonuses, and a very nice little expense account (another of Mr. Wakeman's figures is also recom-

mended to the editors of *Fortune:* the soap company pays
ten million dollars a year for the right to torment the public
with its slogans, and out of that the agency gets fifteen
percent) and he is cynically determined to make a hell of
a lot of money as rapidly as possible. He undoubtedly
would have, too, for he is a young man of ruthless competence and extravagant personal charm, if he hadn't
contracted a species of love affair with a woman of blood-
curdling refinement, though she was not averse to spending a week with him in a Los Angeles flea-bag. This intricate matron, a Mrs. Francis X. Dorrance, has a couple
of swell kids, cuter than Mencken and Nathan, and a husband, a distinguished lawyer stemming from one of those
wealthy old New York families, who is fighting for his
country in the Pacific. Vic (hero's pet name) might have
been willing to take advantage of the absent warrior and
break up his home if he had had any reputable future to
offer a wife. Being in the advertising game, however, and
miserably conscious of his own corruption, he desists,
though only after an exhausting wrestle with his baser self.

"If we did this thing," he tells her by long distance in
the end, "I don't think I'd like myself."

"Don't talk like that," she begs, but unfortunately he
has been talking like that for 306 pages and it is too late
to start editing him. They both hang up, feeling as characters so often seem to on the final page of a renunciatory
novel, not so much noble as just terribly tired and depressed.

This is the skeleton of Mr. Wakeman's book. Our next
concern is the flesh he has selected to cover it. When I
started to write about *The Hucksters* (a title, by the way,
with a rather engaging and old-fashioned innocence about
it, like *The Nazarene* or *The Auction Block*) I considered
a parody and even typed the following sentences:

"Anybody don't like the way I do things," said old Sam
Symbol, "I crush them like a bug."

Mr. Golightly, Yale '35, the third assistant vice-president
in charge of sales, took a small bug out of a sixteenth-
century lacquered box and placed it on the table. The old
man crushed it, using a $250 gold-ribbed Dunhill lighter.

"Like a bug," he said. "Get it?"

"A yak," said Mr. Golightly worshipfully.

"A boffola," said Mr. Penrod.

"You're right on the beam, Mr. Symbol," said Miss
Roundhill, taking another sip of paraldehyde. "You certainly send me."

Hype Insight was feeling very sincere in his hand-
painted Charvet tie and the sixty-four-dollar English shoes.
He had been about to join in the chorus, but now he
changed his mind. Instead, he took a hundred-dollar bill
out of his pocket and swallowed it. It tasted a little like a
counterfeit and he worried about his ulcers, but, what the
hell, it certainly must look pretty sincere, eating a century
right there in the meeting.

This was intended to be a comment, both as to style
and content, on the second chapter in the book, which
deals with the first meeting between Victor Norman and
old Evan Llewelyn Evans, the president of the Beautee
Soap Company and a man apparently with a celebrated
counterpart in life. In this actual version, the old man
empties a pitcher of water on one of his subordinates by
way of illustrating his opinion that some idea or other is
all wet, removes his upper plate with the remark that Vic
seems to have got his teeth into a problem, and spits on
the table to demonstrate the value of the shock technique
in advertising. Up to this point in the book, the word

"sincere," which seems to be a trade adjective, used ironically to describe the public appearance and behavior suitable to an advertising man, has turned up eight times; the
yes-man motif and the intramural slang ("yak" and "boffola," for the benefit of any rubes in the audience, are
variations of the old-fashioned "wow") have been established far beyond the strict necessities of satire if not up
to the limit of reader endurance; and Charvet ties, Dunhill
lighters, sedative drugs, and duodenal ulcers have been
listed so often as occupational phenomena (Vic's immedi-
ate superior is said to suffer from satyriasis but I doubt if
that is really intended to be typical) that the point might
easily be apparent to George Washington Hill himself. It
is not until some twenty pages farther along that Vic
throws eight dollars out of a sixty-seventh-story window
in Radio City to emphasize his sincerity, but it is spirit-
ually part of the same scene, and it marked the spot where
I abruptly abandoned the idea of parody on the ground
that the virility of Mr. Wakeman's humor was such that it
needed no assistance from mine. I am not equipped to discuss the validity of all this as criticism of what seems to be
an achingly peculiar racket; I only know that it is impracticable to try to superimpose parody on broad bur-
lesque, or, to approximate the author's own idiom, to goose
the yak in terms of the boffola.

If it seems hardly feasible to parody *The Hucksters* on
its level of ostensible criticism (the characters the hero
meets in Hollywood are even more relentlessly "satirized"
than old man Evans), it is absurd to think of doing so with
its tenderer scenes. On page 277, for instance, Mrs. Dorrance and her offspring are described as "Sweet, gracious
Kay. Mad, passionate Kay. Grave, serious, manly Hal.
Wild, unearthly little Ellen." Investigating these three
specimens in order, we find Mrs. Dorrance contributing

the following high-toned sentiments to the conversation:

Page 132, in the course of some cultivated literary advice: "Why don't you try a piece of serious writing? You could do a wonderful satire on radio, knowing it so well. With your sardonic slant, it could be a fascinating caricature."

Page 178, with reference to her admirer's appetizing appearance: "I fancy you're a very warm, gentle, passionate man beneath that frozen twentieth-century mask of a face."

Page 238, in a moment of delirium in the flea-bag: "Do other people talk this way? Abandon all other feelings of life this way? I never knew these words, these silly words, could mean so much. . . . But you must sleep, my love. I want to stay awake and love your sleep."

Page 265, more of the same, but *crescendo:* "Hold my foot, darling. It feels so good when you hold it."

Vic's own definitive comment on love starts on page 251 and oozes, so to speak, over onto 252: "A really intense love must be a form of insanity. I think Freud was wrong to pin it down just to the sex urge. The thing that stains and colors all other behavior is love. . . . And when love starts twisting its ecstatic daggers inside you, you soar up to the peaks, the mood of elation is on you."

Somewhere else, Mr. Wakeman himself observes, "Oh, ecstasy, that hoarse and breathless word, that hot and viscous word." As Mr. Evans, that cruel and fearful old man, so often said, he seems to be right on the beam. Beyond any question, "viscous" is the word for the ecstasies in *The Hucksters.*

Grave, serious, manly Hal is probably no more piercing and monotonous than any other little boy—on page 116, we hear him shouting, "Hey, hey, do you know what to do when a crook's pointing a gun at you? You fall on your knee and draw your gun. Kakkkk, kakkk, you're dead. Hey, hey, you see I ducked and your bullet went over my head." And this is the general pattern of his conversation. Little Ellen, however, is certainly as unearthly as they come.

"My not 'ittle Ewwen, my big Ewwen," she says on page 115, for there is some strange disorder in her speech. "Tell my a stowy." A little later, having been obliged, she asks for "anuya stowy." "I wanna stowy about a flutterby," she squeaks, lunatic with whimsy. Ellen turns up off and on for approximately two hundred pages. She is easily the most repulsive literary inspiration, for her age and weight, since Little Eva.

I could quote practically indefinitely from these fascinating types. I was pleased, for instance, to come on a lyric memorandum addressed by the hero to himself while lying sleepless on the Super Chief: "To a restless man on a train, America becomes only a ribbon stretching from his window to the hilltops or the horizon . . . the roads leading like intestines into the hills." Old Whitman never wrote a lovelier line, I thought, murmuring it over to myself. However, I have a feeling that the peculiar treasures of Mr. Wakeman's style and thought have already been sufficiently displayed. I said earlier that they seemed to resist parody; it occurs to me now that they may even be impervious to criticism. *The Hucksters,* by the way, is dedicated to Jed Harris, in his way a character as wild and unearthly as Little Ellen. In some circles, this inscription may easily be regarded as the most successful yak or boffola in the book.

The Personality Kid

It might be interesting, though probably not terribly interesting, to know what a playgoer of generally correct
taste but no information at all about the American theatre
would make of John Barrymore in *My Dear Children*.
Here, some such hypothetical critic might say, is a man
approximately sixty years old, of classic though damaged
appearance, giving a rather ridiculous performance in a
play that really has no particular business on the stage.
Observing an occasional trace of grandeur in Mr. Barrymore's behavior, he might want to qualify that a little. On
the whole, it *is* a ridiculous performance, he would say, but
there are obviously hints that this fossil has been an actor
of considerable ability, in whom the technique is still both
instinctive and highly developed. Even given this qualification, though, how he would account for the hilarious reception accorded Mr. Barrymore and his simple-minded
vehicle I can't imagine.

It is a useless speculation in any case, since there can
scarcely be an adult in North America who doesn't know
Mr. Barrymore almost as intimately as the family doctor
knows his oldest and most bothersome patient. The great
man comes on the stage of the Belasco trailing a thousand
anecdotes, familiar from Bangor to Pasadena. He is love,
alcohol, beauty, and the heir of a dramatic tradition going

back, it often seems, to the Old Testament. He can (and does) act in a way that appears to be a vicious parody of Mr. Walter Hampden, and the audience watches him with boundless delight. Half of this effect lies in simply being a Barrymore and therefore presumably engaged in something supernatural; the other half lies in a very carefully fostered reputation for doing the unexpected.

In this second category, I'm sorry to say, Mr. Barrymore let his first-night admirers down miserably. The manner was all Barrymore, but, with the exception of a few inter- polated lines that I could have improved on myself, there was nothing unexpected—or nothing, at least, until the show had moved on to further triumphs in a night club. In the company surrounding me, this was generally regarded as a gyp. These fashionable people had come, on the whole, in the same spirit they would have gone to a wrestling match. They understood that the show was fixed, and if the star couldn't actually be tight, as advertised by his press agent, they certainly expected him to pretend he was. Mr. Barrymore did nothing of the kind. He threw in a few writhings and grimaces, but he didn't fall down and he remembered his lines perfectly, which was quite a feat since they are among the least memorable lines ever writ- ten. The whole thing was very disappointing, and it was a tribute to his past notoriety and present charm that he got the greatest ovation of the season without so much as throwing an actress at a critic.

Because of the interlocking nature of Mr. Barrymore's private and professional lives, it is hard to say just who will be in the cast of *My Dear Children* by the time this reaches print, although it seems likely that the fourth Mrs. Barrymore, a young woman of remarkable tenacity of pur- pose and almost no reticence, will have supplanted Miss Doris Dudley in one of the leading rôles. The night I went, the associate wags included Lois Hall, Patricia Waters, Tala Birell, and Arnold Korff. A good deal of the time Mr. Barrymore's antics left them quite helpless with laughter, so that I got to wondering now and then if perhaps the wrong people weren't tight.

Adultery Makes Dull Bedfellows

"Sinister chaps, these gods that be, Michael," says Diana, and away we go. The scene is a living room in the home of Mrs. Reggie Williams Browne, the time is a breathing space or vacuum in the history of the world, and the remark is occasioned almost entirely by the circumstance that it has been decided by somebody, though certainly not by me, that what New York really needs at the moment is another comedy by Frederick Lonsdale. I don't know exactly what to tell you about the evening that may be lying in wait for you at the Fulton. There is, of course, an abundant supply of those epigrams with which Mr. Lonsdale has been titillating the Morgan-Harjes set since 1908. The quality of these quips is uneven. Sometimes a cliché has been so ingeniously rearranged that it comes out sounding almost like wit, sometimes the author's gay perversity is such that wicked old dowagers in the audience nudge one another almost out from under their hair, but most of the time, I'm afraid, his record of stylish conversations is just stupefying. At one point, for instance, Diana, a moderately sinister chap herself, offers us a rather involved thought about the double standard. "To a woman," she says, taking a deep breath, "a man's past only means that, thank God, he's had experience, while, to a man, a woman's past only means—that she's had a past." Don't bother to unwrap it. It's just a sample.

294

The real complexity of life among Mr. Lonsdale's power-
fully sexed grammarians can be indicated in a sentence,
though a tough one: Michael, engaged to Molly, is really
in love with Diana, whom he seduced once in Paris; George
can't decide whether to marry Celia or Maggie, both of
whom he has seduced here and there at various times; and
Elsie, though married to Reggie, is still strongly attracted
to her first husband, John, who has seduced practically
everybody and likes to talk about it. Anyway, all these
people, along with a drunken butler and an old family
lawyer, both standard models, are visible on the stage,
sometimes all at once. It is a rich and sophisticated dish,
though not precisely, you might say, the Blue Plate Gibbs.
How Mr. Lonsdale gets everything straightened out in the
end, I won't try to tell you in this fortunately limited
space. An impacted wisdom tooth, the drunken butler, and
a good many dubious coincidences are involved, but the
whole business isn't very clear to me even now, and I think
you'd better just accept my word that everybody winds
up in the right bed. Come to think of it, George (see
synopsis) really doesn't, but the hell with him.

Moving on to the cast, the chief attraction is probably
Roland Young, a good actor but not, apparently, a very
acute judge of scripts. It is Mr. Young's task to portray a
small, neat, harried character, who has had eleven mis-
tresses in the past and is now mixed up with two more. "I
am a dull man," he says gloomily, "with just one way of expressing myself." Mr. Young indicates this unhappy state
largely by popping his eyes and sniffing his mustache, but
he is funny enough and has my respectful sympathy. His
co-star, Margaret Lindsay, a handsome recruit from the
films, with an impressive voice, has been entrusted with
Diana and some of the most staggering lines since *Lady
Windermere's Fan.* Hers is strictly a triumph of beauty

over syntax. Arthur Margetson, as a cynical man of the world, contributes a cryptic smile and a fashionable presence and is, I'm sure, exactly what the author had in mind. Of the others—Doris Dalton, Philip Ober, Henry Mowbray, Augusta Dabney—I can only say that they don't seem exactly right for Lonsdale types, something, praise God, that might happen to anybody. Raymond Sovey's boudoir setting is obviously just the place for a roll in the ermine and the living room is very pretty, too. The name of this piece, by the way, is *Another Love Story*.

The Mantle of Comstock

Of the sixteen Protestant clergymen who signed a resolution condemning Dorothy Baker's play called *Trio*, it appears that only one, the Reverend Dr. John Sutherland Bonnell, of the Fifth Avenue Presbyterian Church, had bothered to see the darn thing. All these gentlemen are members of a society called Sigma Chi, which, for your records, has no relation to that fraternity with the communal sweetheart but is simply a small group of ministers who gather the first and third Wednesday of every month for lunch and discussion. The subject under discussion a few weeks ago was the state of the New York stage and it produced a resolution from Dr. Bonnell demanding that something be done about *Trio*. In a sermon the Sunday before, Dr. Bonnell had specifically denounced a play that "condones, applauds, and even enacts promiscuity," a remark which the congregation obviously took to refer to *The Voice of the Turtle*. For one reason or another, however, he abandoned that crusade and settled for *Trio*. The assembled brethren signed his manifesto with enthusiasm.

In view of these facts, a diligent and gifted worker in this vineyard was asked to telephone the fellowship of Sigma Chi in an attempt to find out just what would move a man to condemn a play sight unseen. I would like to report his conversations, as nearly as possibly verbatim, with fourteen out of the sixteen.

The Reverend W. Russell Bowie, of Union Theological Seminary, said, "I got in at the end of the meeting and was not in on the discussion. I went ahead and signed the letter at the suggestion of the others." When asked if he'd seen *Trio*, he replied, "Well, I haven't given the matter much thought and I'd rather not discuss it."

The Reverend John Knox, also of the Seminary, and in response to the same question, said, "No, I haven't seen the play myself, but I hear it's pretty bad. It ought to be shut."

The Reverend Frederick C. Grant, another Seminary man: "It may be all right for people beyond forty to see a play like *Trio*, but it's terrible when youngsters are permitted to see this sort of thing. Why, a teen-aged girl in Bonnell's parish went to see one of these plays six times; the whole course of her life is now warped. In *Trio*, the subject matter is unduly pathological and the presentation is offensive. No, I haven't seen it."

The Reverend Harold Pattison, retired pastor of Christ Protestant Episcopal Church in Oyster Bay and secretary of Sigma Chi: "The whole thing is too nasty to discuss in a conversation, let alone put on the stage. I'd rather not go into it. Of course I didn't want to see the play."

The Reverend Nolan B. Harmon, Jr., editor-in-chief of the Methodist publications, said he was in a hurry to catch a train but would be delighted to talk about *Trio* some other time. He did, however, add that he hadn't seen the play. "But let me have a chance to think about it," he said hastily. "I'll call you," and went off, presumably catching his train.

The Reverend Howard Melish, of Holy Trinity Protestant Episcopal Church in Brooklyn: "I haven't seen *Trio*, but Bonnell saw it. I was particularly interested in the fact that one or two people Bonnell knew had very definite

Lesbian tendencies—he probably ran into them in his advisory work—well, the play had had a deleterious effect on them. Of course, nobody wants censorship, but it's a question, actually, of the protection of the people."

The Reverend Theodore F. Savage, Executive Secretary of the Presbytery of New York: "The public goes to the theatre expecting dramatic entertainment and gets filth. I haven't seen *Trio*."

The Reverend George P. T. Sargent, pastor of St. Bartholomew's, read over the telephone a portion of his previous Sunday's sermon: "I have a great sympathy for our city officials, who have no desire to be moral censors of our lives but feel a sense of responsibility to maintain moral standards." Part of the trouble, he added, "comes from a tendency in many plays to parade an immoral subject in a beautiful setting with exquisite acting. I haven't seen *Trio* or read the novel. I'm not going to devote Lent to that sort of thing." Mr. Sargent also quoted at length from St. Luke, to no apparent purpose.

The Reverend Joseph R. Sizoo, of St. Nicholas Collegiate Church: "There is no doubt that the stage, just as the press, has a right to narrate tragic elements of life, but in this instance the portrayal of an irregular sex relationship can't be justified because there is nothing in it that *lifts* people. No, I haven't seen *Trio* myself."

The Reverend Lynn Harold Hough, dean of Drew Theological Seminary, Madison, New Jersey: "I haven't seen *Trio*, but I got a very full report from a man who had seen it and who had lived in Paris twenty-five years and had seen everything."

The Reverend Geoffrey W. Stafford, also of the Drew Seminary faculty, hadn't seen *Trio* either, but in the words of Dean Hough: "Stafford was an officer in the British Army in the other war, and he's had a very close contact

with the world in its rougher aspects, as you might imagine."

The Reverend A. B. Cohoe, pastor of the First Baptist Church of Montclair, New Jersey: "I haven't seen *Trio*, but Bonnell saw it and condemned it in a very detailed statement making the subject matter of the drama clear to all of us. I personally would not denounce a play in my pulpit or in my writings without having gone to see it. All we did was to support Bonnell's opinion, which all the members present did without dissent."

The Reverend John H. Powell, Jr., pastor of the Reformed Church of Bronxville: "It was not made clear to us that the thesis of the play is actually a condemnation of perversion, as you tell me. Bonnell has done much psychiatric work and is thought to know something of such matters. I didn't see the play."

The Reverend George Vincent, pastor of the Union Congregational Church of Upper Montclair, New Jersey: "Dr. Bonnell is our spokesman in the matter. He saw *Trio*. I didn't."

The Reverend Arthur P. Mabon, formerly associate pastor of St. Nicholas Collegiate Church, signed Dr. Bonnell's statement. He could not be reached for comment, but his secretary said that he rarely attended the theatre.

The final clerical comment on *Trio* came from one of the above Sigma Chis, who said that it must be pretty bad because it had opened in Paris (*Trio* opened in Philadelphia) and they hadn't let it run there. It was nearly as distasteful, he added, as another French atrocity whose name, as he recalled it, was *La Parisienne*, quite properly suppressed over here under the title of *The Captive*.

Two Very Sad Young Men

Of all the sad young rebels in our literature, which offers a new specimen for our inspection nearly every week, the hero of "Look Back in Anger," John Osborne's play at the Lyceum, is perhaps the one with the most exhaustive set of grievances against the world he has to live in. He is dismayed by his times, because there are no great causes, or illusions, left to fight for; he can take no comfort in belonging to a social class, because he is what might be called a half gentleman, sufficiently a man of the people to hate the soft arrogance of the fortunate and gently bred, and sufficiently educated to despise the ignorant sentimentality of the poor; he has no rational occupation to divert him, being an artist *manqué,* now condemned to the operation of a candy store in some gritty English suburb; and he is, of course, denied the popular consolations of religion and of patriotism, having an almost equal contempt for the dead God and the dying Empire. He is a very young man, as you have probably gathered, and he might easily have been both tedious and insufferable if Mr. Osborne hadn't somehow managed to write about him with compassion and truth, and to endow him with a kind of savage and authentic humor not often found in heroes who consider themselves victims of life, since they are far more apt to be damp with self-pity than bright with rage.

In essence, the play is a furious and almost uninterrupted diatribe against practically everything. The action
takes place in the miserably squalid one-room flat that
Jimmy Porter shares with his wife, Alison, who, being the
daughter of a British colonel until recently stationed in
India, is a symbol of all that her husband finds most
loathsome. A room on the same floor is occupied by a
young Welshman, whose rough exterior conceals the kind-
est of all possible hearts, and who is apparently the only
friend they have left in the world. When the curtain
rises, the lady is ironing while the men investigate the
Sunday papers, and almost instantly Porter finds fuel for
the perpetual fire that consumes him. "The Bishop of
Bromley," he reads, with terrible relish, "has made a very
eloquent appeal to all Christians to aid in the manufacture
of the H-bomb." It is no time at all before he finds occasion to observe that it is "dreary living in the American
age, unless you're American, of course"; to describe T. S.
Eliot, if I heard him correctly, as "a sort of female Emily
Brontë"; and to remark of his mother-in-law that she is
"as tough as a night in a Bombay brothel and as hairy as
a sailor." It is at this point, I believe, that his wife murmurs
wanly, "I think I'll go out of my mind if you don't stop,"
and he replies genially, "Why don't you?" This, in general,
is the pattern of the conversation in "Look Back in Anger,"
and while I can see now that it reproduces only indifferently in print, it sounds quite sprightly on the stage, where
the humor of invective is not customarily so vivid or so ingenious. The serious portions of the entertainment are
perhaps rather less satisfactory. There are occasions when
self-pity does creep in, the hero turning up with floridities
like "I knew more about love, betrayal, and death when I
was ten years old than you will ever know," and there is
a recurring motif having to do with the necessity of think-

ing of oneself as a small furry animal when it is no longer possible to endure the torment of being human. Mr. Osborne states firmly in a program note that this is not whimsey, but I regret to say that it remains too whimsical for me. There is also—probably because of a dearth of natural incident in what is fundamentally a character study—an attempt to contrive incident (the wife, tired of being a victim, leaves; a new and somewhat preposterous victim is supplied; the wife returns, etc.), and I can't help feeling that all this mechanism has a certain desperation about it. By far the greater part of the play, though, is true, touching, and funny in its lively, roughshod way, and I trust you'll take it to your heart.

As Porter, Kenneth Haigh handles his lines with unusual intelligence and obvious enjoyment, and he is nicely assisted by Mary Ure, as his unfortunate wife; Alan Bates, as their friend; Vivienne Drummond, as the other woman in the case; and Jack Livesey, as the colonel, who once says reflectively of his son-in-law, "He has quite a turn of phrase, hasn't he?"—a massive understatement if ever I heard one.

At Home with the Gants

In a modest but impressive way, Ketti Frings has accomplished a miracle in her dramatization of Thomas Wolfe's "Look Homeward, Angel," which opened last week at the Ethel Barrymore. Even after the late Maxwell Perkins, a superb editor, had cut the manuscript almost in half, the book remained a great, roaring torrent of words, muddy, turbulent, overflowing the countryside, carrying a vast amount of debris with it in its passage to the sea. It cannot be said that Miss Frings has completely succeeded in taming this flood—there are still whirling eddies in the current, and sandbars where the logs pile up—but at least she has got it back inside its banks and the water is comparatively clear. The play (I think we've had more than enough of metaphor) is certainly not without its faults, both in structure and in language. Time, for one thing, had to be telescoped enormously, the major happenings of several years being compressed into something like three weeks, and this crowding together of such diverse material as a boy's first love, a shocking death in the family, the final disintegration of a marriage, and the culmination not only of a woman's fierce conflict between greed and her need to be loved but of her son's equally agonized struggle to escape from surroundings that are destroying him both as a man and as an artist sometimes gives the play a rather disorganized aspect. It is also true that some of the lesser characters, such as the hero's girl, his vehemently extrovert sister, a smug, successful uncle, and even, conceivably, the doomed brother, who were fully developed in the novel, have lost their sharp definition on the stage and now seem somewhat blurred and diminished. And it might even be said that the text occasionally goes wrong, partly because of the necessity for turning whole paragraphs of description into dialogue, a process to which Wolfe's prose lends itself only reluctantly; partly because a certain amount of original, bridging material had to be supplied, a nearly impossible task in dealing with a novelist who was unique and inimitable (at least this side of parody) in his idiom; and partly, I suspect, because Miss Frings' veneration for her source was so great that she was unable to tamper with passages that her intelligence must have informed her were "literary" to put it mildly.

Despite these handicaps, some imposed by form and some by temperament, "Look Homeward, Angel" is a fine, moving, and generally eloquent play. Eliza Gant's North Carolina boarding house, an absurd and terrible ruin called the Dixieland, attracts a startling collection of freaks from all over, but none more furiously possessed than the proprietress and her husband, and none as wretchedly trapped as their seventeen-year-old son Eugene, who is, of course, the author's portrait of his youthful self. Like O'Neill, Wolfe had a desperate compulsion to resurrect and understand the past, but his capacity for pity and forgiveness was considerably less, and the elder Gants are, in the main, remorselessly drawn. Eliza's grim passion for collecting land and money, which has had its bitter effect on all her family, has reduced Eugene, in particular, to the condition of a ragged, undernourished errand boy for the tarts, drug addicts, consumptives, and other fragrant personalities who infest the Dixieland, and while we are permitted to see that she is occasionally tormented by shame, regret, and longing for love, the picture remains that of a mean and graceless woman, epic only in the scale of her obsession.

Her husband comes off slightly better, or at any rate more picturesquely. He is a tombstone cutter by trade, but the aura of the lost artist is on him (he dreams of carving a perfect marble angel), and when he is drunk, which is often, his conversation has a thundering magniloquence almost worthy of the Mermaid Tavern. He can be graphic, as when he observes, "I well remember the day your mother first came crawling in here, on her belly, like a snake," or disconcerting, as when, having been reproached for describing his first wife as a miserable old hag, he explains that he does so simply because he is a bastard. In spite of all these charms, however, he is a weak, futile man, unable to help himself or anybody else, and though his son appears to have admired his vocabulary and his reputation for prowess in the local bordello, the ultimate emotion he aroused seems to have been a kind of contemptuous tolerance. Both the elder Gants, in fact, are dreadful people. They are fascinating and unforgettable because they have a completeness of personality, an air of having been drawn from life with scrupulous and passionate care, that is rarely encountered in the theatre. It is uncomfortable to think of Wolfe's looking back on the past with such concentrated loathing, but at least we can be grateful for the concentration. Though the pair it has produced will hardly endear themselves to you, there is not an accent or a gesture that you can doubt, and they are practically guaranteed to chill your blood.

The boy Eugene is a different proposition, since writers

are naturally inclined to take a rather romantic view of their own suffering embryos. We get, therefore, a succession of fairly conventional images—the tortured young idealist lost in a society of yammering barbarians, the adolescent lover wrestling with a lost cause (the girl is twenty-three and engaged to someone else), the son helplessly torn between love and hate, the precocious seeker after truth ("What does it all mean?"), the born writer, aware of his heavy destiny but inflexible in his purpose. If, however, Eugene cannot be said to vary much in essence from a hundred other heroes in literature, he is presented with such fierce and somehow innocent conviction, such a clear, disarming certitude that he is unique, that there is actually an illusion that you are seeing him for the first time. For various reasons, none creditable, I am more immune than most to the pathos of budding genius in a chilly world, but I nevertheless found Eugene deeply touching.

As I've said, the others in the cast come less vividly to life. Eugene's girl, who was not very arresting in the book, is even less so in the play, and it occurs to me that perhaps the first object of a young writer's affection *should* be wan and dull; his older brother, Ben, who dies somewhat protractedly of pneumonia in the second act, is a sensitive man but inarticulate, except in the end, when he is a ghost (I can't help wishing that Miss Frings had resisted this particular flourish); Ben's mistress demonstrates, I guess, that a girl can be fat, vulgar, and rather loose in her ways and still be a comfort to a lonely man; the sister, Helen, unmistakably a Gant but without much of her parents' terrible vivacity, has been triumphant only in breaking her husband's spirit; and the others, who include a stagy old country doctor, a whorehouse madam in the market for a tombstone, Eliza's brother and fellow real-estate shark, and all the grotesque tenants of the boarding house, are, I should say, not much more than surface caricatures, serviceable enough but clearly the victims of drastic editing. It doesn't matter much. The play is focussed on Eugene and his parents, and they are magnificent.